ik Sa   : Senior Lecturer in Media and Commu-
  tior   ry at the Communication and Media
  earch   s.itute, University of Westminster. He is
.ditor of *Arab Cultural Studies: Mapping the Field*
(I.B.Tauris, forthcoming 2011) and co-editor of the
Middle East Journal of Culture and Communication.

LIBRARY OF MODERN MIDDLE EAST STUDIES

Series ISBN: 978 1 84885 243 3

See www.ibtauris.com/LMMES for a full list of titles

92. *Orientalism and Conspiracy:*
Politics and Conspiracy Theory in the
Islamic World
Arndt Graf, Schirin Fathi and
Ludwig Paul (Eds)
978 1 84885 414 7

93. *Honour Killings: International*
Human Rights and Crimes Against
Women in Turkey
Leylâ Pervizat
978 1 84885 421 5

94. *Gender and Identity in North*
Africa: Postcolonialism and Feminism
in Maghrebi Women's Literature
Abdelkader Cheref
978 1 84885 449 9

95. *Kurds of Modern Turkey:*
Migration, Neoliberalism and
Exclusion in Turkish Society
Cenk Saraçoğlu
978 1 84885 468 0

96. *Occidentalisms in the Arab*
World: Ideology and Images of the
West in the Egyptian Media
Robbert Woltering
978 1 84885 476 5

97. *The Army and the Radical Left*
in Turkey: Military Coups, Socialist
Revolution and Kemalism
Özgür Mutlu Ulus
978 1 84885 484 0

98. *Power and Policy in Syria:*
Intelligence Services, Foreign Relations
and Democracy in the Modern Middle
East
Radwan Ziadeh
978 1 84885 434 5

99. *The Copts of Egypt: The Challenges*
of Modernisation and Identity
Vivian Ibrahim
978 1 84885 499 4

100. *The Kurds of Iraq:*
Ethnonationalism and National
Identity in Iraqi Kurdistan
Mahir Aziz
978 1 84885 546 5

101. *The Politics and Practices of*
Cultural Heritage in the Middle East:
Positioning the Material Past in
Contemporary Societies
Irene Maffi and Rami Daher (Eds)
978 1 84885 535 9

102. *The Politics and Poetics of Ameen*
Rihani: The Humanist Ideology of an
Arab-American Intellectual and
Activist
Nijmeh Hajjar
978 1 84885 266 2

103. *The Transformation of Turkey:*
Redefining State and Society from the
Ottoman Empire to the Modern Era
Fatma Müge Göçek
978 1 84885 611 0

Cultural Encounters in the Arab World

On Media, the Modern and the Everyday

Tarik Sabry

I.B. TAURIS

LONDON · NEW YORK

Published in 2010 by I.B.Tauris & Co Ltd
6 Salem Road, London W2 4BU
175 Fifth Avenue, New York NY 10010
www.ibtauris.com

Distributed in the United States and Canada Exclusively by Palgrave Macmillan
175 Fifth Avenue, New York NY 10010

Library of Modern Middle East Studies: 89

ISBN: 978 1 84885 359 1 (HB)
      978 1 84885 360 7 (PB)

A full CIP record for this book is available from the British Library
A full CIP record is available from the Library of Congress

Library of Congress Catalog Card Number: available

Printed and bound in Great Britain by TJ International Ltd, Padstow, Cornwall

Mixed Sources
Product group from well-managed
forests and other controlled sources
www.fsc.org Cert no. SGS-COC-2482
© 1996 Forest Stewardship Council
FSC

For Mohammed Abed al-Jabri
and
Abdelkabir Khatibi

Efforts to structure historical becoming in relation to class alone or nation alone taken as absolutes prove useless, mere tactics and strategies which apparently foreground class to the exclusion of nation, or vice versa…Modernity is best characterized not as an already established 'structure', nor as something which clearly has the capacity to become structured and coherent, but rather a fruitless attempt to achieve structure and coherence.

(Lefebvre, [1984], 1999: 187)

No one today is purely one thing.

(Edward W Said, 1993: 407)

If one is to ask an Arabic speaking intellectual to-day: What are the motivations and ends of Arab contemporary culture, he would feel perplexed as to the motivations, but would immediately answer for the ends by saying: they are to revive our religious Arab history, they are to cement the foundations of Arab nationalism and Arab unity.

(Louis Awad, 1972: 757)

Il faut être totalement moderne pour sentir que la modernité est problématique et l'accepter malgré tout.

(Laroui, 2001: 94)

Contents

Illustrations

Photographs

Charts

Tables

Acknowledgements

I would like to thank Colin Sparks, Paddy Scannell, Winston Mano, Barbara Knorpp and Mohamed Marzouki for their invaluable feedback on different chapters of this book. I am equally indebted to, in no particular order: Philippa Brewster, Fatima Mernissi, Mohammed Abed al-Jabri, Abdullah al-Ghathami, Abdul-Aziz Boumesshouli, Abdessamad Ghabass, Daya Thussu, Naomi Sakr, Marwan Kraidy, Helga Tawil-Souri, Mohamed Zayani, Muhammad Ayish, Peter Goodwin, Sally Feldman, Geoffrey Davies, Dina Matar, Lina Khatib, Myriam Cherti, Gholam Khiabany, Anthony McNicholas, Annette Hill, Zihad Tazout, Rania al-Malki, Layal Ftouni, Jones Alami, Yassir Sabry, Nassr Sabry, Nassir Sabry, Sanaa Sabry, Hassan Sougrati, Knadi Abderrazak, the team at NEWGEN, Annabelle Sreberny, the SOAS Library staff and Aliaa Dawoud for their great help and encouragement. A very special thanks goes to my good friend, Maria Way, an altruist *par excellence,* for making sure the manuscript read well, and to my eternal mentors Paddy Scannell and Colin Sparks for being – always – a great source of inspiration.

I dedicate this book to Shtou, my *Ait Nuhian* grandmother, Helen Sabry, Emma Sabry, Fatima Tazout, Mohammed Sabry and all the people who took part in the research.

1

On Encountering and Modernness

In ontological interpretation an entity is to be laid bare
with regard to its own state of being; such an interpretation obliges first to give a phenomenal characterization
of the entity we have taken as our theme, and thus to
bring it into the scope of our fore-having, with all its
subsequent steps of our analysis are to conform.

(Heidegger, [1962] 2007: 232)

When people say: modern painting, modern music,
modern technology, modern love, they think they know
what they are saying and that there is nothing more to
be said…anyone who utters a doubt or poses a question
is immediately branded as not being 'modern'. He is not
to be trusted, he is not 'with it', not with the movement
which justifies its own existence merely by moving.

(Lefebvre, 1995: 1)

The history of the 'Arab' is a history of cultural *encounters* with
others: in no particular order or chronology, the Greeks, Aristotle,
Byzantines, Persians, Indians, Romans, Jews, Amazighs, Kurds,

Africans, Turks, Chinese, Paganism, Zoroastrianism, Judaism, Christianity, Islam, Sufism, Aramaic, Hebrew, Napoleon, Europe, European colonialism, Empire, Marxism, socialism, capitalism, liberalism, Rock' n' Roll and much more; yet, it seems, all this common cultural universe, this cosmos of *encountering* has never stopped people from searching for that one thing they call a pure and 'authentic' Arab identity. It's like a continuous search for a lost mythical city, the Atlantis of identities, a chimera that will prove forever illusive. What they'll find, if they ever find it, is a mélange or métis of all those things, or/and the different discourses of *becoming* disguised in 'ideological intoxications of the past', nothing more and nothing less. This book is not a search for the certain, pure, absolute or any kind of origin/essence; it is rather a search into *encountering* in its liminal and translucent state, the transient, the intersectional as well as the ironies and, let's add, the contradictions and the possibilities that they bring.

At the age of 7, I suddenly started to have frequent nightmares. Initially, at such moments my mother would kindly give me water and gently caress me back to sleep. Soon, however, the incessant nightmares became more of an ordinary (somewhat annoying) nightly occurrence to which the rest of the family had got accustomed. Some joked I was *maskun or mkahalat* (possessed by *jinn*), relatives to whom my nightmares were no secret decided it was *boughatat*: a helpless feeling of paralysis that happens in one's sleep and which others, being more sensible, simply put down to eating late at night. However, my parents, hitherto staunch Marxist-Leninists and materialists *par excellence*, thought the whole superstitious explanations to be mere traditional poppycock. Once on our way back from Rabat, a trip much of which I cannot remember, at the advice of a friend, my mother decided to stop by the *Khyayta* (holy men who dealt with *jinn* possession and problems of *shur* – 'black magic'). No one had talked with me or had cared to enlighten me as to what happened when one encountered the holy *Khyayta*; was I supposed to keep quiet, scream, close my eyes, bow in awe, I simply had no idea. What's more, having been brought up in a quasi-atheist entourage for much of my childhood, I was almost alien to traditional protocol and could therefore not help the feeling of mortification and *fallnness* that had engulfed me. However, there was no time for hesitation or fear, as my agnostic mother ordered: 'go down, a *fkih* will come to see you, he'll help you with your nightmares'. I remember how my small feet trembled as I went down the high and awkward stairs leading to a stable-like space with hay scattered sporadically on the floor. Two big stones had been intentionally positioned to act as sitting objects. Then there were chains, lengthy ones with rusty handcuffs. The smell was eerie. It reminded one of the London Dungeon's simulations of the inner city's seventeenth-century torture houses. There was nothing holy about the place; not in the least, it was practically a shit-hole, a cave, but what is with the chains I thought? Am I to be jailed, exorcised? Am I really possessed? Have my family brought me here to rid me of my demons? What demons? I did not think Marxists could be superstitious. A psychiatrist with smart spectacles and a cosy sofa would have been more suitable to such 'modern' thinking parents, I thought in hindsight. After a five-minute wait or so, a small thin man, with a long white beard, dressed in a grey-ish traditional *Jellaba* seemed to appear from nowhere. He waddled slowly, but with certainty, towards me and looked me straight in the eyes. He gestured pointing to the stone facing him for me to sit and started putting the rusty chain handcuffs around my hands without uttering a word. I, of course, being taken by the whole spectacle, and the care with which it was performed, conformed willingly to this absurd madness. The man then, all of a sudden, came closer and closer until there was only a few inches gap between our faces. As I made a move to withdraw my face, for the distance between us was so intimately and embarrassingly close, I felt sudden shooting pangs in my cheeks, and slowly in other parts of my face as well. It took me a while to realise that he (I dare not curse him even now) was bloody well spitting at me. I remained frozen throughout the spitting ritual, unable to run for my life, call for help or even wipe my now red and wet embarrassed face. If you remember, I was not prepared for this 'holy' moment. Should I have spat back at him?

That's what the 'modern' Karl Marx would have done, I guess! After a while, the spitting holy-man untied my hands, again with notable care, and asked me not to be afraid. I rushed to my pockets to hand him a modest *Baraka*[1], the only thing I knew I had to do. Maybe it's all in the spit; I tried to reason much later. This old man's spit must be *holy*. He nodded, as if to thank me for the *Baraka* I gave him and asked me to go up the stairs, where my mother was waiting. 'What's the problem with him *sidi* [sir]?' asked my mother from the top of the cave. 'It's television', he replied. 'Make sure he stops watching it for 17 days. That will cure him completely.'

My encounter with the *Khyayta* was my first introduction to 'cultural schizophrenia'. It was a double-encounter: one of a popular traditional ritual in all its colourfulness; the other, my mother's treason towards the 'modern', embodied in Karl Marx, whose *Das Kapital*, and not *the Koran*, took centre-stage in our home library. Does my mother's treason in any way alter or cancel out her state of *modernness*; her *being* modern in the world? Can one be modern all the time? Could my mother have been 'traditional' and modern at the same time? Was she, as Lerner would have put it, a 'transitional'? What does it mean to be both modern and traditional? What are we really talking about here? As for the holy-man's take on *television*, it is strangely McLuhanian, or shall I say phenomenological, *par excellence*, for it was not – according to his diagnosis that is – any specific programming, Arab or Western, that had caused my nightmares or possession, but television itself, as a medium. What's even more impressive about his diagnosis, as I remember quite vividly, is that the nightmares had coincided with the year my father had bought our first black and white television set in 1977. My demons had possessed me at the point of my *encounter* with television, the 'magic box', as the older generation of Arabs would call it. Television is the medium through which a new world with its different *jinns* had come to take possession of my 'natural' state of being in the world. This *double*-encounter calls for a 'double-critique' or to use another of Khatibi's terms: a 'double-semiotics'. The disjuncture between the 'modern' encounter through the revolutionary work

of Karl Marx, the spirit of 'modernisation' it had instilled in my
parents, and the encounter with the *Khyayta*'s 'metaphysical soil'
(Khatibi, 1980) coexist or, shall I say, overlap in the same cultural
temporality without continuity or linearity – what does this mean
and how does it affect our understanding of what it means to be
'modern' in a traditional setting? What does it mean to encounter
something in the world? What happens at the point of the *encounter*? Can we study the *encountering* of the 'modern' as a cultural
phenomenon – that is in a phenomenological way? What structures
and mechanisms underline the encounter with the 'modern'? In
Being and Time Heidegger states that 'the temporal interpretation of
everyday *Dasein*[2] must start with those structures in which disclosedness constitutes itself: understanding, state of mind, falling and
discourse'. (Heidegger, [1962] 2007: 335) How can we make use
of such structures to study *encountering* the 'modern' in the Arab
world as a kind of spatio-temporal disclosedness? To appropriate
Heidegger's structures in the form of questions, we could ask: how
does the 'Arab' understand/interpret encountering 'modern'? How
is this disclosed as a state of *being*? Through what kinds of discourse
is encounter with the 'modern' communicated? Does encountering the 'modern' in any way lead to some sort of fallnness[3]; that
is a crisis in identity or culture? What are we really talking about
when we bring up the subject of cultural encounter/encountering
the modern as an object of study? Through what means do cultural
encounters occur, or what are the facilitators or mediators through
which encounters happen? The corpus that falls under the rubric
of cultural encountering and the mediators that facilitate such an
act are limitless. These include many forms of human interaction,
such as fashion, aesthetics, education, communication, epistemology, music, art, ideas, literature, commerce, popular cultures/visual
cultures, sport and travel. Each of the above-mentioned areas is
important enough to constitute solid components of the historiography of cross-cultural encountering as a phenomenon and can also
be considered as separate intellectual projects in their own right.
My contribution, since it cannot cover any of the above thoroughly

(for the task is evidently impossible in one book), and though it concentrates mainly on the Arab case, can only be a metonym for encountering the 'modern' and its meaning. When mentioning art, aesthetics and other categories from the corpus of 'cross-cultural encountering' what we are really dealing with is general categories under which we can place a whole stratum of sub-areas that can also easily constitute independent and coherent areas of study. To give an example, the historical study of coins and their spread beyond geographical localities is in itself a global act of cultural encounter. As Georganteli and Cook (2006) put it in their introduction to *Encounters: Travel and Money in the Byzantine World* 'the study of Byzantine coins in their archaeological, geographical and historical context offers crucial evidence for the study of medieval economic and cultural encounters' (Georganteli and Cook, 2006: 7). 'Byzantine-derived designs, used on the coins of other lands similarly', they added, 'echo the transmission of Byzantine culture and ideas of kingship' (ibid).

During one of my recent fieldwork visits to Morocco (2007), I spent a week in *Asfi* (a small coastal Moroccan city known for its pottery and very good clay quality), talking to its famous potters (young and old) about their art and how the 'modern', or encounters with Western art and technique, influenced their work. The story that emerged from the interviews was one of 'hybridisation' and cross-cultural exchange rather than 'authenticity'. Even the old school of Moroccan potters I interviewed emphasised the influence of borrowed styles and technique encountered through travel on the development of their art[4]. Whilst jotting down observations on pottery making in Asfi, I was more than tempted to tell the story of Arab modernity through the art of pottery making in Morocco, but such a deviation would have shocked my publisher, to whom I had promised a different kind of story and, to be candid, it would be far more suitable to an art/ceramics historian to pursue such a project. The point of highlighting this episode from the fieldwork is to emphasise, yet again, the vastness of the topic and the rubric that is found under the umbrella of cross-cultural encounter. My concern in this book is with 'modernness' as a phenomenological category and how it is communicated to and expressed by the young Arab through different forms of communication[5]. I do not, in any way, intend that this book be a complete exposé, or even a coherent summary, of the 'modern' condition in the Arab world and how the latter is mediated through mass communication. Nor is it intended as a cultural history or indeed a historiography of the Arab world's encounters with the West or modernity, which would have made for a useful and logical sequel to, especially, Ibrahim Abu-Lughod's *Arab rediscovery of Europe* (1963) and Bernard Lewis's *The Muslim Discovery of the West* (1957) as both pieces were written before the spread of technologies of seeing (mainly television) in the Arab region, nor do I intend that the book should act as a social history of media uses in the Arab world or the Middle East. Daniel Lerner's attempt (1958) at this intellectual task (still an object of critique and debate today) was indeed too premature, as some have rightly argued (see Sparks, 2007; Sreberny, 2008), but it remains, regardless of its known disadvantages, a seminal and indeed a pioneering piece of scholarship. I'd like to take a less fashionable position here and state that Lerner's work on the characteristics of the modern personality or 'self-system', 'psychic-mobility', 'mass mediated experience' or 'vicarious experience/psychic displacement', as he also calls it (Lerner, 1958: 53), has lost neither relevance nor topicality. In fact, these analytic frames, if we can call them that, especially 'psychic-mobility', which I articulated elsewhere as 'mental emigration' (Sabry, 2003, 2005), are central to this book's thesis. My interest in Arab 'modernness' is both ontological and epistemological, and the chapters that follow are nothing other than an attempt to understand the concept vis-à-vis these two distinct yet somehow interrelated interpretive frames. The epistemological interest in the concepts of 'modern' and 'modernness' comes from a conscious intellectual desire to bridge the contemporary Arab philosophical discourse *on*[6] modernity with a new field of enquiry, namely Arab cultural studies, so that the former is able to inform the latter and *vice versa*. The bridging task is not much more than an attempt to rehearse the possible ways in which the Arab cultural repertoire can come to terms with its 'present' cultural temporality creatively. I believe this to be a major concern of this book, as the study and theorisation of modernity in the Arab cultural repertoire has yet (with very few recent exceptions) to surpass its metaphysical stage and open up to the study of man, contemporary cultural life and its transformative character. The ontological interest in this book comes from asking a purely ontological question: What does it mean to *be* modern in the Arab world? Dealing with *being modern* or *modernness*, as I prefer to call it, and what it means, raises a number of questions that problematise the meaning of Arab modernity. What determines modernness – the spatial, the temporal or both? Can one be modern and traditional at the same time? What does this mean? Where is modernness most conspicuous? Does one need to be conscious of one's modernness for him or her to be so, modern that is?

Genealogical research into cultural encountering and its impact on the Arab cultural repertoire is still scarce. A serious and welcome intellectual effort came from Mohammed Abed al-Jabri's philosophical treatise a *Critique of Arab Reason*, especially the fourth volume, A *Critique of Arab Ethical Reason* (Al-Jabri, 2001) that unearths the archaeology of the Arab ethical/moral 'reason' and its many imported aspects, including Greek, Persian, European and Islamic influences. Another work, this time a historical study by Ibrahim Abu-Lughod (1963) entitled *Arab Rediscovery of Europe: A study in Cultural Encounters*[7] provides an interesting analysis of the French expedition to Egypt in 1789 and its effect (as a cultural moment) on the Arab world and its metamorphosis from tradition to modernity (Abu-Lughod, 1963: 7). The Napoleonic communiqué, a cultural text, written by French Orientalists and distributed upon arrival by the French Army was (if we discarded earlier encounters with the work of Greek philosophers) the Arab's first encounter with *modern* concepts, such as *republic* and the *just state* (Abu-Lughod, 1963: 20). The book also explores the influence of the translation movement in Egypt (1800–1936)

and its effect as an intellectual encounter on the Arab cultural repertoire. The School of Translation founded by Muhammad Ali in
1936 was responsible for the translation of around 2000 books into
Arabic, more than all that had been translated for the whole century in the Arab world (Abu-Lughod, 1963: 41). However, unlike
the translations of the ninth century, which covered a wide area of
knowledge, the nineteenth century translation movement, argues
Abu-Lughod, discarded a number of subjects including philosophy, logic and science. This deficit had had a major influence on
the Arab cultural repertoire, especially in the area of philosophy
and critical thinking. What was transmitted through the translations was only 'the superstructure of the cultural manifestations'
and not the intellectual creativity or 'bent of mind' that led to the
establishment of the sciences in the West. Abu-Lughod speculates
that 'early nineteenth-century transmission of European knowledge had only a limited immediate effect on the intellectual out-
look of the Arab world' (ibid, 59).[8] Travel constitutes the act of
cultural encounter *par excellence* and there is a well-documented
compendium on Arab travellers' accounts and experiences of far
away lands (the West included) that can be traced to the travels
of the famous Ibn Batouta and Ibn Khaldun. The most quoted is a
book entitled *Takhlis* by Tahtawi (1834–5) in which he recounts his
voyage to Paris. We can also add the observations of the Arab trav-
eller Marun al-Naqqash (1817–55), credited as the father of Arabic
drama. Al-Naqqash spent time in Italy watching plays and opera
and was the first to direct a modern play in the Arab world (Abu-
Lughod, 1963). Also, in recounting his voyage to Paris, Muhammad
al-Saffar, a Moroccan ambassador in the mid-nineteenth century,
provides gripping observations about French bourgeois politesse,
bosoms, wine, food, time, technology and administrational issues;
and how his encounters changed his view of the temporal and the
spatial (See Miller, 1992). Delving into historical aspects of Arab
encounters with Europe, the 'modern' and modernity unveil a
limitless pool and possibilities for research. My concern in this
book, however, is with the present tense of Arab cultures and the

meanings of Arab modernness. Let's begin with unpacking cultural encountering as a spatio-temporal phenomenon.

Cultural encountering as spatio-temporal phenomenon

What happens to cultural temporality at the point of *encounter* with another temporality? Since the act of cultural *encounter* is of major importance to the thesis of this book, it makes sense to articulate, though briefly, some conceptual categories for thinking about *encountering* as a phenomenological structure. That is, to speak of *encountering* as a matter of fact that happens in time and space without the weight of the theoretical jargon that usually blurs our understanding of what is there in the world, as we witness it or as it discloses itself unto us. *Encounters* are cultural phenomena par excellence, and culture is nothing other than an amalgamation of different *encounters* and the dynamics they produce. The genealogy of Arab 'culture', since this book is about Arab cultural encounters, is a métissage, if not *bricolage*, of different cultural *encounters*. Arab aesthetics, political and ethical modes of reasoning owe so much to these *encounters* (Al-Jabri, 2001). *Encountering* is a spatio-temporal phenomenon – in that it takes place in time and space. What is the nature of the temporality of cultural *encounter*ing? To put it differently: In what kind of time does the cultural encounter happen? Cultural encountering coexists in a three-dimensional temporality: a) the time of the encounter (i.e., when the encounter takes place in real time: e.g., a rock concert broadcast live from London across the world), b) the cultural time of the encountered (what is meant here is the cultural temporality or the time of the culture that is being encountered) and c) we have the cultural time of those who do the encountering. What of spatiality and how does it affect *encountering* in its three-dimensionality? The spatial is a key aspect of any *encountering* and can be either physical or symbolic. Unpicking the spatio-temporal nature of encountering in a world of mass mediated culture is complex and needs to go beyond the three-dimensional structure that characterises it. The interrelation of the three different cultural temporalities produces different and intricate narratives about *self* and the world. Cultural *Encountering* in the twenty-first century, with the spread and 'overabundance', to use Augé's term, of media technologies and floating signifiers of the other, has undermined the role of *place* as a necessary element of encountering. Witnessing or encountering other cultures has now little to do with the physical spaces. It's become more of a symbolic phenomenon. This, however, does not mean that place is no longer important; rather, it is its nature that has changed. Here, the act of encountering and the spatialities within which and through which it occurs tend towards the *phantasmagoric*. As Giddens puts it:

> In most traditional cultures, notwithstanding the population migrations which were relatively common, and the long distances sometimes travelled by the few, most social life was localised. The prime factor that has altered this situation does not lie with increased mobility; rather, place becomes thoroughly penetrated by disembedding mechanisms, which recombine the local activities into time-space relations of ever-widening scope. Place becomes phantasmagoric.
>
> (Giddens, 1991: 146)

Encountering is a human thing. When we talk of *encountering* we are necessarily dealing with something that humans do on an everyday basis. If we can agree on a holistic structure for unpicking *encountering* as a phenomenological and an anthropological phenomenon, then everydayness must be of major importance, for the disclosedness of *encountering* reveals itself as an *everyday* phenomenon (see Chapter 4). Also, cultural encounters are no longer rare events that only travellers or intellectuals can recount or write about. It is now available from practically any part of the world, and 'for anyone as someone', (Scannell, 2000) at the click of a button.

Ontologising encountering 'modern'

What follows is an articulation of the concept 'modernness' and how I intend to deal with it in here. 'What makes it ontologically possible for entities to be encountered within-the-world and objectified as so encountered?' asks Heidegger in *Being and Time* ([1962] 2007: 417). Heidegger's use of the word 'entities' remains rather vague – they are existential phenomena that are 'present' in the world (ibid), but the question he asks remains so important: How do we objectify *modernness* in the Arab case as cultural encounter? Can we separate *modernness* from the time-consciousness through which it acquires its self-understanding? Which time-consciousness are we dealing with: is it the local, the transnational, the global, or is it a combination of these different elements? Since *being* modern and modernity are a matter of concern for '*dasein*': an entity that is able to make an issue out of *being* in the world (Heidegger, [1962] 2007: 231), shouldn't *dasein*'s state of *modernness* or its *being-modern-in-the world* also be part of an ontological enquiry? *Modernness* here, and unlike Heidegger's take on the modern, does not presuppose any sort of *fallnness*, for this would limit not only the structures around which the concept is posited but also the different ontic/anthropological meanings it can acquire. Can we give 'modernness' an ontological interpretation? To further clarify the objective of this book, it is necessary to distinguish between, let us say, modernity, modernisation, modernism and *modernness*. Modernity is a philosophical concept that finds its origins in the Enlightenment as a particular paradigm about a particular narrative of happiness. This paradigm can be broken down into an ensemble of ideas and events, including: individuality, 'the coming into history' of subjects whose fate had hitherto been decided by despotic and theocratic institutions; secularisation, scientific endeavour, reason, man's domination over nature and its resources, freedom of opinion, the coming of the state and the role of intellectuals, not to mention the specialisation of fields of knowledge and the energy attributed to capitalism as a mode of production and a determinant of a new set of socio-cultural relations. Modernity's pathologies and inconsistencies, best articulated by Weber and later Adorno and Horkheimer (1972), have instead led to a 'disenchanted' world, to use Weber's term; an 'iron-cage' that led to the reification and *thingification* of human experience. The unravelling '*dialectics* of the enlightenment' repositioned thinking about modernity and 'subjective-centred reason' (Heidegger in Habermas, 1987: 133); and turned modernity into an object of doubt and 'an expression of 'sociological helplessness' (Beck in Murdock, 1993: 521). The concept 'modern' is equally contradictory and illusive. As Lefebvre observed in his *Introduction to Modernity*:

> When we utter the words 'modern times', 'modern psychology', 'modern art', we think we have used terms and expressions which mean something, whereas in fact we have said nothing at all. We have merely pointed out an inextricable confusion between fashion, the here-and-now, the 'valid', the lasting and the contemporary. In the midst of such confusion, the word has changed meaning several times over. In the way it is used at present it does not refer explicitly to anything definite or mean-ingful. Yet one or other of its meanings will always dominate, and in a curiously unconscious way it will penetrate our consciousnesses.
>
> (Lefebvre, 1995: 185)

'Modernisation' is a *process* and must not be confused with modernity. It is a technical term introduced only in the 1950s, which Habermas (1987: 2) describes as: 'a bundle of processes that are cumulative and mutually reinforcing: to the formation of capital and the mobilisation of resources; to the development of the forces of production and the increase in the productivity of labor; to the establishment of centralized political power and the formation of national identities; to the proliferation of rights of political participation, of urban forms of life; and of formal schooling; to the secularization of values and norms' (Habermas, 1987: 2). For Lerner, modernisation, and its role in the transformation of traditional societies, is no neutral matter: 'the western model of modernization exhibits certain components and sequences whose relevance is global... That the model evolved in the West is an historical fact. That the same basic model reappears in virtually all modernizing societies on all continents of the world, regardless of variations in race, color, creed... Indeed, the lesson is that Middle Eastern modernizers will do well to study the historical sequence of Western growth' (Lerner, 1958: 46). By 'western', Lerner refers not so much to Europeanisation (commonly denoting French and British influence in the region), but to Americanisation, a term imposed by 'recent history'. 'Americanization', he advanced 'became a specific force and the common stimuli of the Atlantic civilization came to be called Westernization' (Lerner, 1958: 45). While Lerner emphasises the role of external dynamics in the process of societal transformation, Mowlana who articulates development/modernisation within a wider integrative 'ontic/emancipatory' framework (that goes beyond Lerner's positivist spirit), strongly argues that 'transformation is not an external object' but that it 'lies deep within the individual' (Mowlana and Wilson, 1990: 212). I argue that societal transformation is the result of both *endogenous* and *exogenous* elements and that it is the dialectical relationship between the two that determines the act of transformation (in fact modernness itself) and not one or the other. In both cases (Lerner and Mowlana), social transformation is ideologised to the point where it becomes a kind of metaphysics, one that stands in the way of understanding the more important anthropological aspects of change as they happen in time and space.

'Modernism' is equally elusive and means quite different things to the Anglo-Saxon world than to the French, German or Spanish[9]. In the Anglo-Saxon world, modernism is conventionally used to describe 'a variety of tendencies within the European and especially, Anglo-American literature, of the early twentieth century'

(Macey, 2000: 257). In visual arts, the term is used to describe 'the process of abstraction associated with cubism' as well as other variations of the avant-garde (ibid, 258). When articulating the concepts 'modern' and 'modernism', Lefebvre stresses the difference between 'immediate consciousness' and knowledge, and 'between representation and concept' (Lefebvre, 1995: 187). 'Modernism' for Lefebvre is an incoherent, self-glorifying, triumphalist and *structureless* concept that confuses newness and creativity: 'a bran tub of exaggerations, justifications, illusions and mystification, where ideologies, myths and utopianism are jumbled pell-mell' (Lefebvre, 1995: 187). 'Modern', 'modernity', 'modernism' and 'modernisation' are intricate and desperately difficult concepts to define. Describing modernism as a constructed metaphor, Lefebvre observes: 'Modernism is determined to impose itself, either without discussion or by being deliberately controversial. It presents its two fold credentials: novelty, imminent access to classicism. Propaganda for modernism is projected in metaphoric form in newspaper articles and radio and television programmes, and its aim is to intimidate. Anyone who does not accept it and dares to challenge it is made to feel and appear old-fashioned, out of date and not "with it"...The actual "creative" struggle is irrelevant, it is being seen at first nights that counts....' (ibid, 186).

In their effort to 'structure historical becoming', to use Lefebvre's phrase, Arab intellectuals have integrated the concepts 'modern' into different discourses and thought systems including socialism, communism, pan-Arabism, pan-Islamism and nationalism none, despite some effect, has proved realisable at the level of consciousness. There is nothing to say, however, and this is a point that must be admitted from the start that modernness as a concept or state of being is or can be illusion free. *Modernness* may be an attempt to deal with 'modern' ontologically, but it is certainly not immune from ontological illusion or the cultural terrorism that comes with it. That is to say, even the most spontaneous self-reflexive narrative can be part of an elusive discourse. Linguistically, when we talk about 'modern' we are dealing with an *utterance*, a signifier that has no relation to the signified – the essence of *being* modern. Their relationship is one of arbitrariness. Dealing with modernness is an attempt to reconcile the signifier and the signified (semantics and *being*) in a more meaningful way. Whereas 'modern' is only an arbitrary description of the state of *being* called 'modern', modernness is about thinking through and reflecting on the very kind of *being*, that thing we call 'modern'. It is difficult and problematic to make sense of modernness as a temporal phenomenon because of its temporal multidimensionality and also because nothing stays the same. Meanings attributed to *modernness* (just as those attributed to 'modern') may thus vary and mean different things in different times or stages of *being*. This book argues that grasping 'modern' through conceptualised knowledge alone is inadequate. An empirical approach to the study of 'modern' is necessary, thus Lefebvre's differentiation between 'consciousness' and knowledge is crucial. Making sense of *modernness* is an attempt to unravel not only semantics of modernity or the underlying mechanisms of modernisation (local or exported) but also, and most importantly for this book, what being modern means to the anthropological subject (as an ontological phenomenon). It is through the ontologising of the *modern* as a phenomenon and a reality that meanings of modernity and modernisation become clearer to us.

'To "be", for the human individual' argued Giddens 'is to have ontological awareness' (Giddens, 1991: 48). To *be modern* is, we may also add, to have ontological awareness of 'modernness', or what it means to be modern in the world. Objectifying *modernness* as a phenomenological category is a way to bring meaning and being together (Luhmann, 1998). It is a way of reconciling *modernity*, as semantics/discourse, with *modernity*, as an ontological category and a lived experience. This is where I think the concept of '*modernness*' has its use, for *modernness*, though related to *modernity* and *modernisation*, is an entirely distinct and different category. 'Modernisation' describes a process; modernness, on the other hand, describes a state of mind and *being* in the world. Modernity, modernisation and *modernness* yield a different kind of hermeneutics and thus require different methodologies. Modernness is a concern for 'dasein', to borrow Heidegger's term, and is, in first place and in essence, an ontological phenomenon about a kind of *being* in the world, which has been termed 'modern'. Attempts to grasp the state-of-mindedness that we call 'modern' have so far been articulated in relation to the institutional, the self-reflexive, 'mobility', the arts and through a study of institutionalised, anti-anxiety mechanisms for coping with the modern condition (Giddens, 1991), but so far this task has been performed in theoretical and non-evidential terms, ignoring the anthropological dimensions of what it means to be 'modern'. 'That period we call modern' observed Heidegger 'is defined by the fact that man becomes the centre and measure of all beings. Man is the *subjectum*, that which lies at bottom of all beings, that is, in modern, in modern terms, at the bottom of all objectification and representation' (Heidegger in Habermas, 1987: 133). *Modernness*, it must be added, is not simply of concern to the intellectual or philosopher; it is also a matter of concern to the ordinary person whose *being* is too woven into the institutional and ontological aspects of modernity. As Giddens puts it: 'The integral relation between modernity and radical doubt is an issue which, once exposed to view, is not only disturbing to philosophers but it is *existentially troubling* for ordinary individuals' (Giddens, 1991: 21). Modernity, for Giddens, is a 'post-traditional order, in which the question, "How shall I live?" has to be answered in day-to-day decisions about how to behave, what to wear and what to eat – and many other things – as well as interpreted within the temporal unfolding of self-identity' (Giddens, 1991: 14). Notwithstanding his attempt at ontologising the 'modern' by bringing it into the realm of self-identity, Giddens often defines modernity as a 'post-traditional order', where fixed-frozen metaphysics give way to a fast changing, 'detraditionalising' and 'runaway world'. The modern world, he argues, is a place where 'not only is the *pace* of social change much faster than any prior system, so also is its *scope*, and the *profoundness* with which it affects pre-existing social practices and modes of behaviour' (Giddens,

1991:16). There is a case to be made here about the use of the prefix 'post', as it presupposes a radical break from a traditional order of seeing the world, which, it seems, Giddens has set as a precondition for the emergence of the 'modern'. This case can only be made when we bring 'tradition' to the fore as a complex sociological category. The prefix 'post' presents us with a notable dilemma when making sense of 'traditional' societies from the developing world that have long embraced modernity's 'axis', but still hang on to a fixed and timeless metaphysics. This sort of continuity defeats the whole point of being modern. To put it in simple terms, what does one call a society like that of the United Arab Emirates or Kuwait where high levels of capitalist consumerism, and the countries of the Maghreb where high degrees of self-referentiality coexist with religiosity and fixed traditional values? I am not sure whether a post-traditional order is at all feasible or coherent enough, either in Western societies or in the so-called traditional societies. The paramount problem with which we are faced here is purely hermeneutic. Although Giddens's attempt to reconcile institutionalised, reflexive modernity with dynamics of self-identity remains very important, he still fails to see modernity and the 'modern' as fluid 'narrative categories' susceptible to different kinds of hermeneutics. 'Modernity', argues Jameson, is 'not a concept, philosophical or otherwise, but a narrative category' (Jameson, 2002: 40). Giddens's insistence (along with many others including a number of Arab intellectuals) that a reflexive modernity is only possible through the evaporation of morality (Giddens, 1991: 145) is only one narrative among many; it is one way of seeing and comprehending modernity. Countering Giddens's take, Taha Abdurrahman (2006) argues that the reality of modernity is not the same as its spirit, even if the reality results from the practice of the/its spirit. Rather, the reality of modernity is specific to a choice from different possibilities or modalities of its spirit. Perhaps a post-Weberian take on 'tradition' is now timelier than ever; for it has become apparent that *being* 'modern' in the world today, either for Westerners or people in the so-called 'traditional' societies means much more and is more complex than the prefix in post-traditional suggests. For, although a radical break with the past was necessary for the development of modern thought, politics and the sciences, the break is not entirely clear-cut from an ontological/anthropological perspective. Is it necessary for one to renounce tradition or any sort of transcendental metaphysics for him or her to claim his or her *modernness* in the world? I have interviewed a number of young people from the Arab region who insist on being both modern and traditional. In fact, many of them insisted, just like Taha Abdurrahman, that being modern does not and should not necessarily mean parting with tradition, morality or God. Here 'the self', to use Giddens's words, is 'as reflexively understood by the person in terms of her or his biography' (Giddens, 1991: 53) at once modern and traditional[10].

What terrain or field can one rely upon to best understand *modernness* in traditional societies or societies in transition? What are the structural items that can help us have a rounded foresight of 'modernness'? I am not after a primordial or a holistic interpretation of modernness – but it is necessary to think of the structure/mechanisms that can help us arrive at a clear understanding of the phenomenon. This book articulates meanings of 'modernness' in the Arab context and focuses on three different structures: *thought, everyday life and self-referentiality.* These three spaces will not be articulated in isolation, but within a relational framework with the hope of guaranteeing a bridging and connecting task that rejoins the modern in Arab thought with the modern in Arab lived everyday experience. For this task to be rooted in a more grounded theoretical and epistemological space, where such a discussion becomes a process rather than an end in itself, the bringing together of modernity as a philosophical category and the dynamics of the everyday in Arab contemporary cultures needs to be conceptualised/articulated, this book advances, within an epistemic intellectual space that is conscious of itself and its aims; a field of enquiry where the study of contemporary Arab media, culture and society is objectified and institutionalised as part of scientific enquiry.

The everyday is where socio-cultural meanings are produced, disseminated and resisted; it is where the carnivalesque, the evasive and the resistant coexist, a site of floating signifiers *par excellence*, where 'modernness' unfolds in liminal forms and shapes. *Self-referentiality* is the next domain or structure through which I intend to make sense of 'modernness' as a phenomenological/anthropological category. Self-referentiality or simply self-reflexivity takes different forms, including televisual encounters with the modern and other forms of artistic expression. Self-referentiality is a way to communicate meanings of being modern. It is a communication of a state-of-mindedness, of individual desire, 'personal disposition' and a way of being different in the world. The verb *to be*, argues Levinas, 'is a reflexive verb: it is not just that one is, one is one-self [*on s'est*] (Levinas, 1978: 28). Self-referentiality, as modernness, comes in the form of style, resistance, signs and symbols, sounds and language and other communicative processes. Most importantly, being modern in the world, or modernness and what that means is a matter of primary concern for people and individuals. It is their articulation of the 'modern' and how it interfaces with the modern institution that should help bring to the surface the meaning of such a phenomenon. As Giddens puts it, modernity 'must be understood on an institutional level; yet the transmutations introduced by modern institutions interlace with individual life and therefore with the self. One of the distinctive features of modernity, in fact, is an increasing interconnection between the two "extremes" of extensionality and intentionality: globalising influences on the one hand and personal dispositions on the other' (Giddens, 1991: 1). Making sense of modernness through the self-referential as it unfolds in the everyday is a way of coming to terms with what modernness means for individuals, and how they in turn use different signs and signifiers to communicate it. The rest of this book is an attempt to concretise the three-dimensional structure described above as the foregrounding upon which we can rely to make sense of modernness in the Arab case: Arab thought, everyday life and self-referentiality. The next chapter: Contemporary Arab

Thought and the Struggle for Authenticity: Towards an Ontological Articulation of the 'Modern', describes a contemporary typology of Arab thought with a focus on key Maghrebi thinkers, and argues for a paradigm shift in Arab discourses on the 'modern', one that takes into account key changes and transformations in contemporary Arab societies. The second task I set myself in this chapter is to rehearse ways in which the bridging and connection between contemporary Arab thought and articulations of the everyday are possible. Chapter 3 entitled: 'Arab Popular Cultures and Everyday Life', problematises the category 'culture' in the Arab repertoire and argues that in order to allow for broader articulations of Arab 'cultures', it is necessary to free this category from fixed, essentialist and ideologised narratives of *becoming*. So the task here is not one of connection or bridging, but one of *dislocation* and disconnection. The aim here is not to dehistoricise or depoliticise discourses of Arab cultures but to separate them from their artificial and discursive relations to make the way for other new and broader articulations. In Chapter 4, entitled: 'The Bridge and the Queue as Spaces of Encountering', I use ethnographic research conducted in Egypt and Morocco to show how examining ordinary taken-for-granted places can unveil useful observations on how certain spaces are used 'tactically' by everyday ordinary people to resist, reconfigure and reorganise hegemonic power structures. The chapter also concretises manifestations of modernness by presenting the everyday as a key component of its foregrounding. Chapter 5: '*Modernness* as a Multiple Narrative-Category: *Encountering* the West' extends the discussion on 'encountering' and modernness by focusing on how young Moroccans from different social and economic strata encounter the West and the 'modern' through television and satellite viewing. It asks: How do young Moroccans encounter the West through television? How does this encounter alter their structures of feeling about the world? And how does stratification in *habitus* and socio-economic strata affect young Moroccans' self-reflexivity about being modern in the world? Chapter 6: 'Still Searching for the Arab Present Cultural Tense: Arab Cultural Studies', articulates the importance of Arab cultural studies as an epistemic space that will allow for a systematic and scientific articulation of transformations in Arab media, culture and society. It rehearses the kind of hermeneutics that would be most suited for such a project and sets the agenda for future work and research in the area.

2

Contemporary Arab Thought and the Struggle for Authenticity: Towards an Ontological Articulation of the 'Modern'

Where is the difficulty or the obstacle? Is it in the hands of a particular person in the state? [Not really] The obstacle is in us, in our minds, our aspirations, our hearts and in our emotions because until now we have not understood the logic of modernity nor have we comprehended all its meanings. We have yet to realize that this concept: 'the modern state' or 'the modern society' is not a threat to either belief systems or power, or even folklore.

(Laroui, 2006: 61) (Author's translation from Arabic)

...the philosophical life is considered superior to everyday life, but when it attempts to solve the riddles of reality it only succeeds in proving the unreality, which is, indeed, implicit in its nature. It requires a realism it cannot achieve and aspires to transcend itself qua

philosophical reality. The philosopher who sees himself qua philosopher as complete wisdom is living in the
world of the imagination, and his weakness becomes evident when he tries to achieve what is humanly possible
through his philosophy. Philosophy is self-contradictory
and self-destructive when it claims its independence
from the non-philosophical, and that it could entirely
be self-sufficient.

(Lefebvre, [1984], 1999: 12–13)

Why Arab thought?

Why do I see it a necessary intellectual task to re-articulate and
situate the project of Arab cultural studies/media studies (see
Chapter 6) and the study of Arab everyday cultures within discourses of contemporary Arab thought? Why go back to Arab
thought, which is, in the main, *Cartesian*? Why be concerned with
Arab thought/philosophy when the main objective of the book is to
actually draw the reader's attention to Arab everyday life as a possible study area? There are other related questions: Why not leave
Arab philosophy and thought to the qualified philosopher or
thinker? In fact, why should the Arab philosopher want to be concerned with what people say in the market, at work or the *shisha*
café, never mind the live concert, the football match, street or
queue? Do these spaces matter? Of course they do, for they are the
kind of places where being manifests itself for us in the world; yet
for the Arab philosopher, they are, in the main, part of an unconscious culture. Everyday experience is itself, in a classic Althusserian
way, inadequate and cannot help us understand the world because
the masses' engagement with the 'everyday' is thwarted by a 'false
consciousness' that only the philosopher and thinker are qualified to expose and analyse. That is the conventional wisdom.
Contemporary Arab thought is part of the foregrounding based on
which I chose to articulate aspects of Arab modernness. The deci-
sion is, of course, not random, for I see (and will later show) how

contemporary Arab thought can inform the study of Arab everyday life and how the latter, in turn, can inform self-referentialities enunciated by young Arabs as anthropological subjects (see Chapter 5), and *vice versa*. The structure is thus relational and derives meaning from its constituents' interaction. Dominant discourses in contemporary Arab thought are more concerned with structuring and orchestrating narratives of *becoming* than with the kind of *being* they are anxious to deliver from wretchedness and ahistoricity. This gap – the ontological/ontologising/ontic gap – is, I argue, at the heart of the Arab intellectual impasse. Arab philosophers/thinkers have forgotten about the world and matters concerning *being*. Is it possible to articulate the phenomenon of the 'modern' or 'modernity' from a purely theoretical/*Cartesian* perspective? The answer is yes, of course, but the kind of repertoire we will generate – what Lalande calls *la raison constituée* – through this choice of method can only tell us about Arab 'modernity' that has been rationalised through consciousness as a form of *transcendental subjectivity*, in the mind of the thinker, rather than what's outside it – the world, that is. The question posed thus far in contemporary Arab thought is mostly concerned with the *whatness* of things – 'What modernity is?' rather than the *howness* of things, that is, 'How do we explain, interpret and analyse how *being* modern in the Arab world manifests itself for us?' What I am proposing here is a paradigmatic shift, a kind of transition from one kind of thinking to another: a dual take on understanding phenomena in Arab cultures that does not undermine the ontic/ontological manifestations of *being*. What is sought here is not a *Kuhnian* paradigmatic revolution (Kuhn, 1996) that does away with the old to make way for the new. What is sought is far more modest: a broader and interdisciplinary approach to the study of cultural phenomena in the Arab world. Why is this shift necessary? Mohammed Abed al-Jabri (undoubtedly the most influential and critical of contemporary Arab philosophers) makes a plausible argument about what he calls the 'problematic' of Arab cultural temporality. Using Jean Piaget's concept of the 'unconscious', Al-Jabri (1989, 1991, 1994,

1996, 2000, 2001) observes in his *Critique of Arab Reason* that Arab cultural time is confused, disorganised and incoherent. This incoherence or 'unconsciousness', Al-Jabri argues, is due to the overlapping of the old and the new in 'Arab culture'. The Arab cultural repertoire is 'unconscious' because it lacks *systematicity*, continuity and linearity. The answer to this problem, for Al-Jabri, is to deconstruct *turath* (Arab-Islamic cultural heritage), reorganise it from within, then modernise it using Western methodology so it can inform questions of the present, forming a linear and orderly structure of thought. I fully agree with Al-Jabri here (even if I am not totally sure about the notion of linearity and its implications for critical thinking), but this alone, I argue, will not solve the problem of the unconscious in Arab cultural temporality. For Arabs to be conscious of their cultural temporalities, they also need to find ways to deal with the present and what it has to offer them. No cultural temporality can be conscious or coherent if it is unconscious of the present – the present tense of its culture – and this means the everyday: television, cinema, art, jokes, communication, cooking, work, the ordinary, anthropological space and all the other manifestations of everyday life. Furthermore, since this book makes the case for Arab cultural studies (see Chapter 6) as a new epistemic space for the study of the everyday in the Arab region, it makes sense to ask, from a purely epistemological point, that is: What are the best possible and available reference points for such an epistemic space? What will it rely upon, hermeneutically, that will make sense of the world? Enunciating Arab cultural studies through a process of negotiation and dialogue with the key *problematics* in Arab thought is an attempt to reconcile thought and being in the Arab cultural repertoire; it is also an attempt to ontologise thought (including the articulations of the 'modern'), guaranteeing a certain level of interdisciplinarity, which, in the long term, will inform both Arab philosophy, its critical project and the field of enquiry into Arab media, culture and society. However, the bridging task is far from straight forward. The question that must be asked here is: what kind of discourses within Arab thought qualify as the best and most useful reference points through which to enquire into Arab media, culture and society? Here, we face two main problems: First, Arab thought is a vast field and accommodates a number of areas, including political, religious and nationalist thoughts. We can also add ethics, aesthetics, theology, epistemology and other such areas. Second, as in any field of study or discursive formation, there are dominant and less dominant discourses within these areas of thought, and opting for certain discourses as a reference point just because they are dominant may not necessarily be the best way to go about this bridging task. To deal with the first problem (the problem of relevance and specificity), I chose to concentrate on discourses within contemporary Arab thought that have articulated the question of modernity, especially the relationship between *turath* (heritage) and *hadatha* (modernity). Another reason for this is the privilege of hindsight concerning historiographies of media studies and cultural studies in the West. Since the latter were reactions to pathologies of modernity (Scannell, 2007), it makes it reasonable for us to argue, in the Arab case, that conceptualising Arab cultural studies necessitates *a priori* an engagement with discourses on 'modernity' as they are thought in Arab scholarship. In dealing with the second problem, I resort yet again to Khatibi's *double-critique* (1980), hoping that such a method will serve as a critical tool for highlighting: a) the problems of key Arab discourses on the 'modern', and, b) unearthing, at the same time, those discourses on Arab identity that remain on the margins of contemporary Arab thought. I use the term Arab thought with some unease, as I am more in favour of a universalistic, *dialogic* approach to thought and thinking. I do not intend to investigate what thought in Arab thought is 'Arab' and what is not, but what I can say with some level of certainty is that what we call contemporary Arab thought is, in the main, the product of close interactions and encounters with Western thought and methodology, and to use Arkoun's term (2006), there are two 'unthoughts' in the Arab cultural repertoire today that play a part in deepening the Arab intellectual impasse: a) a great number of Arab philosophers is indifferent to the role of media and Arab popular cultures as sites of power and change. Philosophy is for many of them beyond the media, popular culture and everyday life, and this is largely due the way they understand culture, which is still very much in an Arnoldian stage – culture is the best that has been said and written, b) the second *unthought*[11] is inherent to the compendium of research into Arab media, culture and society, to which both Arab and Western scholars have contributed. What characterises the latter, to use Abdurrahman's term, is *ebda' mafssul* (disconnected creativity), rather than *ebda' mawssul* (connective/connected creativity) (Abdurrahman, 2002). Debates on the subject of Arab media, culture and society have largely been uncritically contextualised within readily available, often borrowed, conceptual frames of analysis that are detached from *argumentations* and debates inherent to Arab thought and its problems. And even where the creative process has begun to show aspects of connectivity to the Arab-Islamic cultural repertoire, discourses of *ta'seel* (authentication) have unfortunately become *the* main intellectual objective, leaving little space for self-reflection and critique. This calls for another intellectual task – of subverting and troubling its claims to authenticity. I call this process the de-de-Westernising of 'de-Westernisation' theory.

In this chapter, and for practical reasons, my focus will mostly, but not entirely, be on the philosophical discourse emerging from the Arab Maghreb, which, by the respected Egyptian thinker Hassan Hanafi's admission, 'has surpassed the *Mashriq* with its daring thought and methodology . . . and for its prioritizing of method over subject, the new over the old and modernity over *turath*' (Hanafi, 2002: 31). The Arab philosophical discourse on modernity is polarised by a struggle for origins and *models*. The outcome is a binary structure with one group adhering to the *ussuleyat* (originations) inherent to the Arab-Islamic heritage, and the other, to *ussuleyat* inherent to Western modernity (Al-Jabri, 1989). Debate on modernity in contemporary Arab thought is multifaceted and occupies different cultural temporalities. It is framed and discussed within different stages of Modernity's development (as a philosophical concept) and, as such, is at once Hegelian, Heideggerian, Neo-Marxist; Althusserian, Foucauldian, modernist and postmodernist. The 'West', because of its dual nature as 'model' and 'enemy', is presented in contemporary Arab thought not merely as a civilisational alternative but also as a kind of *assl* (originality/origin) that belongs to the future rather than the past (Al-Jabri, 1989). The perpetual oscillation between *turath* and *hadatha* is a key aspect of Arab philosophical discourse on modernity and is what largely motivates the discourses of Arab authenticity. Al-Jabri traces the struggle for authenticity to the Arab *Nahda* (Renaissance) of the late nineteenth and early twentieth centuries:

> Duality of the *exogenous* [the West] into a threat as well as a civilisational model (the enemy and the model at the same time) has led to the dualisation of the 'modern' in the Arab Renaissance's position towards the past and the future. This also resulted in an overlap in the Renaissance mechanism between return to the *roots* and departure from them to the future ... This made the Renaissance of Arab thought problematic. It is also what we have been used to calling the *assala* and *mu'assara* problematic.[12]
>
> (Al-Jabri, 1989: 20)

The *assala/mu'assara*[13] debate continues to be at the heart of the contemporary Arab philosophical discourse on modernity. To bring some sort of order to what is very much a chaotic and disorganised debate, I have, with some hesitation, devised a typology of four key positions. Doubtless, such an exercise always comes with shortcomings. Some of the statements and lines of thinking within the same positions, as I will later explain, overlap and can even be contradictory, making any attempt to typologise problematic, and as with any selective process, some formations will undoubtedly be left out. However, to assuage my scientific guilt, I can say with a good degree of certainty that the chosen positions represent *some* of the most debated and important discourses on the *assala/mu'assara* debate in contemporary Arab thought. These are:

- The historicist/Marxist position
- The rationalist/structuralist position
- The cultural *salafist/turatheya* position
- The anti-essentialist position

Each of the four positions provides a diagnosis and remedy for the Arab intellectual crisis; yet the dialectics they produce, with the exception of the fourth position, which promises to transcend the duality problematic, still find them in a pre-Hegelian stage.

The historicist/Marxist position

The key figure in this position is Abdullah Laroui, a historian who dedicated his cultural/historical project to the question of modernity[14]. As he puts it, in *Mafhum al-'aql* (The Meaning of Reason): 'All I have written so far can be considered as parts in one volume, on the meaning of modernity' (2001: 14). Laroui's call for a radical/ decisive epistemological break with the past, what he calls *hassm*, has been a key contribution to the Arab philosophical discourse on modernity. Progress and development in the Arab world, asserts Laroui, can be achieved only if and when a *decisive* break with the past and its heritage takes place, and also when Arabs are conscious of their own history and their role in it. Western historical materialism (Marxist historicism, to be precise) and its revolutionary politics, for Laroui, is the only viable strategy to get away from cultural *salafism*, the superficialities of liberalism and technocracy, and the only route to modernity (Laroui, 1973). However, Laroui's radical break with the past (Laroui, 1973, 1996, 2001) must not be confused with an outright rejection of *ussul* or cultural heritage. For Laroui, this still remains a very important object of enquiry. What he rejects, however, are the Arab-Islamic heritage's value systems. As he puts it: 'If, as the theologian/philosopher thinks value is the absolute, then the modern man is the man of non-value, he who expects nothing to be definitive'[15] (Laroui, 2001: 72). For Laroui, the main reason for Arab intellectual digression is the Arab's inability to realise the historical split that took place between the secular realities in the Arab world and cultural heritage (1973).

The rationalist/structuralist position

Mohammed Abed al-Jabri (who represents the key voice in this position) has a different take on *turath* (heritage). Rather than breaking with the past aesthetically, ethically and epistemologically, Al-Jabri refutes Laroui's 'universalism' (Western historical materialism) arguing for the historicisation of *turath* by modernising it from within, so that it reconciles with the present and the new realities of Arab cultures. Al-Jabri calls for *al-infissal min ajl al-ittissal* (to disconnect in order to reconnect) as a strategy to solve the problem of the 'unconscious' in Arab cultural temporality. For Al-Jabri, the main problems with Arab thought and the Arab intellectual crisis are inherent to a structural/epistemological problem in modes of Arab reasoning. The *turath* and modernity problematic, observes Al-Jabri, is not moved by class struggle but 'by cultural and conceptual issues dealing with thought and its structure' (1989: 24). Al-Jabri, like any intellectual, is the product of historical moments. He, like a number of predominant pan-Arab intellectuals, Laroui included, has had his intellectual formations shaped by key historical events: the occupation of Palestine in 1948, the nationalisation of the Suez Canal by Nasser in July 1956 and the Arab-Israeli wars of 1967 and 1973. These events have shaped a whole political consciousness and dictated the kind of hermeneutics relied upon to interpret 'Arabnness' and 'Arab culture' by a whole generation of Arab intellectuals. The pan-Arab interpretation of culture's function is an interesting one. The term 'Arab world' is divided into two unifying terminologies: *Al-watan al-Arabi* and *al-ummah al-Arabiya*. The first term denotes geographic unity; and the second alludes to some sort of spiritual ('Din' religion) common experience (Al-Jabri,

1994: 25). According to Al-Jabri, the main historical characteristic of 'culture' is inherent to its function as a unifier. Here, the awakening of Arab consciousness is predicated on culture's ability to unify. Culture's historical function and purpose, according to Al-Jabri, a pan-Arabist *par excellence*, is to help transform the Arab world from a mere geographic space (*al-watan al-Arabi*) to *al-ummah al-Arabiya*, a space bound by common experience and consciousness (Al-Jabri, 1994: 25–7)[16].

The cultural salafist/turatheya *position*

Arab-Islamic heritage is a key component of Arab culture and makes for the best, if not the only, possible and coherent civilisational model. This position is intricate[17] and contested and can easily be unpicked through a dozen different positions, some even contradictory. The term *turatheya* is derived from *turath*, meaning heritage. Taha Abdurrahman (2006) differentiates between *turatheya* and *turathaweyah*. The former refers to schools of thought that privilege *turath* (cultural heritage) as a civilisational model and reference point. The latter (*turathaweyah*), however, is a more orthodox position within *turatheya* that takes Islamic heritage as the *only* acceptable narrative for happiness and vehemently/defensively rejects all others. There is no room for otherness, tolerance or double-identity in this position. He also distinguishes between *hadatheyah* and *hadathaweyah*. A *hadathi* is an intellectual who embraces modernity as a necessary phase of human development and is prepared to negotiate a local narrative of the modern (Al-Jabri being a good example). A *hadathawi*, however, is a kind of radical intellectual, perhaps like Laroui, who is not afraid to argue for a decisive break with the past. The cultural salafist position varies from the *turathi* to the *turathawi*. What gives the cultural salafist position some sort of coherence, as a discursive formation, is its adherents' hanging on to the 'utopian idea of a recoverable past', (Al-Azmeh, 1993: 51) the thinking/methodology; perhaps illusion, which answers to the Arab/Islamic world's present problems can be found in a past/timeless temporality (the golden Islamic era of *Ahl al-salaf al-saleh*[18]). From this position the struggle is driven by the privileging of the past over the present and an illusory *authenticity* over *difference*.

The anti-essentialist position

Parallel to these three dominant positions lies a fourth discourse that has remained almost unnoticed at the margins of contemporary Arab thought. Its advocates call it *tajawuz* – a philosophy promising to surpass the duality problematic between modernity and heritage. This group may hold the key to the Arab intellectual impasse, but they face both endogenous and exogenous obstacles, and the two are interrelated. Historically, when under outside threat (and here I refer to imperialism), Arab scholars have tended to move from being enlightened rationalists to becoming traditionalists (Laroui, 1976). The first casualty here is thought itself, as it shifts from the rational to the dogmatic. This also explains why the work of contemporary Arab thinkers such as Abdelkabir Khatibi[19] (1980), 'Abdel-Salam Binabdal'ali (1983, 2000, 2002), Abdul-Aziz Boumesshouli (2001, 2003, 2005, 2006, 2007), Fatima Mernissi and the late Edward Said has never found the same resonance or reception in the Arab intellectual scene as work that is embedded in essentialist ideologies of cultural unity – nationalism, pan-Islamism and pan-Arabism – does. The threat of imperialism prompted defensive reactionary positions, justifying intoxicated discourses of unity and salafism. Imperialism, it is important to add, is a system that subverts not only consciousness and institutional structures but also thought and its development. The fourth position can be encapsulated in the philosophy of *tajawuz*[20]. Its key intellectuals reject ideological discourses of identity and situate both heritage and even modernity within a position of différance, where both tradition and philosophy become objects of critique and subversion, thus Khatibi's famous call for a double-semiotics and *double-critique* as *double-death* (death here implying the birth

of difference as the source of new questions and ways of knowing). The advocates of this position, headed by Khatibi, constitute
a very small minority in contemporary Arab thought. They champion otherness, alterity, pluralism, fragmentation, non-linearity
and the constant questioning of essentialised Arab discourses of
becoming. *Turath* for them, to use Khatibi's phrase, is nothing but
'the return of the forgotten dead' (1980: 17–18). Khatibi finds the
'savage difference' vis-à-vis the West and what he calls 'blind identity', naïve, patriotic, nationalist, ideological and leading to nothing
but a theoretical trap. Instead, he calls for critical work that dis-
turbs the metaphysical soils monopolising Arab thought, mainly:
the metaphysics of God or *lahut*, the metaphysics of sects or *maz-
ahib* and the metaphysics of technique (Khatibi, 1980: 17–18).
Khatibi's take on history and *turath* is different from Laroui's, as
he refuses to articulate *turath* through any philosophy of History
(Binabdal'ali, 2002: 60). He critiques Laroui's ideological take on
history for its generalisations (*shumuleyat*) and considers it a type
of metaphysics that champions organisation, continuity and *will*,
but does not consider difference, otherness, chaos or non-linearity
(1980). Binabdal'ali, on the other hand, stresses that Arab thought
cannot move forward lest its problematics are framed within key
changes or 'revolutions' in world contemporary thought: a) a semi-
ological revolution that led to a re-examination of *interpretation*
and the creation of meaning; b) an epistemological revolution
that disturbed the philosophy of the *cogito* and c) the philosophical revolution that reversed Platonism, championing the truth of
the body (2002: 18–19). Thought in the Arab cultural repertoire
has become stagnant, affirms Binabdal'ali, because it was disconnected from the event (1983) and thus calls for a reconnection
between Arab philosophy and *event*. Both Khatibi and Binabdal'ali
champion universalism and the de-territorialisation of thought.
Binabdal'ali uses Heidegger's take on *metaphysics* and Derrida's
deconstructionist approach to articulate his position in relation to
turath and other key aspects of thought in the Arab philosophical
repertoire. He calls for a rereading of *turath* with différance as a

way of surpassing it. His take on différance, as a way of dealing with essentialised forms of identity and *turath*, can also be traced back to Hegel's *dialectics*. However, Binabdal'ali argues for a different kind of *dialectics*: one that liberates difference from fixed and absolute forms of oppositionality. He calls for a distancing of the two opposites so they are brought nearer – and that is exactly what Heidegger means by '*ontological difference*' (Sheikh, 2007: 44). Binabdal'ali and his followers from the same intellectual position seek to surpass not only naïve *metaphysics* as we live it in the Arab-Islamic world but also philosophical metaphysics (Boumesshouli, 2007: 45).

Problematising the four positions

These positions are, of course, not fixed, since some of them overlap. The rationalist/structuralist position does not make the historicist or *turatheya* positions either less rational or irrational. In other words, these positions are not anti-rationalist. It is the insistence of the *turathaweya school* on finding solutions for the present using lessons from the past, and its defensive/critical stance towards the modalities of Western rationality, that positions it within the discourse of *turathaweya* and cultural salafism. Giddens captures this position succinctly in his *Modernity and Self-Identity*, arguing that the 'fixity of tradition does not derive from its accumulation of past wisdom; rather, coordination of the past with the present' (Giddens, 1991:145). It is odd, however, how *the turathaweya* position and its authenticators accept contemporaniety – a product of modernity – when it comes to technology, economy and other spheres of life, but not when it comes to the intellectual sphere. As Al-Jabri puts it:

> The problem that faces us does not lie in choosing which civilisational model to opt for: modernity, or *assala*, or the reconciliation of the two, but the problem, in truth, lies in the duality of our position

towards this duality. We accept this duality at the
level of modernisation and the need to modernise the economy, and other contemporary sectors,
political, social and educational ... However, at
the same time we refuse this *duality* on other levels: spiritual and intellectual life.[21]

(Al-Jabri, 1989: 13)

Aziz al-Azmeh problematises this *duality* further by pointing out
that debates on authenticity/turath and contemporaniety/moder-
nity take it for granted that *authenticity/assala* is monolithic,
when it is, in fact, a discourse with different and competing voices
(Al-Azmeh, 1992: 18–21). Al-Azmeh provides a nuanced critique
of *assala* in contemporary Arab thought by calling into question
not only the claims to *assala* but also the nature and *structure* of
the claimed *authenticity/assala*. Here, authenticity is unpicked as
discourse that cannot be tied to one meaning or paradigm but to a
multiplicity of complex and, at times, conflicting voices. Al-Azmeh
thus objectifies *assala* as discourse and calls for its deconstruction
and subversion. *Assala* in its twentieth-century pan-Arab and
pan-Islamic sense, as Al-Azmeh interestingly observes, finds its
origin, not in the Arab-Islamic tradition but in the Western repertoire, particularly in its meanings of *dialectics* (Al-Azmeh, 1992:
24). So, what often presents and defines itself as *assil* (original and
authentic) frequently camouflages the very identity of the *assala* it
advances. The opposite of contemporaniety, argues Abu al-Majd, is
not *assala* but *salafiyya*[22] and *turatheya* (Abu al-Majd in Al-Azmeh,
1992: 26). Al-Azmeh also demonstrates how authentication as
Islamisation often takes place within a discourse that largely serves
the *telos* of the *authenticator* rather than Islam. In this case, it is
not Islam that determines the particularity of a certain institution
or history but the history and institution that determine Islam and
its culture (Al-Azmeh, 1992: 28). Taha Abdurrahman divides cultural heritage *turath* and its past into two elements: the past events
and the past of values (Abdurrahman, 2002). Khatibi, on the other

hand, provides a more nuanced interpretation using a distinction between *originalité* (originality) and *originarité* (origination). Khatibi favours dealing with heritage as a moving *source* (or source in flux), rather than that which is 'authentic' and static. However, to frame all attempts at *authentication* as *salafist*, or as purely ideological, would be misleading. Taha Abdurrahman, the Arab philosopher who advocated the Arab right to philosophical difference (2002) provides a more critical discourse of Arab authenticity that privileges the spirit of modernity over that of Western modernity. According to Abdurrahman, the spirit of modernity has three main aspects that can be summarised into three principles: *Rushd* (based on independence or liberation and creativity), *critique* (based on the transition from belief without evidence to an evidence-based critique) and *Shumul* (moving from the particular to the general). The historical reality of modernity, argues Abdurrahman, is not the same as its spirit, even if this reality results from the practice of this spirit. Rather, the reality of modernity is specific to a choice from different possibilities or modalities of the spirit of modernity (Abdurrahman, 2006). Reason, he argues, is not static; it is fluid and constantly changing. There is not just one kind of rationality, but different rationalities[23]. Abdurrahman (2006) also critiques the limitations of Western rationality in privileging physical, worldly and objective phenomena over ethics or values. His call for the '*ethicisation*' of modernity is a double-edged critique, directed at both the Western rationalist project and voices from within Arab philosophical discourse on modernity (known as the rationalists), which, according to him, propagate Western modalities of rationality, with little care for critiquing its limitations. What Abdurrahman calls for is not merely a rational society, but a rational-ethical-society.

Ontologising the 'modern'

The ongoing argumentations within the duality problematic, however, are not specific to the Arab world or to Arab philosophical discourse on modernity, as they have also formed part of the debate in the West and elsewhere. Dealing with the issue of heritage (religion or tradition and modernity) in Western philosophical discourse of modernity can easily be traced to Hegel, who was against both religious orthodoxy and the religion of reason (Habermas, 1987: 25). Other examples can also be given from Walter Benjamin's take on tradition (ibid) and Baudelaire's harmonising between Modernity's 'fleeting transient' and the 'immovable' sacred (Baudelaire in Habermas, 1987: 10). However, what the Arab discourse on modernity is not about, as yet, is humans and lived experience. We simply cannot make sense of modernity in the Arab world today without making sense of what it means to be modern (modernness), and if living in a mass mediated world is part of modern experience, then a philosophical discourse that ignores this surely lacks contemporaniety – a key component of modernity. Furthermore, the cultural time-consciousness of Arab modernity cannot be reassured of its time and consciousness solely through *Cartesian* doubt or through its historicist/rationalist/salafist schools. And, if we are to make use of Arab discourse on modernity as a bridge to understand contemporary Arab, media, culture and society, then we must begin by removing it from its discourse or, should I say, metaphysics, making it an object for critique before it can become a tool of critique. As the Arab discourse on modernity is heavily influenced by Western thought and methodology, (especially the 'rationalist' and 'historicist' positions), it has unwittingly inherited a much debated problematic in modern Western epistemology, which can be traced to Descartes whose starting point in thinking the world was not 'the facticity (the actual matter-of-factness) of the actually existing living world', but 'the contents of his own mind' (Scannell, 2007: 3–23). This is, to quote Scannell, a *Heideggerian* par excellence, 'where an awful lot of modern philosophers and others start' (Scannell, 2007: 3–23). The Arab philosophical discourse on modernity has yet to ontologise or humanise its take on modernity; that is, to become able to deal with its sociological and anthropological significance.

Those who threaten to do just this (the anti-essentialist position) are sidelined as ahistorical and marginal. Although their attempts to ontologise Arab thought and Arab discourses on modernity are still at their 'pre-conceptual stage', their philosophy of *tajawuz* (transcendence) brings with it a cannon of hope, not only for Arab thought but also for Arab critical philosophy, as a whole. The kind of work with which the anti-essentialist position thinkers have so far engaged grapples with what the Arab philosopher Mohammed Arkoun describes as the 'unthinkable' and 'unthought' in contemporary Arab thought. (Arkoun, 2006: 31). How we deal with this marginalised, yet exciting, school of Arab thought calls for what Arkoun articulates as 'emergent reason' or 'reason in crisis', that is: 'meanings, effects of meaning and horizons of meaning do not emerge only where hegemonic reason is active, along with its unequalled means of action, creation and invention; we have to be able to hear voices reduced to silence, heterodox voices, minority voices, the voices of the vanquished and the marginalized, if we are to develop a reason capable of encompassing the human condition' (Arkoun, 2006: 33).

Manifestations of the *duality* problematic in recent discourses of media theory 'de-Westernisation'

The old/new *dual* debate on *assala* and *mu'asara* (tradition/ modernity) is not unrelated to the ongoing attempts by some Arab-Muslim scholars to *de-Westernise* media and communication theory. In fact, this discourse of authentication is nothing other than a reflection of the *duality* problematic described earlier. It is essential that the Arab discourses of the 'de-Westernisation' and 'internationalisation' of media theory are understood and articulated within the *assala* and *contemporaniety* problematic, and within the broader discourse of Arab modernity. No serious discussion on Arab media, culture and society can ignore such debate, for I see the 'de-Westernisation' discourse as an extension of it. Relatively recent pieces of work by Mohammad Ayish, entitled *Beyond Western Communication Theories: A Normative Arab Islamic Perspective* (2003), and by Basyouni Hamada, entitled *Islamic Culture Theory* (2001), are two attempts at 'de-Westernisation', which also reflect the *duality* in Arab thought articulated by Al-Jabri. On the one hand, Ayish provides us with an interesting and insightful analysis that theorises Arab-Muslim communications and their audiences, while tracing and making use of characteristics inherent to Arab heritage that date back to the *jahiliya* (the period predating Islam). Hamada, on the other hand, adduces what he considers to be a coherent set of Islamic cultural principles, which he recommends as a normative framework for governance of the media in a 'just' and democratic Islamic society. Hamada's point of reference is Islam and particularly the Koran, a text that satisfies (and in fact preaches) all the prerequisite elements recommended by the author to guarantee a democratic Islamic 'public sphere'. Both the authors' attempts to de-Westernise media and communication theory – and, in Hamada's case, to formulate an Islamic *Shura*-based public sphere – are useful, but if we are to remain faithful to Khatibi's proposed *double-critique,* such an intellectual process (that of authentication) has to be accompanied by de-authentication and de-de-Westernisation. Although I make the case elsewhere that the hermeneutics upon which we rely to interpret media, culture and society in the Arab world ought to be broadened to include a category that precedes both the 'social' and the 'cultural', namely the 'existential', I also believe that the latter category should be articulated in ways that do not put it above debate or critique. 'Islamic culture', as it appears in Ayish's and Hamada's work, is a taken-for-granted category. It is articulated as *thinkable* and part of a closed process when, if anything, conceptualisations of 'Islamic culture theory' are possible only if and when we are prepared to objectify 'Islamic culture', making it open to an ongoing process of re-articulation and reinterpretation. A reworking of the idea of Arab and Islamic culture is fundamental and should precede all attempts to theorise media, culture and society in the Arab and Islamic worlds.

Conclusion

I have no doubt that aspects of modernness can be found in all the intellectual positions discussed above, with the exception of the orthodox salafist position, of course. The problem lies not with the *hadathi* (modernist) or the *turathi* (cultural heritage) intellectual, but it is with the more orthodox positions within these lines of thought: for example, the *hadathawi,* who maintains that only Marxist historical materialism or Western modalities of rationalism will work and the *turathawi,* who strongly rejects any form of dialogic conversation with the other. Modernness in thought should not necessarily be predicated on the annihilation of tradition or *turath*; a post-traditional world 'where all that is solid melts into air' (Marx in Berman, 1983). In other words, it would be facile to read modernness as a post-traditional order that does away with morality and all aspects of traditional societies. The aspects of modernness, as I will later show, are more visible in the ceaseless and perpetual, Baudelairian negotiation between the modern, the transient and the sacred, the new and the old. The philosophy of *tajawuz,* led by the fourth intellectual position, and which claims to transcend the duality problematic (tradition/modernity) through the championing of difference, alterity and the de-territorialisation of thought, may have to accept that what is being transcended here is not the duality *per se* but how we conceive of it and deal with it, and the two things are entirely different. By making both the modern and the traditional subject to a *double-critique*, we are not really abolishing the duality problematic, but we are undoubtedly changing how we think it, and that is an aspect of modernness *par excellence.* Here *double-critique* as 'double-death' makes both modernity and tradition vulnerable, championing critical reason instead of authenticity, difference instead of sameness and creativity instead of orthodoxy.

3

Arab Popular Cultures and
Everyday Life

What is the difference between you and us, and you, you
and me.

> (Nass Al-Ghiwan, an Arab-Moroccan pop band from
> the 60s and 70s)

It's been five months since we met
Love passed through here S Loves M

> (Graffiti from Qassr Nile Bridge, Cairo, 2007)

Nass Al-Ghiwan's famous lyrics cost them, according to popular
folklore, a brief jail sentence because they used it in their theatrical,
hippy fashion to address government officials sitting in the front
row during one of their live concerts. This event symbolises the
moment when the 'popular' (*sha'bi*) speaks to power. At the heart
of their simple yet politically charged lyrics lie questions of class,
cultural stratification and resistance through art. The 'us and you'
dichotomy, masterly put by this young Moroccan band, echoes
Hoggart's *The Uses of Literacy* (1957), especially the chapter entitled: '"Them" and "Us"' where he famously articulates the 'they' as

'the people at the top', 'the higher-ups', the people who give you your dole, call you up, tell you to go to war, fine you... 'aren't really to be trusted', 'talk posh'... treat you like muck' (Hoggart, [1957], 1992: 72–3). These are exactly the kind of people at whom *Nass Al-Ghiwan* were pointing the finger, shaming them by the intoxicated delight of the live concert audience who cheered their heroes, the heroes of the Moroccan working classes. The government officials represented an oppressive and corrupt system and, therefore, by pointing the finger at them, *Nass Al-Ghiwan*, young, poor Casablancans from *Derb Al-Kabir* were rebelling against the whole power system. What do we know about the cultures of the Arab working classes – the classes who, incidentally, make up the majority of Arab populations? Who speaks for them? What determines Arab popular cultures and how can they be objectified as systematic fields of scientific enquiry? How and in what ways are discourses of modernness played out in the everyday of Arab popular cultures? There are dozens of books, theses and journal articles on 'Arab culture', its modes, problems and future. The majority of these are written in the Arabic language, though there are also numerous publications on the subject in French, English and other European languages. The Centre for the Study of Arab Unity[24] alone has produced dozens of books (both single-authored and edited collections) that attempt to deal, through different capacities and specificities, with the future and challenges that face 'Arab Culture'[25]. Although, the number of publications that deal with the challenges facing 'Arab culture', and here I use the category 'Arab culture' in the most generic and unreflexive fashion, demonstrates the importance that this category occupies in the contemporary Arab cultural repertoire, it would be facile and simplistic to use 'abundance' or quantity as a measure for, or an assessment of, the quality of this repertoire. The undeniable richness and diversity of such work is undermined by key problems that have prevented the study of Arab culture's metamorphosis from a fragmented whole into a conscious and conjunctional intellectual project. When I say 'conscious', I do not exactly mean 'political consciousness', for much of the work on

'Arab culture' is driven by a clear historicist telos. What is some-what ironic is that while the historicisation of the category 'Arab culture' has made it into a politically conscious and coherent intel-lectual project, it has simultaneously alienated other types of her-meneutics about 'culture', especially those competing for broader and non-essentialist definitions, thus limiting what could be said about this category beyond the prism of the ideological and the kinds of *metaphysics* this brings with it. The framing of 'Arab cul-ture' within pan-Arabist, nationalist, Islamicist and Salafist dis-courses has indeed contributed to the historicisation of the category, but in the meantime, I argue, this process has led to an *epistemo-logical* impasse, underlined by the dominance of very few interpre-tations of 'Arab culture'. Here, the political historicisation of 'culture' becomes a mere philosophical metaphysics, as it limits what can be said about Arab culture or identity to a narrow and fixed frame of analysis. Therefore, by the 'unconscious' in the discourse on 'Arab culture' in the first instance I am referring to an epistemic and par-adigmatic deficit and not necessarily to a political one (although the two are, of course, not entirely unrelated). Just as there are mul-tiple discourses on the 'modern' and 'modernity' in the Arab cul-tural repertoire (some more dominant than others), there are also different discourses on 'culture'. These two contested thought posi-tions are relational, since those discourses that dominate debate on the *assala* (tradition)/*hadatha* (modernity) duality (see Chapter 2) also dictate how the category 'culture' is articulated, thought of and appropriated. All the three dominant positions in Arab thought (the historicist, the rationalist/structuralist and the cultural salafist) articulate the category culture within frames that justify the posi-tions' ideological *telos*. This leaves the fourth and less dominant position (the anti-essentialist position), discussed earlier, on the margins of Arab cultural/identity discourse yet again. The domi-nant discourses on 'Arab culture' are still frozen at a metaphysical, *Cartesian* and, one might add, an aesthetic/elitist stage, almost oblivious to the anthropological factors and the socio-economic and cultural transformations that determine contemporary Arab cultures. What is required here is not so much a task of bridging, as attempted in Chapter 2 between Arab thought and everyday life, but one of *dislocation*. Here, the intellectual task is to expose the artificial, discursive conjunction between Arab thought (the philosophical repertoire/its historicised discourses of becoming) and its articulations of culture – that is, to break and unveil this artificial conjunction by removing it from its discourse. The point of dislocating/disturbing the conjunction between articulations of culture and the discourses of Arab *becoming* should not be confused with an attack on any possible form of Arab historicity. This would be to miss the point. Nor should this be confused with an attempt to depoliticise Arab cultures or, indeed, discourses on Arab cultures. If we are to treat 'Arab cultures' as objects of scientific enquiry, we must be prepared for the archaeological task that comes with it. We must be prepared to implement Khatibi's *double-critique* (1980) by questioning, interrogating and disturbing the continuities, totalisations and teleologies inherent to Arab discourses on culture and identity. Defining Arab cultures through the prism of 'Islamicism', 'historical materialism' or 'Arab nationalism' limits what can be said about 'culture'. Such limits, usually borne out of quiet and undisturbed continuities, must be troubled and exposed. The task of *dislocation* is useful here, as it will open up space that allows for broader and less totalising articulations of Arab culture/identity to emerge. *Dislocation* is also a way to accommodate and free new political expressions and new spaces of resistance. Therefore, *dislocation* rather than being a tool of de-historicisation or de-politicisation may lead to the creation of new and alternative discourses of *becoming*. The epistemic deficit in the study of 'Arab culture' is also the result of a web of interconnected sub-deficits that are inherent to the Arab cultural repertoire and to the quasi-hegemonic apparatus of the Arab states, including their intelligentsia, media and educational systems (see Hussein, 1975). Furthermore, conceptualisations of 'Arab culture' remain largely non-linear, without coherent structure or sense of direction. There are three key methodological problematics, not detached from those described above, which I think stand in the way of a broader and more engaging interpretation of 'Arab culture'. Framing 'Arab culture' within essentialist discourses of *authenticity* and unity masks differences (social and cultural stratification) and undermines anthropological interpretations of the everyday. Arab intellectuals' attempts to mobilise the masses through a historicised articulation of culture have ironically failed: a) to recognise the role of 'popular culture' as a site for the production of political meaning and also, b) by downplaying the centrality of 'the everyday' to the Arab masses and their cultures. The second problematic is an outcome of the first and is manifest in the analytical vacuum that exists between 'official', homogenising mediations of Arab cultures and the extraordinary range of contemporary and resistant heterogeneous forms of artistic and carnivalesque expressions, which remain notoriously understudied. What's more, and to highlight a third methodological problematic, I am not convinced that Arab popular cultures have been thought through a concrete structural framework that acknowledges the problematic conjunctions and the fluid, yet interdependent, moments that determine their nature. Arab popular cultures have yet to be rationalised within a relational structure, or through a concretised foregrounding that explores conjunctions between the social, political, economic, existential, anthropological, as well as the dynamics that result from the interface between the 'local' and the 'global'. Both rationalist and salafist positions attack popular culture. While the latter sees popular culture, especially mass mediated culture, as an extension of Western capitalist discourse and its consumerist culture (see Johnson, 1987: 165), the former sees everyday popular culture as 'unconscious' and ahistorical (Al-Jabri, 2001). In these conditions, the culture that prevails, though always been resisted in different ways, is 'the culture of the ear' (Binabdal'ali, 1994: 7–8), that is, that of deference to the state, its intellectuals (both rationalists and salafists), their 'multiplex ideologies' (Johnson, 1987: 171) and different discourses of *becoming*. The result is rather predictable: Arab popular cultures and lived experiences remain, not only on the periphery of Arab intellectual discourse but also on the periphery of political discourses that, ironically, champion the Arab working classes and their concerns.

The recent resurgence of philosophy in contemporary Arab thought (especially in Maghrebi countries, particularly Morocco) is a welcome event. However, as shown in Chapter 2, this development is, for historical reasons, fraught with the dominance of the essentialist, dualistic discourses of Arab 'culture' and 'identity', displacement, or should I say relegation, of anti-essentialist thinking to the margins of Arab intellectual thought. Due to the external threats from Western imperialism and Zionism, it was, and still is, much more fashionable for Arab intellectuals to contextualise their work on 'culture' and 'identity' within frames of nationalistic, pan-Arab and pan-Islamist discourses. Arab intellectuals who have sought to transcend these positions by broadening the notion of 'Arab culture' have been sidelined as *ahistorical* and therefore irrelevant. Attempts to de-essentialise Arab 'culture' and 'identity' have also been equated with treason, abandonment of the Palestinian question and the pan-Arab project (Boumesshouli and Ghabass, 2003)[26]. What is ironic is that it is the anti-essentialist discourses within Arab philosophical thought that hold the key to both the cul-de-sac in which Arab philosophy finds itself and to the reconciliation of Arab philosophy and the everydayness of Arab cultures. Here, I must reiterate, yet again, that the task of *dislocation* is purely epistemological, dealing in the main with an epistemological problem. It is also a way to accommodate the position of the fourth and less dominant school of thought within the Arab intellectual repertoire, which asserts that no discourse is above critique. Locating discourses of Arab culture within fixed ideologised histories of becoming, limits what can be said about culture. It is also the cause of a large discrepancy, or gap, between contemporary articulations of Arab 'culture' and developments in contemporary Arab literature, art, theatre, cinema, television and other forms of artistic expression, whose popularity is due, in the first instance, to their relevance to the questions and problems of everyday life.

Khamissi's novel, *Taxi*; Aswani's novel and its film adaptation, *Ya'kobyan Building*; the Arab version of the reality TV programme, *Star Academy*, and the novel *I Want to Marry* by Abdal'ali (2008), based on the diaries of a female, Egyptian Blogger; not to mention, a range of new Arab film and music genres are extremely popular with Arab audiences because, as texts, they deal with issues relevant to everyday: Arab popular cultures.

Towards a *double-critique* of the everyday

The everyday, asserts Lefebvre, is 'not only a concept but one that may be used as a guide-line for an understanding of society' (Lefebvre, [1984], 1999: 28). However, 'doing everyday life' as we learn from Lefebvre and, much earlier, Adorno, who urged us to distinguish between popular or folk culture and the culture industries (1991), can also be a site of control and ideology. Modernity and its institutions, argues Lefebvre, are responsible for the reification of the everyday by detaching leisure from its festive nature and replacing the latter with a mere 'generalised display': television, cinema and tourism (Lefebvre, [1984], 1999: 54). It is not difficult to find examples from within Arab 'popular cultures' where the 'popular' is reified to serve the state's ideological telos. Work by Laila Abu-Lughod (2005) that explored Egyptian television drama as a form of encounter with the state's hegemonies and its elites (see Chapter 4) is a good example of an interface between the 'popular' and the 'political'; the state and the masses. In dealing with the question of pan-Arabism, Hammond (2007: 66) also asserts that though the latter may have failed as an ideology, it still survives in popular cultural discourses, including those emanating from satellite programming. Although this is true in the case of certain Arab satellite channels that intentionally champion the Arabs' frames of common injustices, for example, Israeli occupation, American imperialist interventions in the Arab region, corruption of Arab regimes, such discourse is so intertwined with the political economy of these channels that it renders them impotent – *une terre brûlé* – to use Ferjani's more radical term (2009)[27], a 'fetishized-catharsis-sphere' that has, for more than a decade, failed to become translated into any concretised form of historical consciousness. However, to limit articulations of the everyday within discourses of reification, or 'false consciousness', is itself a kind of ideological positioning that needs to be questioned? Lefebvre's account of the everyday (and here we could add the accounts of two key Arab intellectuals: Laroui and Al-Jabri, hugely influenced by French philosophy.) draws much from French structuralism; to be precise, from Althusser whom Scannell (in Sabry, 2007a) satirically calls the 'Pope of structuralist Marxism'. For this position or positioning of the everyday, 'lived experience cannot be taken as the ground for anything because it is unconscious in a double sense: it is unreflective (unselfconscious if you like) and therefore gives no account for itself. And it is also unconscious in psychoanalytical terms, and therefore cannot *account* for itself' (Scannell in Sabry, 2007a: 12). Positioning everyday and lived experience along this line of thought clearly limits what can be said about the everyday, popular culture and certainly has serious implications for the ways in which the media and their audiences are articulated. Perhaps, a more nuanced and useful critique of the everyday – one that combines ideology critique with a more culturalist positioning – is advocated by Raymond Williams, who takes lived experience as the ground for a conscious and reflective analysis of culture. Such a paradigmatic reconciliation was the objective of Hall's article: 'Cultural Studies: Two Paradigms' in *Media, Culture and Society* (1980), but where, according to Scannell, Hall fails in his attempt in privileging Althusser over Williams. What I find more exciting about Lefebvre's critique of the 'quotidian' is his insistence on objectifying it by rediscovering it as a crucial arena for study, and also his prompting to find a new language or discourse to do so. For Lefebvre: 'The answer is everyday life, to rediscover everyday life – no longer to neglect and disown it, elude and evade it – but actively to rediscover it while contributing to its transfiguration; this undertaking', he notes, 'involves the invention of a language...the transfiguration of everyday life is the creation of something new, something that requires new words'. Reducing manifestations of the everyday, or everyday popular culture, to mass media is to also limit the everyday and its dynamics to the realm of the institutional. The 'everyday' or 'quotidian' is certainly a much wider and more varied phenomenon as it encompasses a whole set of human activities and non-institutional social settings, from shopping to cooking, having sex, following fashion, queuing, worshipping and dancing. These spaces of the everyday and other mediated experiences in Arab culture are also the parameters and the sites within which structures and aspects of Arab modernness are disclosed (see Chapter 4). What kind of language, semiotics and even hermeneutics do we rely on to study everyday Arab popular cultures? Inventing a new language to deal with them can only succeed if preceded by another intellectual task, that of democratising and freeing the category 'Arab culture' from: a) the grip of the aesthetic as *discourse* and b) the discourses of *becoming* that downplay all other forms of artistic and carnivalesque expressions. The latter, an emancipatory project, is still in its infancy and is mainly led by a small group of Arab thinkers. I classify this project under the fourth and less dominant position within Arab thought, whose thinkers are now convinced that it is only by ontologising lived experience that Arab philosophy can survive as a critical project. Arab thought, according to the anti-essentialist position, cannot move forward beyond its non-dialectical, cyclical structure lest its problematics are contextualised within key changes in modern human thought (see Chapter 2). The former task is well encapsulated in Al-Ghathami's[28] archaeological project: to unearth the *aesthetic*, mainly in Arab poetry, as a discourse that camouflages a hidden and seldom critiqued ugliness. This ugliness, he argues (2000), is embedded in a system that feigns modernism, yet ceaselessly reproduces old and fixed-frozen discourses about gender, youth, the 'other' and 'Arab culture' as a whole.

From literary criticism to cultural criticism

How does Al-Ghathami propose that we democratise 'Arab culture'? To answer this question, I turn to his most important work, *Al-naqd athakāffi* (*Cultural Criticism*, 2000) in which he argues for a shift in the Arab cultural repertoire from literary criticism to cultural criticism. His aim is to make a jump, or *qafzah*, as he calls it, from a critique of texts to a critique of the systems (anssaq/discourses) embedded in the texts, thus reversing the role of the critic, as defined by the celebrated poet Nizar Al-Qabbāni[29] in *Childhood of Nahd*: 'the critic must stand in front of the object of art as a worshipper and not as a judge' (Al-Ghathami, 2000: 128). The divide between Arab 'high' culture, mainly the literary tradition known as *adab*, and Arab 'popular' culture, argues Al-Ghathami, is the product of a process and an embedded system he calls *nassaq*, ceaselessly engineered by an official elitist discourse that privileges certain aesthetics and forms of artistic expression over others. Using examples from Arab poetry (both old and 'modern'), Al-Ghathami shows how the system (*nassaq*) inherent to Arab literary aesthetics is laden with a largely anti-modern and chauvinistic culture (*takkafat al-fahl*) that is so old that it predates Islam. Arab literary aesthetics, he advances, need to be freed from both institutional rhetorical discourse that reproduces them, and from 'aesthetics' as official discourse. Literary criticism failed as a tool of language and analysis because it focused on the text's beauty and ignored the hidden meaning system camouflaged by the text's aesthetic quality. Al-Ghathami proposes that we remove the aesthetic in Arab culture from its discourse and expose it to constant critique and subversion. The reproduction of *nassaq* and its cultural meanings, observes Al-Ghathami (2000), infiltrates not only *adab*, but also aspects of Arab public and social life and therefore urges the literary person (*adeeb*) to resist the official institutional imaginary by rethinking the question of aesthetics, and by exposing the variety of the discourses it represents (Al-Ghathami, 2000: 59). Al-Ghathami's call for an intellectual jump from Arab *literary* criticism to

Arab *cultural* criticism is an attempt to broaden the notion of Arab culture and its creative processes. It is also a concerted effort to democratise the Arab cultural text and to find the new kind of language necessary to understand and critique Arab cultures (ibid, 61). For Al-Ghathami, liberating *adab* (literature) from its official form of aesthetics and the ideas that it propagates is the necessary first step towards liberating *adāt* (the critical tool). The proposed transition from literary to cultural criticism is best achieved through an operational system constitutive of four elements or jumps: a jump in the critical terminology, a jump in the meaning of *nassaq* as a system, a jump in role/assignment (*wadeefa*) and a jump in appropriation (ibid, 62). *Nassaq* is a central concept in Al-Ghathami's operational system. It is usually communicated through different aesthetic forms behind which it hides, and it unconsciously spreads them into everyday culture. *Nassaq*, unless exposed by the cultural critic, warns Al-Ghathami, is capable of hiding forever. He describes four key poetic modes that are prevalent in Arab poetry and points out how they have become engrained in the Arab cultural imaginary. They are: a) the personality of the eloquent beggar or poet as a eulogiser; b) the personality of the hypocritical intellectual or poet as a eulogiser of those in positions of power; c) the personality of the dictator/despot, and d) the personality of the feared evil, whose enmity must be avoided at all cost (ibid, 99). The emergence of these personalities in Arab poetry have, according to Al-Ghathami, led to the reification of the Arab poetry's original purpose and of the authentic tribal values it carries, mainly: hospitality (*karam*) and courage (*shajā'a*) (ibid, 144). The radical shift in Arab pre-Islamic poetry came about through the emergence of the poet as a eulogiser (*mādih*) and of the eulogised as absolute king/ruler, traced by Al-Ghathami to the latest period of *jahilyia* (pre-Islamic era). Al-Ghathami attributes the popularity of this phenomenon to the emergence of the Arab city and city rulers, as well as to encounters with Persian and Roman cultures where eulogising autocratic kings/emperors was a common practice. With the appearance of the poet as a eulogiser, came an uncritical culture of silence, hypocrisy and fear, leading to a radical shift in Arab cultural and social values (ibid, 144–5). To give an example, *karam*, one of the values of the desert nomadic tribes, was an act performed by both men and women, yet with the emergence of *madh* poetry, the object of *madh* was concentrated mostly on male *karam*. Here, argues Al-Ghathami, change in the significance of *karam* as a socio-cultural value affects the whole structure of Arab ethics. As he puts it: 'since *karam* is a central value in the Arab ethical system, any change that occurs in the meaning of the concept is likely to affect both the mental and behavioural systems of Arab identity' (Al-Ghathami, 2000: 152). The poetic system, as it stands, privileges silence over opposition, old age over youth and male over female. In his book *Taaneet al-qassidat wa al-quāri' al-Mukhtalif (Feminising the Poem and the Different Reader,* 1999), Al-Ghathami advances the notion that the emergence of Arab free verse in the early twentieth century was a significant cultural event and a resistance to conventional official discourses and their hidden cultural systems. It was a reaction against chauvinism and its system. Free verse championed the marginalised, the popular and the feminine, paving the way for a whole new creative and critical discourse. Al-Ghathami's contribution to Arab cultural criticism and to the broadening of Arab 'culture's' meanings is considerable. *Cultural Criticism* not only provides an analytical model to unearth cultural systems but also broadens the scope of the Arab cultural text from the poetic and the literary to the image and the televisual. Al-Ghathami's most recent work, *Television Culture* (2006), is an extension of this project.

What is the 'popular' in Arab popular culture?

There is a sociological distinction between the use of the term 'popular' in the Arab and Western contexts. In the former, a 'popular' or *sha'abi* person does not necessarily denote a successful or rich person, but denotes someone accepted as being from, of and for the people. In the Arabic sense of the word, the linguistic sign 'popular' connotes meanings of belonging, modesty and humility. A *sha'abi* person can either be rich or poor, educated or uneducated. To be 'popular' is to be one of the people. A rich man wins *sha'beyah* 'popularity' not only through his material possessions but also through his modesty and acceptance of the poor and their way of life. If one is rich, what wins him or her popularity with the Arab working classes is not money or wealth but the capital of sociability: the ability to mingle with the poor, speak to them, joke with them and eat with them as an equal and not as subordinates. Implicit in this conception of the 'popular' is a 'care-structure', which distinguishes it, though not entirely, from conceptualisations of the 'popular' as they appear in the English language. Another example, which explores meanings of the 'popular' even further, is when we talk of newspapers, cinema or/and music in Arab popular culture: popularity in this context must not be confused with the 'quantitative' which, according to Sparks, can be used in a Western context 'to correspond more or less exactly with the size of the audience' (Sparks, 1992: 24). A *sha'bi* 'popular' cinema, for example, is not popular because it draws larger audiences than other cinemas do, but because it is situated in a *Hay sha'bi* – 'a working class quarter' and frequented by working class audiences. Arab rulers and politicians often address their people as *sha'b* (people). The term is used here in an abstract and absolute form that renders it entirely unrealistic, if not meaningless, for there is in fact no *sha'b* as such but rather different social groups, who live in different areas, with different tastes, languages and interests. This possessive unifying use of the word *sha'b*, which appears to be innocent on the surface, is part of the workings of a discourse through which feelings of unity, harmony, reconciliation and stability are constructed. Hence, to speak of Arab 'popular culture', or cultures, in a general fashion is to mask the particularities of the very voices, heard or unheard, which make up Arab popular cultures, thus concealing dialectics of local power relations that are at work within Arab societies. Discourses of unity and reconciliation mask *difference* and competing antagonistic forces that are inherent to Arab societies. Their purpose is one of fetishisation and control. This invites the following questions: Who speaks for and about Arab popular cultures? Who speaks for the 'popular' person in Arab popular cultures? Why should intellectuals play the role of uniting and cementing what is diverse, when instead they could work towards unearthing the mechanics of power dialectics inherent in the discourses of unity that they are ceaselessly pushed to fabricate? I raise these questions to provide readers with a critical account of Arab popular cultures that will engage them in a deeper and not a celebrated mosaic reading. Suffice it to say: discourses of 'unity and reconciliation' that are inherent to conceptualisations of Arab popular cultures are built from above, not from below. They are the product of a managed 'publicness'. Salah al-Rāwi distinguishes between 'popular' (*sha'bi*) discourse and 'public' (*jamāheeri*) discourse. He defines popular discourse as a summary of popular culture that is produced by the popular group as part of its class struggle and as a reaction to its realities. However, 'public discourse' is an 'official discourse *par excellence*… a hyperactive ideological mix, articulated by the 'official' institution, as part of a general ideological project, using a variety of tools that include education, media and the role of intellectuals' (Al-Rāwi, 2001: 54). The ontological positioning of Arab popular discourse is largely undermined and reified by the very elite who purport to care and speak on behalf of the 'popular'. Most Arab intellectuals, who consider it their legitimate role to speak for the popular man or woman, are educated men and women from the middle classes, who unfortunately have little in common with the base structure of Arab society. 'The word "people" in our country [Egypt]', observes Saadawi, is 'glorified or even sanctified in the dictionaries of the ruling class… regardless of whether the elite is liberal (believing in the free market and privatisation), Arab nationalist (believing in socialism or Nasserism), Islamic (believing in the *Qur'an* and religious tradition) or Marxist (believing in class struggle and the public sector) all these types of cultural elite glorify the great Egyptian people. However, their glorification is but empty words. Rarely do they try to get to know the people in their daily reality or to know the different categories of women, youth, workers, peasants, soldiers, artisans and others.' (Saadawi, 1997: 180). The 'popular' in the Arab world is outside ruling mechanisms and its different apparatuses. The vernacular, for example, whether in Egypt, Tunisia or Saudi Arabia, is outside French, English and literary Arabic and is therefore outside official language/discourse. Many voices that constitute Arab popular culture remain unheard and thus become subordinate to a cultural structure that is mainly led and dominated by an authoritarian polity and its apparatuses. Who speaks for the Nubians, Amazighs, Kurds or their subordinate cultures? Who speaks for *Jbala* 'tribes living in Northern Morocco' and their culture? One might venture to say that the 'popular' in Arab popular culture is not at all 'popular'. It is rather a pseudo-popular culture that speaks not with its own voice but with the voice of the centre, its ideas and choices. It is the ruling elite and their apparatuses who have control over the means of production in the Arab world and control over cultural production as well. As Belkbir puts it: 'the culture that prevails in any society is mostly the culture of the groups that rule that society economically and institutionally... those who prevail economically and socially are in possession of strong and efficient means through which they communicate their culture... popular culture, in this case, is nothing other than official culture...'[30] (Belkbir, 1991: 16).

Arab oral Popular cultures (*turath sha'bi*), including storytelling, poetry and other creative forms, it is important to add, not only precede the era of *tadwin* (publishing) during the Abbasid rule but also constitute an important element of the cultural heritage that made it into the written word. Although it is sidelined by many intellectuals and, indeed, by scholars working on Arab culture, oral Arab popular culture has had a great influence in the shaping of the structure of written, modern Arabic literature, the modern Arabic novel being only one example (Mahmmoudi, 1998: 28–77). Popular culture, Nawal Saadawi observes, is 'a mixture of the conscious and the subconscious in the past and in the present. It is a merger of the organic and the inorganic within the body, a merger of matter, spirit and mind. That is why popular culture is more expressive of experienced reality than the culture of the ruling elite or the intellectual elite, which usually stems from books and from scientific, religious or cultural texts' (Saadawi, 1997: 179). Can we move beyond the descriptive to find new and concrete means to articulate the unarticulated, to foreground the analytic structure and objects of study that can make this task possible? How do we study the everyday in Arab popular cultures, and what do we study? The answer can in no way be possible outside the development and institutionalisation of two fields of enquiry: anthropology and cultural studies. Studying the everyday in Arab popular cultures depends on the development of these two fields in the region. Anthropology will provide the methodological terrain for the study of the manifestations of the everyday as they unfold in ordinary popular cultural spaces and the ways these produce different kinds of social and political dynamics. Cultural studies can use ethnography to do just this, but it can also extend the enquiry into the study of different cultural texts, the ways they are encoded and read by different audiences.

In search of Arab subcultures

Dislocating different articulations of Arab cultures by detaching/ disconnecting them from their ideological/metaphysical relationships opens the way for new voices of expression, or even resistance, which have yet to be studied or analysed in any concrete or systematic form. How are hegemonic discourses of Arab cultures subverted, troubled and resisted? What do we know about Arab youth subcultures and their styles? How are they mediated and/ or communicated? What rituals are involved, and where and how do they disclose themselves to us? These questions are yet to be rehearsed in any organised way and can, with the help of ethnographic research, form a whole intellectual project. Just as in the case of Arab popular cultures, work on 'cultural resistance' in the Arab world lacks coherence and continuity. Since these questions are beyond the objective of this chapter, I would like to opt for a preliminary task: to problematise the category 'subculture' and its appropriateness in the Arab context through an articulation of some of the historical and cultural specificities that may distinguish Arab subcultures from others, especially those that originate in the USA and Britain. Is 'subculture' a universal category that discloses itself in similar ways, regardless of differences in historical moments or cultural geographies? Or is it inextricably linked to particular historical moments and cultural specificities? Fifty years of 'subculture theory' in the West have provided a rich repertoire, which saw a paradigmatic shift from the 1950s and 1960s, where the dominant readings focused on 'the sociological' as a determining factor in the study of youth culture, to cultural, 'predominantly Marxist, class-based and ethnographic approaches in the 1970s; to an emphasis on semiotic readings of subcultures in the late 1970s and 1980s, and on to a postmodern identification of 'post-subcultures' (Bentley, 2005: 66). The concepts 'youth' and 'teenager' are Western phenomena *par excellence*, determined by historical events, including changes in geopolitics and a transition from the economies of scarcity to the economies of abundance. This change brought with it a commodity that had until then been monopolised by a small elite: 'leisure time'. There was also a large increase in mass mediated cultural artefacts. The emergence of 'youth culture' was a clear indication of the interdependence of the socio-cultural and the economic. Readings of youth subcultures in the UK and the USA were also 'intricately bound up with general anxieties and concerns in the 1950's culture' (Bentley, 2005: 65). Youth culture was seen as a symptom of the rise of consumerist society. 'Subculture' Hebdige argued, 'is always mediated: inflected by the historical context in which it is encountered; posited upon a specific ideological field which gives it a particular life and particular meanings' (Hebdige, 1979: 80). In this context, subculture must be seen and understood as a reaction to specific moments (historical, economic, cultural and political) and anxieties that are driven by modernity's pathologies, including class, gender and the idea of the nation. It was these moments

and the anxieties that they brought that determined the specificities and the conjunctions, if not the styles, of Western subcultures.
Are there cultures in the Arab world that fit the description of a
subculture? If so, to what moments or anxieties are they reacting?
Are they particular subcultures, reacting to particular moments?
What are these moments? What is the relationship between Arab
popular discourse and Arab subcultures? Popular anger, observes
Saadawi, 'expresses itself from time to time in labour strikes, in
student and youth demonstrations, in feminist movements, or in
peasant revolutions ... written laws often crash those movements
of anger, and popular anger seeks other forms of intellectual resistance by way of axioms and proverbs, of political and sexual jokes
launched against the elite or the ruling minority' (Saadawi, 1997:
179–80). However, what Saadawi describes here, as 'popular anger'
must be distinguished from 'subculture'. The Punk Movement in
Britain, as an example, was aimed at subverting, transgressing and
resisting the 'naturalness' of bourgeois national culture, but this
was not an act performed only through anger but also, and most
importantly, through the use of style as signifier and as an intentional form of communication, which because of its spectacular
nature, attracted the media and subsequently a mass audience. It is
'the subculture's stylistic innovations', argues Hebdige, 'which first
attract the media's attention' (Hebdige, 1979: 93). There are a myr-
iad of subcultures in the Arab world, but because of the traditional
and still rigid authoritarian structures of Arab societies, these are, in
the main, functional and operational only in private spaces: clubs,
houses, saloons, derbs, concerts, mosques and the like. As long as
Arab subcultures are confined to the realm of the private, they will
lack the confrontational and transgressive styles that made Western
subcultures most effective in subverting narratives of 'naturalness'.
In looking at the Hip Hop and rap scenes in the Arab world, one
finds an interesting combination of style, imagery and lyrics, used
interchangeably to subvert both the local and the global power. The
baggy trousers, caps, even gold chains, hands on the crotch, hands
in the air, the yo-yos, the trainers, the attitude, a borrowed one, of

course, combined with lyrics in Arabic dialect, create a complex discourse, floating from new forms of nationalistic ideology to the denouncement of imperialism and Israeli occupation[31]. Arab rap, in all its diverse and intricate styles, represents new kinds of spaces, unprecedented spaces of Arab youth culture, where the young and the 'popular' (the working classes) are given a momentary voice that speaks to different forms of power, both local and global.

Conclusion

The present tense is a powerful temporality; it is the arena where the everyday, culture and power relations are played out. A call for a semiotic of the everyday in the Arab world is an attempt at making the obvious and the ordinary more visible, making it count as part of our intellectual curiosity and as an object of study. Dailiness and daily spaces of human interaction are often associated with the banal and the ordinary, and this is largely due to their repetitive and uneventful structures. The everyday is boring because it happens everyday. Whatever happens on the street, in the souk, the queue, the bridge, the work place and the café is common and has a daily structure that makes it appear, at first glance, to be nothing special, not worthy of our curiosity, yet these human settings are the very spaces where much of our existence and everyday politics are played out. The young unemployed in Algiers, Cairo, Casablanca, Beirut and other Arab urban cities spend considerable amounts of time on street corners (*derbs*) and in cafés. This is where their dailiness is acted out; this is where they chat, joke, fight, smoke, watch and discuss the news. In other words, this is where their dailiness unfolds. These anthropological spaces, regardless of their ordinariness, can also tell us a lot about the region's working class cultures and social stratification. The next chapter uses ethnographic research, conducted in Egypt and Morocco, to concretise some of the ideas discussed here about the 'everyday'. The intention is to take the study of the everyday in the Arab world to another stratum of analysis; one based on empirical evidence.

4

The Bridge and the Queue as Spaces of Encountering

If we linger for a moment on the definition of anthropological place we will see, first, that it is geometric. It can be mapped in terms of three simple spatial forms, which apply to different institutional arrangements and in a sense are the elementary forms of social space. In geometric terms these are the line, the intersection of lines, and the point of intersection. Concretely, in the everyday geography more familiar to us, they correspond to routes, axes or paths that lead from one place to another and have been traced by people; to crossroads and open spaces where people pass, meet and gather... defining a space and frontiers beyond which other men are defined as others, in relation with other centers and other spaces.

(Augé, 1995: 56–66)

If authors have become more prominent in ethnography (as the construction of texts also takes the foreground of analysis), in a curious sense places have disappeared – or at least the boundaries around them have become deeply problematised as connections between culture and territory, identity and fixed community, are challenged.

(Coleman, Simon and Collin, Peter, 2006: 2)

Arabic *adab* (literature) oozes rich and, in many instances, beautifully choreographed depictions of place, such as souks, streets, *hamams*, country-houses, landscapes, cafés, buildings, scents and many more. One has only to read the late Naguib Mahfouz[32] to note this great old Arab literary tradition. Though many literary depictions of place are inspired by detailed, non-fictional observations, they are still enunciated within a fictional world that is, in the main, galvanised by fictional characters and woven into a narrative structure, intended for a specific artistic/aesthetic purpose: to create worlds and places that demand our curiosity, attention and, most importantly, our admiration for the author as a storyteller of place – as an artist and *flâneur*. Regardless of the anthropological detail, spatial objectification is, in this case, limited to the literary and to the storytelling as a craft. There are, however, other stories we can tell about place, moving our gaze from the aesthetics of the text to the realm of the social/anthropological. Here, place moves from being a purely fictional subject, serving a fictional purpose, to being an object of ethnographic/scientific enquiry. I use the word 'scientific' with some hesitation, not because I have an issue with ethnography as science, but because of the somewhat irritating truth that even the most accomplished and 'thick descriptions' of place – anthropological place, that is – could only have been told through some sort of storytelling, a kind of *poetics*, making it at times, difficult to distinguish between the 'real' and the 'fictional', the fiction writer and the ethnographer as a 'writer of culture'. This is part of a known and a well-rehearsed problematic in the discipline of Anthropology (Geertz, 1973; de Certeau; 1984; Fetterman, 1989; Clifford and Marcus, 1986; Hannerz, 2006) that finds its origin in an old and as of yet unresolved phenomenological problem – that of the reconciliation between meaning/semantics and being (Husserl, 1973; Luhmann, 1998). What follows is an ethnographic account of two popular cultural places, not by an ethnographer as such, but by a cultural studies person using ethnography as a method. The first is a bridge in Cairo called Qassr Nile; the other, a series of queues formed by Moroccans waiting for visas outside different Western embassies in Casablanca. The objective of stopping at these two different places is two-fold: a) it is an attempt to concretise my analysis of the everyday in the Arab context, a way of investigating what the study of taken-for-granted popular cultural places in the Arab region can teach us about the structures of feeling of the people being observed and about the stratification of their societies, and b) since I have chosen the *everyday* as part of the foregrounding of the comprehension of modernness, I look into these two places for signs and manifestations of how 'being modern' discloses itself as an everyday, daily occurrence.

Qassr Nile Bridge and the detraditionalisation of everyday space

During my last fieldwork trip to Cairo in April 2007, I walked daily, sometimes twice a day, from *tal'at harb* to one of my favourite *maqhas* in Cairo, called the Qassr Nile Café. The *maqha*, which served the most exquisite apple-flavoured shisha, had a stunning view of the magical Nile and its colourful *feluccas* (small boats). The sight of the *feluccas,* the euphoric sounds of *sha'bi* (popular) Egyptian music to which men, women and children clapped, sang and danced[33], together with the apple-shisha scent, and the late lazy afternoon jasmine-laden breeze, were enough to move the most wretched soul to an ecstatic state of being. This is where my experience as a romantic tourist ends. En route to the *maqha*, I had to cross a rather long bridge (about 382 meters long and 20 meters wide, just in case you are wondering, I did not measure it! I read about it) called Qassr Nile Bridge, at the entrance of which stood two grandiose bronze lion statues that, I later learnt, were created by the French sculptor Alfred Jacquemart (1824–96). The bridge was built by a French architect called Bellfond and first opened to traffic in 1872. However, by the 1930s the structure of this narrow bridge became weak (especially since, by then, around 31,000 vehicles of all categories were licensed in Egypt). The bridge had to be demolished and a new one was built, this time, by a British company called Dorman, Long and Co, using 3,701 tons of steel manufactured in Middlesbrough[34]. Standing by the bridge at night, overlooking the river and the skyline in the distance brought back immediate memories of London, the South Bank and the good old Thames. It was as if the British had intended to recreate a piece of London in Cairo – Karl Marx was perhaps right about the bourgeoisie and its plans to recreate the world in its own image! There is something about the relationship between colonialism, the temporal and architecture that remains unconsidered, even today. However, there is also something about the Nile, something verging on the sacred, that the Thames can never match or equal. My primary observations: my interest in the length and width of the bridge, its history, were not exactly the main attributes that attracted me to it (even if they were my primary encounters with this place). There was something else, more significant. The bridge was about to metamorphose from a structure of steel and cement, colonial history to a human setting and an ethnographic object of study, but this took some time. At this point during my stay in Cairo, I was not sure what aspect of Cairean cultural life I wanted to study. There were so many distractions, so many competing, bustling human settings, floating signs and signifieds, images and sounds, and scents. I walked long distances, took long taxi rides, had long conversations with taxi drivers (as one would in Cairo), went to mosques, souks, museums, theatre, old buildings, shopping malls, universities, cinemas, music concerts, I frequented a dozen or more shisha cafés, read newspapers, novels, sat in bars and each of these places presented themselves, rather competitively as potential anthropological objects of study. But in the end, it was Qassr Nile Bridge that preoccupied me the most and eventually metamorphosed from cement, iron and car traffic to an ethnographic space; a socio-cultural setting. Time is the privilege of the *flâneur* and I had loads of it. I spent a lot of time going up and down the bridge, aimlessly, not knowing what to focus on. It was the love graffiti painted on the bridge and the sight of young Egyptian lovers holding hands and admiring the Nile that captivated me the most, not the steel structure or even Alfred Jacquemart's imperially imposing bronze lion statues. I took pictures of different graffiti, most of which was in white paint, ranging from short poems to inscriptions of different lovers' initials. I also took pictures of heart engravings with arrows going through them (a universal sign for being in love). Qassr Nile Bridge is a place where young Egyptian lovers unite, hold hands, kiss when no one is looking and eternalise their *encounter* in written form on steel from Middlesbrough. This was, for me, the point at which the bridge became an ethnographic space: a trans-local space. This metamorphosis brought with it immediate questions and problems of meaning, what did it all mean, this public 'lovenness'? What was this space? Why are the passers-by completely indifferent to the sight of cuddled up lovers. Why is this kind of behaviour not tolerated in other public places in Cairo, such as the souk or even the street? The sight of two lovers holding hands or cuddling was extremely rare, if not absent, in other public places. Why was it OK to do this on the bridge or by the edges of the Nile and not in any other public space? What I encountered on the bridge did not tally with the theses I had read and heard on cultural change in contemporary Egyptian society, especially those which spoke of increased levels of conservatism, religiosity and radicalisation. It is true that more Muslim Egyptian women are wearing the hijab today than in any previous period of Muslim Egyptian cultural history, but these women are also lovers who are not afraid to hide their emotions or cuddle up to their lovers. The reasons for the increase in hijab wearing cannot be put down solely to religiosity. That would be facile as an interpretation. The increase must be articulated within a complex relation between gender discourse, identity politics and also by looking at the wearing of the hijab as an object of female empowerment (Amin, 2004: 83–90), construction of virtuosity, piety (Zuhur, 1992) and even middle class respectability (Abu-Lughod, 2005: 130). However, if we were for a moment to assume that conservatism or radicalisation were winning ground in Egyptian society, how does one then explain what goes on on the bridge, by the Nile, in Zamalek and, most important, its being tolerated as an act of premarital love? I kept coming back to the Bridge, sometimes three times a day, and the nagging questions returned with me. However, for a long while I failed to move beyond my primary observations to a more contextualised, cultural interpretation of the bridge. Methodologically, only a covert participant–observation strategy could be pursued. The last thing I wanted to do, although I confess I was tempted, was to approach a young couple, intoxicated by the romantic experience, and ask in my fake Egyptian accent (the one I learnt as a child in Morocco watching Egyptian television drama) 'Are you in Love? 'Do you kiss?' That's what Annie Kate, my late Irish grandmother in law, God bless her soul, asked me, to my mortification, when my wife first introduced us. Somehow, I do not think this would have gone down well. This meant, all I could rely on to make sense of this place was my observations. And in this case, the method was one of participant–observation *par excellence*. The only thing I could do was to walk up and down the bridge at different times (during the day and at night), rereading most of the graffiti and gazing, like a pervert, at the lovers standing next to each other, holding hands and always facing the Nile. There was not much to go by in terms of the construction neither of an ethnographic narrative nor, to use Abu-Lughod's words, 'the right point of entry' (Abu-Lughod, 2005: 31). Making sense of the Bridge as a human setting was hampered by what appeared to be an inadequate method. There was only so much one could interpret from looking at the graffiti and by gazing at the couples, as they stood close, chatting away and looking longingly at each other. More meaning was to derive, not so much from denotative signs but from seeing the open 'lovenness' on the bridge as both constitutive and product of more subtle interpretations inherent to socio-economic and cultural transformations in Egyptian society. How and in what ways is the bridge and what happens on it part of social change in Egypt? How much of it is about the emergence of the modern subject? How much of it is about class, economic change? The consistent questions have to remain: what kind of a place is it? Is it real? Of course, I did not dream it, but is it or could it be a different kind of public space, a private–public space, an in-between space or even a hyper-real space? How and in what ways could the bridge be a case of '"mad hypertextuality", a "postmodern condition" in which reality and images blur into each other, perhaps even define each other?' (Armbrust, 1996: 3). Were the passers-by tolerant because they were simply indifferent, or was it because they were under the spell of this very postmodern condition: a blurring of the fictional and the real? Could it be that the lovers and the place they embodied were extensions of other people and other spaces, an acting out of romance by fictional characters?

Photograph 1 Arabic graffiti on Qasr Nile Bridge saying 'Love passed through here'

Photograph 2 Two young Egyptians cuddling and overlooking the Nile river from Qasr Nile bridge

Photograph 3 Arabic Graffiti on Qasr Nile Bridge by a lover saying: '5 months have passed since we last met'

Photograph 4   White graffiti (a love poem) in Arabic

Photograph 5   White graffiti in Arabic written by two lovers saying: 'I love you and me too, I swear to God'

Reading Qassr Nile Bridge as
a geometric/intersectional 'space'

To use Augé's terms (1995), the bridge is 'geometrical', 'intersectional' and can only be made intelligible through conjunctional
moments/points where different 'axes' and 'routes' intersect. The
point of intersection does not happen on the bridge as such, but in
the mind of the ethnographer/participant observer. This includes
multiple, fluid and, at times, contradictory disjunctures between:
two kinds of 'romance' (institutional/ontological); public space/
private space; tradition/modernity, traditional space/romanticised
space; the lovers as performers of 'lovenness'; the passers-by as
onlookers; the social; the cultural and the economic. It is the
combination of all these elements and their interaction with one
another that gives meaning to the bridge as an anthropological
space. How? Let us first tackle the question of class and see how
this might tell us more about Qassr Nile Bridge. In my shameful
gazing at the couples, I could not help but notice that, in terms
of dress, it was not difficult to deduce that the majority of the
couples (both the men and the women) had come from working
class and possibly lower or poor middle class backgrounds. A lot
of the girls dressed modestly, in most cases, with headscarves. As
for men, most wore plain shirts, T-shirts and trousers. There was
nothing trendy about the clothes. Hardly any Western dress labels
were observed and most of the couples had made their way to the
bridge on foot. After a period, judging mainly from clothing (in
the case of men the state of their shoes), it became clear that the
young people who frequented the bridge, were in the main, from
the Egyptian working classes. I later learnt that the middle and
upper middle classes used membership-only *salonaat* (saloons/
private clubs) and other private places for such intimacies. I have
already hinted at the possibility that the romanticisation of the
bridge as a place could be part of an acting out, a performing of
what Abu-Lughod calls the state's 'sentimental education of the
modern citizen' (Abu-Lughod, 2005: 231). To suggest that being in

love and showing it is an immediate effect of media consumption alone is, of course, absurd, for we all know that romance predates television and all other forms of media. It is the naturalisation / neutralisation, the performative element of romance, so to speak, that is of concern here. The act of 'lovenness' as it manifests itself on the bridge and along the Nile, I argue, is the product of inter-play between two intersectional discourses of romance: one is a natural human act, performed as a kind of self-actualisation and the product of natural human desire. The other is the result of a carefully constructed hegemonic, 'developmentalist' discourse produced by the Egyptian elite through the medium of television as part of a nation building process. In her articulation of the role played by Egyptian soap actors/stars in the process of 'emotional-ising' the nation, Abu-Lughod observes:

> These actors are...instrumental in perpetuating the generic conventions of emotionalized acting that...may play a role in the sentimental educa-tion of the citizen. They animate the individuali-zation encouraged by the focus on the emotional states of the characters they portray. Their loca-tions in domestic settings, usually consisting of small nuclear families, often middle or upper class, are largely due to budgetary and logistical issues not unrelated to the hiring of characters. Both features of the serials – the emotionalization and the domestication – communicate certain values subliminally, whatever the plot or overt messages; they construct naturalized models of personhood, which actors bring to life.
>
> (Abu-Lughod, 2005: 231)

This is where modernness, like 'modernism', falls into the trap of illusion, what Lefebvre calls 'cultural terrorism', for it is not clear what is driving what here; modernness as an 'institutional reflexivity' or modernness as a self-ontic reflexivity? The latter is a performative, self-reflexive way of saying: 'I am in love with you, or I like you so much, I'd love to marry you, but cannot afford it just yet', 'I engrave your name's initials next to mine, I draw a heart, I put an arrow through it, I look at you longingly, then at the Nile, I hold your hands' – 'I am, in an ontological way, performing/expressing *being* in love with you/ *being* romantic, regardless of what the passers-by might say – '*bahebak*' (I love you). The former is an act of premeditated televisual romance, institutionalised romance, romance as a modernist/nationalist project, a kind of 'institutional reflexivity' that undercuts traditional habits and naturalises bourgeois norms, tastes, *habitus* and more. The latter process, or form of reflexivity, does not necessarily reify the former, rather it naturalises it, making it more acceptable. At the point where the two reflexivities intersect (as they do in the case of the bridge), they become inextricably linked. In their convergence, the televisual and the ontological create a third space, which, perhaps, only the lovers can articulate. Since modernity 'is inseparable from its "own" media' (Giddens, 1991: 24) and since 'the transmutations introduced by modern institutions interlace with individual life and therefore with the self' (ibid, 1), attempting to separate the two reflexivities (the self-ontic/institutional) is very much a pointless exercise. It is, in fact, in the convergence of the two reflexivities that the modern subject (performing being romantic in a traditional setting) comes to light. How about the other intersections, and how do they affect our understanding of the bridge as a 'geometric' human space? How does the intersectional structure of the bridge affect the kind of space it is? Here, using the bridge as an example, I'd like to rehearse ways of seeing 'tradition' as a spatial phenomenon, and argue that tradition does not just manifest itself in social relations, institutions, discourse, time, protocol, the mind, ritual, but it also imposes itself on place/space[35], dictating how one behaves/performs in the house, church, mosque, school, university, street, shopping mall and in other public places. In private places (the bedroom, the private party, the house, all of which are protected from the gaze of the stranger or intruder) tradition can easily be subverted. However, because of the per-formative rules one is expected to uphold in everyday public place (Goffman, 1959), tradition (or how tradition dictates one should behave in public space) is more difficult to trouble or subvert. What goes on on the bridge reverses this rule and makes that which is private public, blurring, in the meantime, the relationship between the two spaces (see Meyrowitz, 1985). What also occurs here, which I find even more significant, is a kind of decolonisation and detraditionalisation of space, that is to say, tactically imposing on it (space) a different narrative of spatialisation, where tradition (not all of it, of course) is undermined. The bridge is, in this case, an everyday 'tactical' space (de Certeau, 1984), which reconfigures and reorganises the functioning of tradition and its power.

Desegregation of the sexes in modern Egypt, and in the majority of Arab countries, a result of the change in women's status, has problematised old, fixed gender structures dictated by tradition. The bridge can, in this case, be seen as a symbolic manifestation of socio-economic and cultural change in Egypt and as a subversion of imposed narratives of 'publicness', driven, in the main, by bourgeois hypocrisy and cultural salafism. The bridge is a working class popular cultural space; a temporary outlet for repressed libido, of desire and the desire to be desired, and where romance is acted out, just as in the tragic 'structures of feeling' (Abu-Lughod, 2005: 117) emanating from the Egyptian soap. The bridge is a liminal amorous space, an extension of the fictional, a 'mad hypertextuality' where such extensions are permissible. It is a display of tolerated intimacy, where lovers could be just that: lovers, eying each other, holding hands. Romance, in this case, is acted out, just as in televisual scenes from Egyptian serials, as a daily occurrence, irrespective of what religion, the Imam, or the traditional societal code dictates as the norm. This is an act of modernness *par excellence*, (a double-modernness) fuelled not just by the human desire for love and 'lovenness' but also through *encounter* with the televisual, as a modern project. The bridge is, as such, a multi-sited space, an extension of other things/axes/routes/paths: a way of carving modern forms of selfhood, momentarily de-spatialising tradition and fixed-frozen moral systems. The bridge, as romantic space, is fuzzy and liminal. It not only defies tradition but also scientific certainty. It is, to quote Coleman and Collin (2006: 11), who misquote Walter Benjamin, a syndrome of 'The Work of Ethnography in the Age of Postmodern Production'.

The queue

Moving on from Qassr Nile Bridge to queues outside Western embassies in Casablanca, I carry on with the same task: exploring taken-for-granted popular cultural spaces and attempting, in the meantime, to find the kind of new language that Lefebvre asked us to discover in order to make sense of the 'quotidian'; its relational structures and how these produce meaning for us. Making use of ethnographic research conducted in Morocco, concentrating on different, taken-for-granted, non-institutionalised, popular cultural spaces, here I focus on the queue outside Western embassies, ordinary talk about migration, and argue that emigration in Morocco is not an isolated social phenomenon, but a pervasive part of the make up of its popular culture. The queue, as I will later explain using evidence from participant observation, is no ordinary space. It is a complex space of encountering, unveiling different characteristics such as: stratification, hope, intimacy, alienation and modernness.

The *queue* is not an Arab *thing*.[36] It is a product of encounter with Western modernity. After living in England for more than 20 years, I must confess that not only have I mastered the art of queuing but also have developed an aggressive disposition towards queue jumpers. I like to call this disposition queue-rage. The mere detection on my part of anyone, man or woman (with the exception of the elderly, pregnant women and people with disabilities) hinting at, or trying to jump the queue, instantly transforms me from the gentle person I think I am to a monster. I protest ruthlessly, for I see such an act as an unpardonable infringement on and violation of my civil rights. It is undemocratic, uncivilised – it is wrong! In Morocco, however, and indeed in much of my beloved Arab world, this is an often-abused right, whether waiting for the bus, in the bank, the souk or at the cinema – no one seems to like to queue. I would like to recollect an incident that happened 18 years ago, an incident that remains as vivid in my mind as if it had happened yesterday. It taught me a cultural lesson I will never forget. I was standing outside a 'popular' (working class) cinema in Morocco where a newly released, American film, *Homeboy*, starring Mickey Rourke was showing. The cinema had its iron shutters down. Against them, more than 300 desperate young Moroccans jostled like cattle, waiting for the shutters to open. But beforehand, the people who worked inside the cinema had openly allowed their friends entry. How despicable and humiliating, I thought. They walked through us, we who, packed like sardines, waited so patiently and in they went. The passivity and inertia of the people outside the shutters disturbed me; not one of them dared to protest. My friend Khalid, who then lived in the *Old Medina* (a very rough working class quarter of Casablanca), could see that I was outraged and advised me not to complain. However, the 'queue-rage' took over and I began to shout uncontrollably at the queue jumpers, 'You have to queue, whom do you think you are, you fucking scum!' Before I knew it, three stocky, well-built men jumped over the cinema shutters and started to throw punches and kick us. No one came to our rescue. On the contrary, others too joined in. Regretfully, my friend took all the bad punches; he had a nosebleed and a bruised face. As for me, I learnt, though violently, that the queue and *queuing* remain alien concepts in Morocco.

Doing ethnography in the queue[37]

This section reflects on methodological issues that I encountered while doing fieldwork in a series of queues outside different

Western embassies in Casablanca. It provides a rationale for the research strategies and addresses the ethnographer's positionality as a native researcher. *Entrée* to the queue was open. To use Goffman's terminology, it was a 'front stage' and not a 'backstage' human setting (see Jorgensen, 1989: 43). As such queues outside Western embassies in Casablanca were open to me to enter as a 'queuer', my identity as a researcher was unknown to the rest of the queuers. In total, I have queued outside four Western embassies in Casablanca, which I joined at different times during the day and at night over a period of five weeks. I did participant–observation outside the American, French, Italian and Belgian embassies. For the purpose of this chapter, I will give examples from the French and Italian embassies alone.

Doing ethnography in the queue was accidental. As a young boy living in Casablanca, I had encountered queues outside Western embassies on a daily basis. They were so common and everyday that they had become almost invisible to me, just as the pictures we hung in our sitting rooms: they are there, we encounter them daily, yet after a while, no matter how appreciative of them we are, they become as good as not existing to us. It was only after I had returned to Morocco following a long stay in London that the queues became visible to me again. I was so taken by them. But this time, I saw them differently. I saw them as ethnographic spaces. As I entered the world of the queue as a human setting and after spending long periods queuing, rather sporadically outside different Western embassies, it became clear to me that the talk about migration/emigration/immigration was only one element of what I now believe to be a complex structure and a very much-taken-for-granted, everyday, popular cultural space. As I queued for long hours, I learnt more about the queue, the queuers and queuing. I then became interested in the relationship between the queue and the queuers, the queuers and their encounter with the 'other', (the French, the American, the Italian and so on), the queuers and their intermediaries, and the people who made careers out of the queue, such as the information-men (unemployed young Moroccans who make a living by selling information to the illiterate and confused). All these elements later became as important as the *talk* that unfolded in the queue. It became apparent to me that the queue encompassed two structure-systems or worlds: the world of the *queue* as a Western colonial imposition and the world of the *queuers,* who displayed cultural particularities, which were inherently Moroccan. The world of the queuers also reflected the stratification of Moroccan society. As I was interested in ordinary talk about emigration as it unfolded in the queue, I decided not to interact with the queuers, for doing so would have interrupted the very ordinariness I was seeking to record. For the same reason, my identity as a researcher and the intentions of the research were also not revealed to the queuers. As such, methodologically I thought it more efficient to deploy a *covert* rather than an *overt* strategy. It is important to note, however, that this strategy may not have worked had I been a Westerner. The queuers, I have no doubt, would have been very suspicious of a Westerner queuing with them. So, the fact that I am Moroccan and look Moroccan was indispensable for the success of the covert strategy. However, my strategy also had its limitations. Once I joined a queue, I had to respect the rules. I could not jump the queue just because a fight was unfolding 20 meters ahead; I had instead to rely on the 'communication chain' (what others in front of or behind me heard or saw). Using a covert strategy meant I was restricted to talk and to conversations that unfolded immediately behind or ahead of me. As such, I was never in the queue, but only in parts of the queue. Several hundred conversations were on, yet it was possible to follow only one or two at a time. In the eyes of the queuers with whom I queued, I was but another Moroccan who wanted to emigrate to the West. The narratives I am about to introduce are part of my fieldwork diary. They describe talk, people and happenings as they unfolded. I have selected these notes with the hope that they will bring the queue and its people to life for the reader. I am also hoping that the style in which the narrative is written will help the reader capture events in their preserved temporal dimensions.

The queue outside the Italian Embassy

I arrived at the embassy at 10.00 am. There were about 300 people gathered in front of me, almost all of them engaged in some sort of talk. Those in the queue had formed into sporadic small groups. As the sun grew strong, some men and women took refuge under shady trees. There were boys selling single cigarettes and some selling cake. There were young children, boys and girls in their teens running about, and some women who had brought their toddlers with them were now placing them under the trees. There were middle-aged people and those in their 60s. 'Mohamed got a visa last week, he just phoned me from the boat', said a woman in her 50s to a group of people who appeared to take the news with great joy. 'We will all meet in the plane *'Insha' Allah'* (God willing), said a man in his 30s. There was laughter. Two things bring together all the people I was observing: they are all Moroccan and they all want to leave Morocco. Everyone was carrying a file with them that had all carefully placed documents needed to apply for the visa. 'Murad got the visa, he's left', said a man to two other men who had come to shake hands. A big Italian man makes his way to the embassy door accompanied by an attractive young Moroccan woman. The whole queue, including those who had been queuing since three o'clock, looked on in despair as the girl made her way in quite effortlessly. There was an angry, incomprehensible murmur, but no real protest. In Morocco, it is accepted that those with money do not queue; only poor Moroccans queue and most of them queue in vain. There was a great camaraderie between those waiting to apply for a visa, those who had come to keep them company, those who had been refused a visa and those who already had one. Not only did they share *talk* about migrating, they also shared the same *hum* 'big problems, anxiety' or *humum* (plural of *hum*), because they are 'popular' people in the Moroccan sociological sense of the word. They represent the working class of Morocco: the Moroccan people proper. Said, a Moroccan in his early 40s whose job is to liaise between the Italian Embassy and Moroccans queuing for visas, proved to be, in both the English and Moroccan sense of the word, a very 'popular' person. He was followed everywhere like the Messiah, constantly smothered by confused and frustrated people from the queue. 'Hold on, hold on, I can only speak to one person at a time. I cannot speak to all of you at once. Where is that young woman who was angry with me a while ago? I got her file. She got a visa.' There was no response. At least 20 people of all ages followed Said. They turned when he turned, they stopped when he stopped, they talked when he talked, they shouted when he shouted. Said was handling the situation quite well, until he erupted: 'Let me tell you something, things are changing; there are no jobs in Italy. There are hundreds of Moroccans in Italy who sleep in the streets, hundreds who make a living washing cars in the streets. I am telling you, there are no jobs left.' I am not sure whether Said truly cared for his people, or if he was simply trying to dishearten people waiting in the queue in order to make the Italians' job easier. A young man with short black curly hair and a half-buttoned shirt that revealed an expensive gold chain, rose to challenge Said: 'That is not true', he said quite loudly so others could hear him. 'There are jobs in Italy if you look for them. I have my own business in Italy; some of my employees are Italian.' Said did not answer, but moved his head to and fro as a sign of disapproval. Another man did. He had a beard and what Moroccans call a *Dinar*, a dark patch on the forehead that appears as a result of years of praying. 'Does saying this make you feel proud?' he demanded of the young Moroccan. 'What would happen if all young Moroccans like you left the country? Look at you; do you think the vulgar little gold chain you're wearing makes you superior? Morocco is better than Italy.' 'You do not know what you are talking about', replied the young Moroccan in a rather defeated voice. The quarrel disintegrated and with it the crowd, who had perhaps thought this the beginning of a fight, only to follow Said as he started to make conversation with an old

Moroccan peasant. 'I won't get your dossier until you tell me where you come from', demanded Said, teasing an old peasant wearing a traditional Moroccan *Jellaba*. The old peasant had been pestering Said for a while. Everyone around Said, and many of those queuing, waited rather impatiently for the peasant's answer. There was a long pause and then the peasant, looking sheepishly at Said, uttered '*Ben Meskin*'. This sent everyone into stitches. *Ben Meskin* is a Moroccan *Aroubi* tribe; notorious for the emigrants who generally make their money in Italy selling carpets and watches on beaches or in the street. Said, too, burst out laughing, slapped the old man's head, then held it with his hands and kissed it violently. Said's action triggered yet another hysterical fit of laughter, after which he held the old man's hand and said: 'Now, I'll go and fetch your dossier.' Said, and perhaps all the people in the queue, had known exactly where the old man had come from. His clothes were a give away. It was the confirmation they enjoyed. A small street separated the Italian Embassy and the queue from The Centre for English Language. I stood outside the Centre on two occasions when students were coming out and made the following observations. Young Moroccans gathered in very small cliques where a Parisian French accent prevailed, an indication that these young Moroccans belonged to the middle and upper classes of Moroccan society. They wore very fashionable Western 'gear', Nike trainers, Calvin Klein, Armani and *Lacoste* T-shirts. Some of the girls wore fashionable torn blue jeans; others wore skirts. Parents and *chauffeurs* stopped their cars outside the college to pick them up. The cars matched the expensive clothes and the French accent. There was a stream of BMWs, Golfs, Mercedes, 4x4s and others. What I found striking was the fact that these young people were nonchalantly indifferent to the world of the queue, its people, the police and the dramas unfolding only 4 meters away. Perhaps they did not care, or maybe they had seen these queues so often that they had lost their attraction. Not one of the people I observed turned to look at the queue or the people in it. It was as if the queue was not there.

The queue outside the French Embassy

The French Embassy was only at 15 minutes walk from where I was staying in Casablanca. It was 4.00 am when I arrived. No one was queuing by the embassy, but as I walked a 100 yards towards the *Amala* Park, I came across a gathering of about 150 people or more. There was a man with a list in his hand shouting: 'you have to register with me first before you queue at the Embassy. The queue will start here and we will then move you, so you can queue beside the Embassy at 6.30 am.' There was already a queue forming in the park. I joined the queue like everyone else did. Some men and women, who must have been queuing since the previous night, were still sleeping on the grass. Except for those who were still asleep and a young boy who sat on a bench, almost everyone else was talking. Groups of two, three, four and five people had formed, everyone engaged in some sort of talk. The group ahead of me consisted of five students who had applied for visas to pursue studies at French universities. I heard one of them say: 'The English are much better; they do everything on the same day. They do not make you wait like the French.' On the bench to my left, a man in his forties was talking to a girl in her early twenties. I overheard him say to her, 'The Spanish are the purest racists I have ever met. They hate Arabs.' At exactly 5.30 the man with the register asked everyone to stand and form a proper queue. I was already in the queue. A man whose age I could not tell, as his face was covered with a pink towel, was laying on a bench some 5 metres away from where I stood. He wore an old beige suit, which was falling to bits because of incessant use. The registrar's shouting had woken him up. He was calling names loudly and allocating numbers to each of us. Indifferent to the people around him, the man with the beige suit began to scratch his groin. He did this for about three minutes, and then with one of his eyes, he took a peep at what was happening before him. He dragged his body off the bench lazily to reveal a burned face and a bushy, dirty-looking brown moustache. He then faced us with a pair of amazed, lazy eyes that he was struggling to open. Looking at the people in the queue before him, he uttered almost in disbelief, 'Is this the army?'

Notes from the next day

'I have been here since 4 a.m., why don't you queue like the rest of us?' a man shouted angrily as people started to jump the queue. I moved from the queue and stood under a tree, facing the door of the French Embassy, which, without exaggeration, looked like the door to heaven. I do not know what the door to heaven looks like, but this must be close. The queue was more than a 150-meters long. There were four Moroccan policemen by the door, two each side of it. An arrogant looking Frenchman in a uniform stood at the door. He hardly talked. He stood firmly looking down at *Les misérables*, jostling to enter his 'paradise', from behind his dark sunglasses. From time to time, he literally pushed people away from the door, which made him look superior. At about 10.00 am two *Garraba* (traditional water salesmen in red, traditional Moroccan costumes) roamed the place with their black sheepskin water containers on their backs. Ringing their brass bells to attract people's attention, they fill their brass pots with water from time to time and spill it on the floor, as if this would make people thirsty. Maybe it does. You could hear young boys selling single cigarettes: 'Marlboro, Marquis, Winston.'

After having queued for just three days outside different Western embassies, I realised that queuing had given rise to new opportunities for the jobless. From the cake boy to the cigarette boy to the water salesman, not to mention the information-men, everyone seemed to be making a living from the queue. There were also people who made good money queuing overnight for other people. At one point, I sat beside an information salesman who shouted from time to time: 'Information, information, all kinds of information, *majeur, mineur, étudiant*!' These mostly young, well-dressed Moroccans who have created unofficial jobs out of nothing are called: '*Hassrafa*'. 'Are you educated? Have you got a bank account?' asked the information-man. 'No', replied a girl to both questions. 'Don't waste your time', he replied, information for which he demanded no money. 'How much money do I need in my bank account before the French would accept my *demande?'* asked another girl. 'You need to have 5000 Dirhams in your bank account; your work manager has to write an official letter to confirm it. He must provide you with a letter confirming the date of your holiday; otherwise they won't give you anything.' 'Information, information, student visa, working visa, *mineur, majeur,* all sorts of information', shouted the information-man and said to himself as if he had gone mad: 'nobody wants to live here anymore. This is a nice country, but its people are difficult. I left this country a long time ago, left my job, family and everything. I went to France. Look at me now, selling bits of information on the street.'

Talk of and about emigration in the Old Medina of Casablanca

It was summer in Morocco and many Moroccan émigrés had come home from different Western countries to spend the summer holiday with their relatives. Talk of and about the émigrés, their spouses, cars and other material possessions, as I learned from fieldwork in the Old Medina (a poor borough near the port of Casablanca) was unavoidable. Many young people from Old Medina have emigrated or 'burned' (see table below) to Europe. Some of them have become legends and therefore objects of talk in this working class area of Casablanca. 'Hassan burned to Italy and after three months he came back with a car and his papers. He managed to take all his brothers and sisters back with him to Italy. They are all living there now. He is what I call a man,' said Murad, a young Moroccan from Old Medina. There were times where talk of the émigrés altered to become talk about the émigrés. In other words ordinary talk transformed into gossip. As another young Moroccan from Old Medina confirmed, 'Sometimes you cannot help but talk about the *zmagrias*' (émigrés) wives, how good looking or ugly they are. We also talk about how changed some of the people we know have become.' Arrivals of émigrés from the West become the talk of '*Derb*'. From the car, clothes, presents to the appearance of the émigré, all is scrutinised, all becomes an object of gossip. In the Old Medina, talk of and about burning is inescapable. As Nassir, a young Moroccan from Old Medina commented, 'There are young people here who wake up and go to bed talking about *burning*.'

New words emanating from ordinary daily conversational interactions about emigration are ceaselessly enriching the Moroccan *Dareja*[38] vocabulary. This has created a new *speak*, which finds its origins in French, English, Spanish, Portuguese and Arabic. These are some of the migration-related words recently incorporated into Moroccan popular *Dareja*:

New *Dareja* Word	Meaning
Hrig	From the Arabic word *hareek,* meaning burning. In Moroccan *Dareja*, it means to emigrate illegally.
Harrag	Burner, an illegal emigrant.
Lourak	From the Arabic word *awrak*, meaning papers. In Moroccan *Dareja*, it is used to refer to legal documents.
Dock	This English word is used to describe the place from where the burning takes place (inside the port).
Watchman	This English word is now commonly used among *burners* and young people in Old Medina to signify the person who is responsible for the security of the cargoes.
Kwan	From the French word *coin*, meaning corner. A place where one hides in wait for an opportunity to *burn*.
Contonaire	French for container, a hiding place many illegal emigrants use to migrate illegally to Western countries.

(Continued)

New *Dareja* Word	Meaning
Tarrack	From the Arabic word *tarrak,* the person responsible for closing containers.
Lhih	A *Dareja* word meaning 'there'. To burn 'there' is to burn to the West.
Hatt	A *Dareja* word meaning to land. It is a synonym for burn or emigrate illegally.
Meeka	A *Dareja* word, meaning plastic bag. In the popular culture of the Old Medina it is a plastic bag where the burner carries food for his journey (usually nuts and water).
Speciale	French for special, a police station in the port that deals only with illegal emigrants.
Zmagri	A *Dareja* word from the French émigré. Plural: *Zmagria.*

These words constitute a new *Dareja* vocabulary that has become a pervasive part of ordinary communicative interactions among young Moroccans in the Old Medina and which has spread to many parts of Casablanca. Different areas of Morocco have adopted different migration-related words into their original vocabularies. In north Morocco, for example, where many Moroccans are fluent in Spanish, a lot of Spanish words, related to migration, have been incorporated into daily conversations of Moroccans living in the North.

On 'Burning'

The most commonly used word to refer to illegal migration in Morocco and much of the Arab Maghreb is '*hrig*', literally meaning burning. The latter has become a very common and recurrent word in everyday speech in Arab Maghrebi popular culture. People whom I asked gave two interpretations of the word. According to one group, a *burner* is someone who destroys/burns his passport and all his identity cards before emigrating illegally to a Western country, so that if they are caught their identity will not be revealed (making it difficult to deport them back). The other group traces the etymology of the word to an historical event in 711 when Tarik Ibn Zayad, an *Amazigh* soldier, burnt all his fleet on approaching Spain so that his army would have no choice but to fight to conquer Spain. At the rock of Gibraltar, Ibn Zayad delivered his famous speech: 'the enemy is in front of you and the sea is behind you, where is there to run?' To burn in Moroccan popular talk is therefore a reference to a one-way journey where one attempts to enter a Western country illegally. As the Moroccan joke goes: *After the building of the Great Mosque of Hassan II, an architectural wonder and the second biggest mosque in the world, was finally completed, the King of Morocco offered to give it to the Americans as a token of friendship. All efforts were made by the Americans to remove the Minaret from the ground, but it just would not budge. As the Mosque was built on the sea, the Americans sent their experts to find out what was happening under the water. To their shock they found thousands of young Moroccan burners holding on to the base of the Minaret. They all wanted to burn to the States.*

To explore meanings of burning even further, one also needs to place the term in its cultural context. One needs to think of burning not merely as a physical action but also as a pervasive part of Maghrebi popular culture. It is for many young Moroccans the only way out and only alternative to their lived realities. I heard a story about a pupil aged 8 who told his teacher, 'What is the point of all this homework and hard work, my brother has a degree and sells single cigarettes in the street. The only solution is burning.' Burning needs to be understood as a phenomenon, as well as part of a popular culture that is symptomatic of indifference and defeatism, one that is, moreover, becoming increasingly common among young Maghrebis, especially those from the working classes. Burning as a phenomenon is illuminated by another Moroccan joke, which goes: *An American scientist from NASA was sent by the American government to explore how the Moroccan brain functions. In his laboratory, the scientist took the brain of a young Moroccan and placed it into the head of an American. He then placed the latter's brain into the Moroccan's head. The Moroccan with the American's brain stayed in Morocco, while the American with the Moroccan's brain was taken back to the States. One year after the experiment, the scientist decided to check on the two young men. In Morocco, the Moroccan with the American's brain had become a successful businessman with successful projects all over the country. Back in the States, the American with the Moroccan's brain had been reported missing. When they finally found him he was sitting by the port in New York looking rather sad. When they asked him what he was doing there, he said: 'I want to burn to Italy.'* The other commonly used word in migration-related jokes and in ordinary daily interactional conversations in Moroccan popular culture is *Loorak*, meaning papers. The majority of Moroccans, who become legal residents in different Western countries, whether in Europe or the USA, do so through marriage to either a European or American citizen. When these émigrés return to Morocco for holidays, their spouses are often satirically referred to as the 'papers': *A young zmagri 'émigré' was strolling along the beach with his Western wife when she tripped and fell in the sand. A young boy playing football with his friends saw the incident. He approached the husband who was contemplating the sea and said, 'Your papers dropped sir.'*

The queue, queuers and the politics of hope: mobility within immobility

The queue is a colonial imposition that reflects the power of Western modernity. Its dynamics constitute a taken-for-granted cultural space of everyday Moroccan culture, ceaselessly displaced by its encounters with this alien 'other'. Queues outside the French and Italian embassies divulge a dual cultural structure that is intrinsically paradoxical. On the one hand, we have the rationalised world of the queue as an institutional, bureaucratised product of Western modernity. On the other, we have the world of

the 'queuers', which accommodates Moroccan, non-institutionalised cultural particularities that are manifest in the closeness of
cultural distance, the sociability and intimacy shared by queuing
Moroccans. Attempting to bridge the gulf between these two-
world structures are native intermediaries, who work for Western
embassies and the *information*-salesmen. What the queue epitomises is the shock of Western modernity. This shock is manifest
in the queuers' sense of chaos and disorganisation. Most of all,
they feel displaced, unwanted and humiliated by the powerful
'other'. The queuers are trapped. This is how I felt, trapped with
them. Extraordinarily, in their entrapment, the queuers joked,
shared food, blankets and talked incessantly. I confess, to my
mortification, that I have hardly used the word 'mobility', in its
written form. I have, of course, used similar terms to describe
different kinds of movement, such as migration, emigration and
burning. Here, I am more concerned with rehearsing, or shall I
say toying with, the idea of 'mobility as immobility' or mobility
within immobility, as a way of concretising the kind of experience Tomlinson describes as 'the paradigmatic experience of
global modernity', where most people, and I mean most people,
stay in one place but experience 'displacement' brought about by
global modernity (Tomlinson in Morley, 2000:15). Much of what
I discovered from fieldwork conducted in Morocco, especially in
the poorest parts of the country, has less to do with movement
and mobility and more to do with immobility and its different
kinds. The interesting thing about these immobilities is that in
a desperate search for hope, they create the illusion of movement and mobility. The queue is that kind of symbolic space: a
resource of hope. Queuing for many is the nearest point to being
there in the West, encountering it beyond the phantasmagoric,
touching it. The queue, in this instance, is about hope. It is the
nearest point to the plane, the boat, to crossing the border. It is
a way of *being*: feeling mobile within a world of social, cultural
and economic immobility. Every step made in the queue towards
the door of the embassy is a step towards hope. The queue is a

space where both hope and entrapment coexist. The unbearable feeling of possible or, in some cases, certain rejection, is eased by the cultural closeness of the queuers; their intimacy, jokes and shared *humum* (problems). The hope is also fed, kept alive, by occasional queue gossip about such and such a Western country desperately seeking migrants, or about so and so lucky ones who have just received visas. The queue creates the illusion of mobility: it is a simulacrum, a chimera of the immobile. It allows the immobile to feel mobile, albeit momentarily. I can observe queuers, hear what they have to say to others they have befriended in the queue, but I do not know what goes on in their heads. What do they think? What do they feel? How humiliated are they, really? Knadi, a young Moroccan from the working class quarter of the Old Medina, with whom I conducted long interviews about his desire to emigrate to the West, has been denied a visa by almost every Western embassy in Casablanca. His immobility is compensated for by the mediation of the Western music text, a place where he feels mobile. For him, Western music is a kind of alternative *heimat*[39], allowing him, even if momentarily, to dwell in an imaginary spatial-temporality. As he said: 'Western music helps me forget the fact that I live in Morocco. It makes me feel as though I were there in the West.' The utterance 'there' indicating the West has connotations that are deeply seated in the Moroccan popular imaginary. The 'thereness' of the West, here, does not merely signify distance or location but also, and most importantly, 'unreacheablity': the geographic, economic and cultural unreacheablity of the West.

Mobility of the dead

Is our world truly one of 'mobility', as many social and cultural theorists from the West suggest? What is often unspoken in discourses of 'mobility' is the very immobility, or perhaps immobilities of the 'other', who resides outside the boundaries of 'Fortress Europe' (Morley, 2000). According to an official government statistics, approximately 500 Moroccans drown every year trying to cross to Spain (this is without adding the number of others from the rest of the Maghreb and the sub-Sahara). 'Mobility' that so many scholars take for granted is, sadly, a prize for which 'the wretched of the earth' are prepared to die. As one young Moroccan told me, 'I'd rather a shark than stay in Morocco.' The seldom asked question is: 'Whose mobility are we talking about?' Most of the world's poor, and the poor outnumber the rich, simply cannot afford to be mobile. Hence, drawing a picture of a de-centered, globalised world, characterised by mobility, is dangerously occidental and must be questioned. We ought also to be concerned about the structures of immobilities, which extend from physical to mental (symbolic) trajectories (see Chapter 5). This can be said not only of young Moroccans or Arabs but also of most of the developing world's youth. Europe is, for many of them, both desirable and unreachable. Europe, as Ang and Morley argued, 'is not just a geographical site, it is also an idea: an idea inextricably linked with the myth of Western civilisation.' (Ang and Morley, 1989: 133) 'Fortress Europe' may be closing its borders, but Europe's symbolic geography is, thanks to transnational communications, borderless. In fact, it is a welcoming one! The West's symbolic geography ceaselessly invites others to cross its borders, whereas its physical geography is ceaselessly trying to get rid of and cleanse its home from unwanted dirt.

I watch the corpses of young Moroccans, Algerians, young people from the sub-Sahara, the forgotten *misérables* of global modernity, moving gently with the silent waves of the deep, Mediterranean Sea, and I cry. These brave ones who gave up hope of getting visas, of queuing outside Western embassies. How many times did they queue and how many times were they rejected? I watch as the Spanish coastal police drag their 'mobile' bodies (some wearing two pairs of jeans, expecting the worst) with a long metal hook. Their mobility, as they float before my eyes, is that of the dead who, even in death, refuse entrapment and immobility. How powerful the idea of the West still is!

Conclusion

While the queue is a place of encounter with the local and the Western 'other', it is also a manifestation of a desire for hope, the kind of hopes and possibilities that the physical mobility promises. It is a space where encounters with the West and its institutions are played out, refuted, critiqued and negotiated. The diary notes and the narrative they weave also tell the story of class and local cultural stratification and, most importantly, the story of the Arab working classes, their hopes and aspirations. The story of the bridge, regardless of its methodological inadequacies and 'openness' as a text, shows how certain 'places' intersect with different routes, axes, roads, the fluidity of which allows for an acting out of the self and of desires that contradict conventional and fixed ideas about gender and love in an Arab society. The acting out of romance is, in this context, an act of individual modernness; a desire to normalise, just as in the Egyptian soap, the act of premarital love as a human natural act. The bridge and the queue are the spaces of the unheard and unseen: those of the unemployed standing in the corner of the *Derb*, the visa queuer, the information-men, the cigarette boy, the burner, the Taxi driver and the young lovers who cannot afford marriage. What I have also tried to show here (by default, perhaps) is that to comprehend Arab popular cultures it is imperative that we examine not only mass mediated popular culture but also the unmanaged and often taken-for-granted ordinariness of everyday experience.

5

Modernness as a Multiple Narrative-Category: Encountering the West

Modernity is not a concept, philosophical or otherwise, but a narrative category.

(Jameson, 2002: 40)

In conditions of late modernity...Everyone still continues to live a local life, and the constraints of the body ensure that all individuals, at every moment, are contextually situated in time and space. Yet the transformations of place, and the intrusion of distance into local activities, combined with the centrality of mediated experience, radically change what 'the world' actually is. This is so both on 'the phenomenal world' of the individual and the general universe of social activity within which collective social life is enacted. Although everyone lives a local life, phenomenal worlds for the part are truly global.

(Giddens, 1991: 187)

> What is remarkable about television is that it is doubly
> *world-disclosing*, in its technological form *and* in what
> it opens up when we turn it on – the life of the world,
> life-as-lived by the generations of the present as shown
> *live* on television.
>
> (Scannell, 2009)

Couscoussière as a *technology of encountering*

Couscoussière is French for *Cass-Cass*, a symbol of Moroccan
cuisine and the pride and joy of millions of Arabs and *Amazighs*
throughout the Great Maghreb. The *Cass-Cass* is necessary to
cook the 'authentic' thrice-steamed Moroccan *couscous*. It has two
parts: the lower an oval-shaped pot where meat, sauce and vegetables are cooked, and an upper round structure with holes at the
bottom to let the steam from the meats, the vegetables: carrots,
cabbage, courgettes, chickpeas, pumpkin, coriander and the like
through to the *couscous* on the top. *Couscous* is a dish that has
travelled far and now is a part of international cuisine; a dish readily available in the West and other parts of the world. In Morocco,
couscous is a mix of semolina with meats (in Tunisia, fish is also
used) and vegetables. In the West, *couscous* is a 'hybridised' dish,
added to salads and other dishes, strangely associated with healthy
eating! There is a popular cultural story about the *Couscoussière*
that goes like this: Overlooking the Old Medina of Casablanca
(in an area also known as the *Mellah*, formerly a Jewish quarter)
stands the imposing structure of the Hyatt Regency Hotel (still
there today), on the roof of which appeared a gigantic satellite dish.
The *Mellah*'s young people were fascinated by the structure of the
dish, more so when they heard it could 'bring the whole world
to their sitting-room.' Owning such a 'phantasmagoric' technology in 1989, at a time when most Moroccans only had access to
one channel (RTM), was a very exciting prospect to the *Mellah*'s
working class youth. One day, a young Moroccan from the *Mellah*,
standing with his unemployed friends, and joking, as one would,

in the *Derb* (see Chapter 4), likened the image of the satellite dish on the roof of the hotel to the shape of the *Couscoussière*. In fact, he went further and experimented with the idea by attaching his mum's beloved *Couscoussière* to the television antenna on his own house-roof. To his amazement, when he turned the TV on, he could hear voices that were neither Arab nor French: they were Italian, Spanish, English and German – according to the story, that is. The picture was fuzzy, but this did not spoil the euphoria at the mere thought of having access to sounds and images of the *Gur*[40] in one's sitting room. He returned to the antenna and readjusted the *Couscoussière* several times until the picture became clearer. This young Moroccan, a modern Robin Hood, a hero of the Moroccan working classes, had single-handedly reinvented satellite technology and was about to disseminate it so the poor could have access to it. The news travelled fast and in just few weeks later, the *Mellah's* rooftops were littered with *Couscoussières*. This was the day Moroccans gave up their couscous for satellite! The story of the Couscoussière is a story of encountering *par excellence*. It is also, as I will later show, a story about modernness, cultural temporality and double-identity. This chapter must be read as a further attempt to concretise the three-dimensional structure around which I articulate meanings of 'being modern'. Here, I focus on the third and final part of the foregrounding: the self-referential. To do this, I revisit the theme of *encountering* by looking at the role played by television in the process of young Moroccans' encounter with the West and how this produces different understandings of modernity and 'being modern'.

Problems of meaning

In his short, yet seminal work, *non-places*, Marc Augé (1995) advances that the ceaseless growth in media and communications in the late twentieth century had led to an 'overabundance' in the temporal and the spatial, leading thereafter, to a crisis of meaning. Earlier on, Jean Baudrillard (1983) expressed the same view when he observed that we now inhabit a world with more and more signs, but less and less meaning. The crisis of meaning that Augé and Baudrillard alerts us to, also resonates when one looks at the language used by social theorists/cultural theorists to make sense of the world in which we live. If our world today is, because of the spread of the mass media, one of 'globalisation' and 'hybridisation', how do we, then, make sense of such phenomena? How useful have 'globalisation' theories been in helping us understand, let us ask, for the purpose of this chapter, what the cultural consequences of 'globalisation' are? It is not the purpose of this chapter to sift through or attempt to organise the chaos of globalisation theories, nor do I intend to engage in a phenomenology of 'meaning'. I set myself a far more modest and less laborious task. This is inspired by the viewpoint that globalisation theories, especially those Sparks (2004, 2005, 2007) categorises as 'strong' ones – those which make 'culture' and the 'media' central to their enquiries – remain largely over-abstracted and 'non-evidential'. Sparks argues: 'if we are to make any serious intellectual progress, we need to... develop the insights of social theory into the kinds of propositions about the mass media that we can subject to an evidential critique' (Sparks, 2004: 4). The 'newness' often attributed to the cultural consequences of 'globalisation' is rarely challenged. Here, I argue that for a better understanding of globalisation's cultural consequences we need to investigate not only the ways in which institutions of modernity have altered the 'ordinariness' of culture (Sreberny-Mohammadi, 1997) at the periphery but also how they have altered the 'structures of feeling' of people about the world. Using qualitative and quantitative data from fieldwork conducted in Morocco (2001–7), including 11 unstructured focus groups[41], life histories, a survey targeting 1000 young Moroccans and participant observation, I investigate how long-term consumption of Western media texts, other factors included, play a role in producing different, self-reflexive narratives of modernness. Here, I contend that young Moroccans (a microcosm for youth in the Arab world) are able to emigrate mentally to the West, being in Morocco, through their long-term exposure to 'globalised' Western media texts and so expand the West's symbolic geography and its project of modernity. Using material from focus groups and participant observation, I rationalise the dynamics of 'mental emigration' (Sabry, 2003) as one of the cultural consequences of 'globalisation' and argue that the intersection between its non-fixed reference points, together with young Moroccans' contradictory structures of feeling and *habitus*, allows for different articulations of *being* modern. It is within this conjunction, I argue, that aspects of subjectification and modernness are negotiated. This chapter also demonstrates how difference in socio-economic and cultural strata among young Moroccans produces different readings of and reactions to modernity. These I classify as 'incoherent acceptance', 'coherent acceptance', 'negotiation' and 'coherent rejection'.

Young Moroccans and media access

Young Moroccans are part of an increasingly young Arab population where more than 56 per cent of the region's population is under the age of 20 and 78 per cent under the age of 35 (see Talal, 2005: 102). Their construction as a political generation, and their role as agents of change, is significant not only for Morocco but also for the rest of the Arab world. This section introduces findings from a survey that targeted 1000 young Moroccan students, between the ages of 16 and 25, from 6 colleges situated in different areas of Casablanca. The main objective of the questionnaire was to obtain general information about young Moroccans' access to media technology (television, satellite, computer, Internet) and gain information about their consumption of these media (preferred channels, programmes, genres, and the time spent using each medium). The six chosen colleges were divided into public and private schools so as to reflect stratification of socio-economic status[42]. Although a substantial number of young Moroccans were targeted by the survey, and although it had a very good respondent success-rate (891 of 1000), this survey does not claim to be representative of Morocco, or even Casablanca. However, it was sampled so as to reflect social stratification within Casablanca.

Media access and consumption

Chart 1 illustrates that 99 per cent of the respondents said they had access to television in their household, making it by far the most accessible medium of entertainment. Eighty per cent of the respondents said they had satellite, 33 per cent said they had a PC and 15 per cent said they had access to the Internet at home. The chart shows a massive increase in access to satellite technology with 80 per cent of the respondents saying they had access to satellite in their household. The chart also shows a clear case of stratification in access to media technologies amongst the respondents. Although 80 per cent of the respondents from category A said they had access to a computer in their household, only 18 per cent from category D and 16 per cent from category E said they had. As for the Internet, 47 per cent from category A said they had access to the Internet at home, whereas only 11 per cent from category C2, 8 per cent from category D and 3 per cent from category E said they had. As for satellite access, 100 per cent of respondents from categories A and B said they had access to a satellite in their household, but only 63 per cent from category E said they had access to the technology. The respondents' average television viewing-time

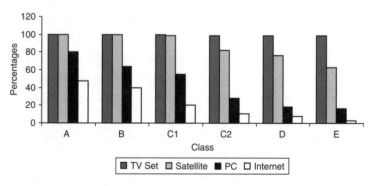

Chart 1   Access to media technology according to class

is between 3.4 and 3.5 hours a day, with male and female respondents consuming far similar amounts of time daily.

As Chart 2 illustrates, female respondents consume far more Arabic programmes[43] than male respondents do. These are mainly Egyptian films and soap operas. The chart also illustrates that female respondents consume far less Moroccan programming than male respondents and that an almost equal amount of male and female respondents prefer Western programmes. The difference between the two is a mere 1 per cent. Chart 2 reflects the low quality of Moroccan programming most conspicuously. Only 28 per cent of the 891 respondents said they liked to watch Moroccan programmes. According to the survey, Western programmes are the most popular amongst the respondents. However, Moroccan programmes remain the least popular with only 19.6 per cent of male and 9.2 per cent of female respondents saying they preferred them to Western and Arabic programmes.

Chart 3 shows respondents from the upper middle and middle classes to be the most prolific consumers of Western media texts. Sixty-seven per cent of respondents from the upper middle classes or category A, 49 per cent from category B and 55 per cent from category C1 said they preferred Western programmes. Although, the chart shows that respondents from the working classes consume far more Arabic programmes than respondents from A, B and C1, the Chart surprisingly shows that more respondents from category A consume Moroccan programmes than respondents from class E, but not more than those from B, C1, C2 and D. Arabic programmes

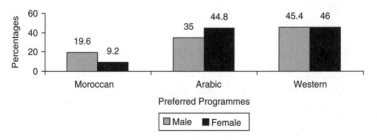

Chart 2 Programme preference according to gender

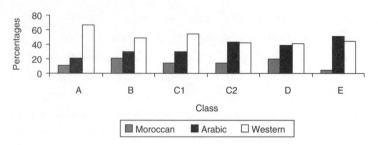

Chart 3 Programme preference according to class

become more popular as we go down the social ladder, whereas Western programmes are popular in all categories. However, C2 is the only category where the respondents consume almost an equal amount of Western and Arabic programmes. In case of category A, there is a remarkable disparity between the respondents' consumption of Western programmes and Arabic programmes.

Chart 4[44] shows a clear gender disparity in the viewing habits of male and female respondents. The Egypt and Nile TV channels both show a large number of Egyptian films and soaps and this makes them far more popular with female than male respondents. Five per cent of female respondents said they watched the Nile TV channel, whereas only 1 per cent of male respondents said they did. There is also a clear gender disparity in the consumption of the Egyptian satellite channel Egypt. Although 9 per cent of female respondents said they watched Egypt, only 4 per cent of male respondents said they did. Al-Jazeera, the Qatari based satellite channel, shows no films at all and is, as the chart shows, more popular with male respondents (14 per cent) than it is with female ones (11 per cent). It would be misleading to extrapolate from this data, however, that male respondents watch more factual programmes. More number of female respondents (13 per cent) said they watched TV5, the French satellite channel that places heavy emphasis on news and current affairs, than male respondents (9 per cent). The chart also shows that almost an equal number of male and female respondents (3 per cent each) watch the Islamic, Saudi, privately owned channel Iqraa. The latter is a 24-hour channel, mainly broadcast in Arabic,

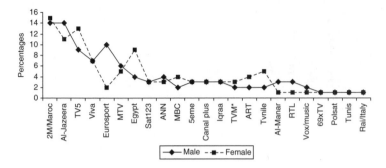

Chart 4   Satellite and local (national channel)* viewing according to gender

the largest proportion of which is, besides news, dedicated to religious broadcasting. Al-Manar, the Lebanese channel and the voice of *Hizb Allah*, is more popular among male than female respondents. Of the two local Moroccan television channels: 2M and TVM, the former is the most popular. The commercial channel 2M, which broadcasts most of its programmes in French, heads the list of preferred channels among respondents. TVM, the first national Moroccan television channel, which broadcasts most of its programmes in Arabic, is, as the chart shows very unpopular with both male and female respondents. Al-Jazeera is by far the most popular Arab channel amongst the respondents. There are, however, in the consumption of Al-Jazeera and other Arab satellite channels, some acute differences in class, which I will address later. Ten per cent of male respondents said they watched Eurosport, whereas only 2 per cent of female respondents said they did. As for the consumption of Western satellite Music channels, such as MTV and Vox, the chart shows a very marginal difference based on gender.

It is important to note how local* and Arab satellite channels (with the exception of Al-Jazeera) are the least popular amongst the upper and middle classes (categories A and B), especially TVM, the first National Moroccan television channel, Iqraa and Al-Manar. None of the respondents from categories A and B said they watched TVM, Iqraa or Al-Manar. One per cent from category A, and 5 per cent from category B said they watched both

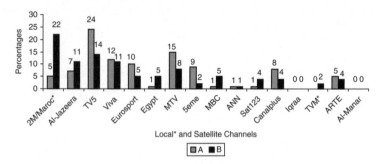

Chart 5 Local* and satellite channel viewing according to groups A and B

Egypt and MBC (Middle East Broadcasting Corporation). One per cent from both categories said they watched ANN (Arab News Network). Al-Jazeera, as stated earlier, is by far the most popular Arab channel with a viewership of 7 per cent from category A and 11 per cent from category B. 2M, the local channel, mainly broadcast in French, is watched by 5 per cent audience from category A and 22 per cent from category B. Categories A and B consume far more Western channels than Arab or local* channels, with the exception of the Moroccan channel 2M. More respondents from category A watch the French channel TV5 than 2M or any other Arab satellite channel. Furthermore, 2M is the most popular channel among respondents from category B. More respondents from categories A and B watch MTV and VIVA (German), two Western music satellite channels, than any other Arab channel.

Chart 6 demonstrates that (with the exception of MBC and Egypt) category C2 respondents watch more Moroccan and Arabic channels than respondents from category C1 do. However, on the contrary, C1 respondents watch more Western satellite channels than Moroccan or Arab channels. Disparity between the categories is especially conspicuous in the consumption of Al-Jazeera, MTV, VIVA and Al-Manar. Though 18 per cent of respondents from C2 said they watched Al-Jazeera, only 4 per cent from C1 said they did, and while only 3 per cent from C2 said they watched MTV, 10 per cent from C1 said they did. Transition from category C1 to C2 marks the shift of taste and preference from, mainly, the Western channels, as we saw with the A, B and C1 groups to the viewing of more Arab and Moroccan channels, as we saw in the case of C2, and as we can see below in categories D and E (in Chart 7).

As charts 5, 6 and 7 illustrated, more respondents from categories D and E said they watched Moroccan television 2M than respondents from the rest of categories A, B, C1 and C2 did. Respondents from categories D and E (as Chart 1 illustrated) have less access to satellite than respondents from the other categories do, which could be one of the reasons why more respondents from the working classes watch more Moroccan television than the respondents from the upper and middle classes do. The most popular channels amongst groups E and D are Al-Jazeera and the commercial Moroccan channel 2M. In fact, as Chart 7 shows, more respondents from category D preferred watching Al-Jazeera to both local Moroccan channels. Furthermore, it is important to note how Iqraa and Al-Manar are more popular among respondents from categories C2, D and E than they are among respondents from categories A, B and C1.

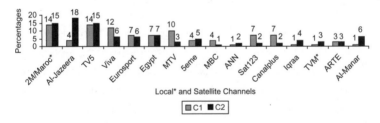

Chart 6 Local* and satellite channel viewing according to groups C1 and C2

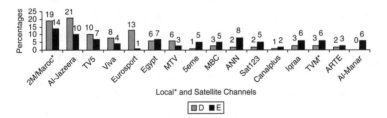

Chart 7 Local* and satellite channel viewing according to groups D and E

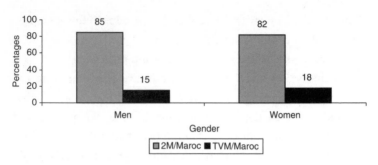

Chart 8   Local channel viewing according to gender

Chart 8 illustrates the unpopularity of TVM (the first Moroccan national channel) with both male and female respondents. Only 15 per cent of male and 18 per cent of female respondents said they watched TVM, whereas 85 per cent of male and 82 per cent of female respondents said they watched the Moroccan commercial channel 2M. The latter was the first private commercial channel in Africa and the Arab world, which has recently been entirely bought by the Moroccan state. It broadcasts most of its programmes in French.

Young Moroccans' conceptions of the West

A total of 11 unstructured focus groups were interviewed and they were made up from five different subgroups of young Moroccans, drawn from different socio-economic and cultural strata: Young *Amazighs* from the Atlas Mountains, young Islamists[45] from Casablanca, young political activists from USFP (*Union Socialiste des Forces Populaires*), young people from the Old Medina and Olfa (two working class quarters of Casablanca)[46] and young people from *Gautier* (a middle class[47] quarter of Casablanca). In their response to the question: 'What is the West?' the participants gave a number of definitions, which I divide below into mythical and negative significations. The West or *Gharb*, as it is known in Arabic, means different things to young Moroccans. The body of young Moroccans' conceptions of and about the West, as empirical evidence from fieldwork will show, is contradictory and ambivalent, containing different readings and based in different geographic spatialities. For some the West exists in Europe, for others it is in the USA or, in the case of young *Amazighs* from the Atlas, the West is only in France. Moreover, while some believe the West to exist in the *outside*, others, reflecting Khatibi's 'double-identity' discourse, feel there is a West both within them and within Morocco. The West is paradoxically conceived as both a dominating and an emancipatory power. It is, at the same time, a *paradise* and an *octopus*[48], which also seems to replicate the duality in which Arab intellectuals position the West and its cultural repertoire. Just as we saw with the four intellectual traditions of Arab thought described in Chapter 2, even within the same, carefully sampled subgroups, conceptions of the West were neither fixed nor entirely homogeneous. I have divided young Moroccans' conceptions of the 'West' into two different types: 'mythical' and 'negative' (here meaning critical). Negative *significations* of the West came mainly from the young Islamists, and from a small number of the Socialist Youth Group. Mythical *significations* of the West came mainly from the rest of the subgroups: young Moroccans from the middle class, from the working class (politicised and non-politicised) and young *Amazighs* from the *douar*[49] of *Ait Nuh*[50].

Table 1

Mythical significations versus Negative Significations

The West signifies freedom/ The West signifies domination

The West signifies safety/ The West signifies killing

The West signifies happiness/ The West signifies ambivalence

The West signifies wealth/ The West signifies octopus

The West signifies progress/ The West signifies decay

The West signifies praxis/ The West signifies colonialism

The West signifies virtue/ The West signifies interests

The West signifies paradise/ The West signifies deprivation

The West signifies individuality/ The West signifies cultural hegemony

The West is without/ The West is both without and within

Since myth depoliticises speech and empties it of history, I may be criticised for stipulating that conceptions of the West, such as *freedom* and *happiness*, are *mythical* significations, which may in turn be misread as enforcing a presupposed truth about the West. However, such *significations* of the West are mythologised and de-mythologised, as will later become evident, by nothing other than the mere existence of the critical/negative *significations* with which they enter a dialectical relationship. Still, in the same vein, I could be criticised for not choosing to deal with *negative* (critical) significations, such as *colonialism*, *killing* and *domination*, as mythical significations of the West. Such a critique, however, can only reinforce the critic's naiveté, for significations such as *colonialism* (coming from the 'oppressed') are usually unpurified, full of history, and therefore unlike *myth*, which relies for its existence precisely on inflexion, purification, de-politicisation and, we should add, the masking of history. This is encapsulated succinctly in the following passage from Roland Bathes's *Mythologies*:

> The speech of the oppressed can only be poor, monotonous, immediate: his destitution is the very yardstick of his language…he has only one, always the same, that of his actions; meta-language is a luxury…the speech of the oppressed is real…it is a transitive type of speech: it is quasi-unable to lie; lying is a richness, a lie presupposes property, truths and forms to spare.
>
> (Barthes, 1972: 148)

If one looks carefully at the content of the table, it will become apparent that what we are in fact dealing with are not merely 'conceptions' of the West as it is encountered but a complex system of significations that presupposes a signifying consciousness: a kind of knowledge about the West that takes place at the point of encounter, not only with the televisiual but also with *history* (encounters with the West as a colonial and a dominant power). Islamists, most of whom came from a poor working class area of Casablanca, were by far the most educated, critical and assertive. This might take some Western readers by surprise, as in the West these aspects are usually ascribed to the middle rather than the working classes. A young Islamist responded, when I asked him to define the West:

> In the name of Allah, the bountiful and merciful, first on the meaning of the term 'West', I do not think we could find a precise answer or definition of the term. Geographically, the West is not part of the Arab Islamic world... and so we think of it as being outside. Then we have the cultural meaning of the West. We think of a culture that is not Arab or Islamic as Western. Politically, the West lives in our memories and what we recall is colonialism, killing, domination and so on. There is another perspective and that is the West's economic hegemony and the draining of resources from the Arab and the rest of the world. But this idea of the West, how is it built? The accumulated culture we have gives us a short conclusion – that the West is an enemy. Of course this enmity is not absolute; there are ways in which we could say we could and do have a relationship of reciprocity with the West. However, such reciprocity is merely based on 'interests'. The relationship of the West with the rest is that of interests: It is not built on a pure cultural, religious or historical exchange. Take away interests and what remains is *adaa* 'enmity' and struggle.

It is crucial to point out, however, that while Islamists' conceptions of the West were the most critical, their reading of the West was not the most dominant. The dominant and prevailing reading of the West among the majority of young Moroccans remains positive and uncritical. What distinguishes Islamists' conceptualisations of the West from those of other subgroups is not merely their sense of history or their linguistic superiority but also the fact that their conceptions are framed and structured within the context of power relations: an historical struggle they think is taking place between them (as young Islamists) and the West. The most conspicuous manifestation of this is in the use of symbolic significations, such as *silb* (denying someone their rights)[51], *Octopus* and other *negative* significations such as *killing, domination, maslaha* 'interests' and '*adaa* 'enmity'. What is the structural nature of the associative relationship between young Moroccans' *mythical* and *negative* significations of the West? The binary examples: freedom/domination; safety/killing, progress/decay, within/without, show how *mythical* and *negative* significations of the West enter a relationship of opposition, one of mythologising and de-mythologizing. However, because the opposing significations are not held equally within the same consciousness or 'structure of feeling', cancellation is never complete. Significations of the West, as young Moroccans encounter them/cultivate them, be they mythical or negative, are not fixed. Islamists' conceptions of the West, for example, were not entirely homogenous. In an Islamist focus group discussion, a female participant strongly and openly criticised her 'brothers' and sisters'[52] critical stance as being hypocritical and urged them to be realistic and learn from the West as a superior civilisation:

> In the name of Allah, the bountiful and merciful, the West is superior and it is not only protecting its culture but propagating it. Why don't we just acknowledge the fact that the West is superior? When it comes to praxis, the West is leading, that is why Westerners are in front and we are behind. They give importance to women and to

the individual. I am proud of them, we must learn from them.

The West as a symbolic and a physical geography

The different *significations* of the West, as they appear for us in Table 1 and Table 2, show us that the geography of the West occupies divided and dual spatialities: one symbolic, the other physical, both are inextricably linked (see Chapter 4). The symbolic geography of the West exists in mental *mythical* and *negative* conceptions thereof. Significations of the West, such as *freedom*, *happiness*, *progress*, *safety* and others, are the invisible maps and the basis on which a symbolic geography of the West is built. Reacting to the question: 'Where is the West?' participants from different subgroups placed the West in different spatial geographies.

As Table 2 shows, for young Moroccans, the spatial geography of the West dwells in and is limited to a number of countries or physical geographies, such as the USA, Europe, Canada, England, France, London, Germany and Spain. These, regardless of their

Table 2

Spatial significations of the West

The West signifies the USA
The West signifies Europe
The West signifies Canada
The West signifies France
The West signifies Germany
The West signifies England
The West signifies London
The West signifies Switzerland
The West signifies Scandinavia
The West signifies 'There'

physicality, not only dwell in the physical geography of the West but also in its symbolic geography. In other words, they cannot be thought about outside their symbolic significations. Europe, for example, is not only a continent but also an idea, and the same applies for every country mentioned. London, to give another example from Table 2, is not a mere physical geography, for it also accommodates an *ensemble* of imaginative narratives, such as 'coolness', 'freedom', 'lights' and pop music/Rock 'n' Roll. We, therefore, have Europe and the idea of Europe, the USA and the idea of the USA, and so on.

Relocating the term 'structure of feeling' within the postcolonial

In one of my earliest field trips to Morocco, my old friend Hassan, with whom I went to university 20 years ago, insisted that he took me to a karaoke bar he frequented in the centre of Casablanca. He said, 'it would be a nice place to reminisce about the past'. As Hassan told me to dress smartly, I put on my best clothes and we headed for a taxi. The bar, which turned out to be in a Sheraton hotel, was beautifully designed with marble and brass. Hanging from its ceiling was an extravagant, luminous chandelier and, on the ground floor, an imposing fountain, the trickling water of which created an immediate soothing effect. Hassan chose the table nearest to a four-man Moroccan jazz-band that was performing and called the waiter. He greeted us in French and asked: '*Messieurs, bon soir, vous voulez boire?*' '*Un Heineken*' replied Hassan. I ordered the same and spread my eyes across the room, as Moroccans would say. In the bar, there were some 50 or more nicely tanned young Moroccans, male and female, most of whom were wearing recognisably Western label-wear: *Tommy, Lacoste, Gucci, Levi's, Nike* and others. From the neighbouring tables came sounds of well-spoken Parisian French. The tables displayed Western cigarette brands, which included Marlboro, Benson & Hedges and Camel, as well as expensive looking mobile phones, Western beer, cocktails and whiskies on the rocks. When the jazz band finished playing, some-one who appeared to be the Karaoke motivator took hold of the microphone and started welcoming everyone in French. All this seemed normal practice, this language thing I mean (even if most of the audience was Moroccan!). As the audience started choosing songs from the Karaoke catalogue, the Karaoke motivator started singing 'Hello', a famous Lionel Ritchie love-song. Though there were 35 Arabic songs listed on the catalogue, every song sung that night was either French or English, except for one, which was Tunisian. Ironically, it was stopped half way through, as the singer was too drunk to finish it. To save embarrassment, the jazz band took over and played a racy and feel-good Western melody. The most popular song of the night by far was 'Losing My Religion' by *R.E.M.* Late at night, the audience, some tipsy, some drunk, excited by the lyrics and the melody of the song, lifted their beer and whisky glasses high and joined my friend Hassan who, by this time, had the microphone in his hand and was singing: 'Losing my religion...but that was just a dream ... that was just a dream.'

What do I mean when I refer to young Moroccans' 'structure of feeling'? I am aware of Raymond Williams's use of the term, defined in *The Long Revolution* as 'the culture of a period...the particular living result of all the elements in the general organisation ... I think it is a very deep and a very wide possession, in all actual com-munities, precisely because it is on it that communication depends' (1961: 64–5). But what will the term 'structure of feeling' mean if detached from its Western context (or at least Williams's post-war Britain) and applied to other cultural contexts, in our case, the 'postcolonial'? I use the term 'structure of feeling' differently from Raymond Williams, that is, in a context where the structure of feel-ing is not merely the result of dynamics inherent to one culture, one 'general organisation,' one 'culture of a community' or one 'culture of a period', but it is used rather in the context where it is the prod-uct of a dialectical interaction between at least two different sets of cultural 'general organisations'. I also use it where its context is best described not only as the product of the 'culture of a period' but also as the product of an interaction/intersection between at least three cultural temporalities: the 'culture' that is being encountered, the 'culture' in which it is being encountered and the 'culture' of the person doing the encountering (which of course varies according to *habitus*). Furthermore, I do not content myself with merely studying elements of the two 'general organisations' separately but also explore the dialectical relationship and the dynamics resulting from their interrelation and intersection. It is, I argue, the relationship between at least two repertoires: Moroccan/Arab-Islamic 'culture' and Western modernity that form young Moroccans' structures of feeling about the world. The interaction between these two worlds and the ways in which they are encountered in the temporal gives rise to a complex set of 'Self-identity'[53] dynamics, oscillating between different and competing cultural temporalities, thus creating new ones. It is within this complex conjecture that manifestations of modernness (*being* modern) are demarcated, expressed and negotiated. The young Moroccan's desire to be different in the world, as the fieldwork material will later show, is helped by the existence and the encountering of an 'alternative' cultural temporality, a 'disembedding mechanism', inherent to television and its *phantasmagorical* 'worldliness'[54]. What television, the postmodern magic box, brings to the young Moroccan are not only the images and sounds of the *Gur* but also the temporalities within which the culture of the *Gawri*[55] operate. So, what is being encountered through television is not just 'cultures' but also the temporalities of the encountered 'cultures'. In what follows, I illustrate the variety and complexity of the different positions that can be adopted on this spectrum though examples from discussions with young Moroccans from different social groups.

Young *Amazighs* of Ait Nuh: *modernness* as an incoherent project

Ait Nuh is situated some 9 kilometres from the Atlas Mountain town of *Khunifra*. The *douar* cannot be reached by car, as it is quite high up the mountain. Over the eight-year period during which I was in contact with young people of Ait Nuh, I was able to converse with many of them and take part in a number of events. In the summer of 2002, when I was in Ait Nuh, young people of the *douar* invited me to a wedding. *Ait Nuhian* weddings follow formal ritual proceedings that have been passed on from one generation to another for centuries. All members of the *douar* are invited to take part in the proceedings, which last for three days. On the first day of the ceremony, a selected number of young men are set the task of finding a good, long bamboo stick, which they bring to the home of the husband-to-be, chanting and dancing on the way. Then, the most skilful is given the task of turning the long bamboo stick into a money collector. How is this done? The long bamboo stick is carefully incised from the middle throughout its length to create a crack that would accommodate bank notes from the people of the *douar*. This experiment is repeated many times until the notes are firmly and securely placed inside the bamboo stick. Once this is successfully completed, the young men, followed by children, carry the now-bamboo-money-collector in turns, chanting and playing with their *bendirs*[56], stopping, from time to time, to perform well-choreographed, folkloric dances. They move from house to house to collect the money. The process is very democratic, for each family in the *douar* gives exactly the same amount of money. In the case of this wedding, a 10 *Dirham* note (about 70 pence, 1$). All the notes are placed vertically within the crack so that there is a procession of them. The young *Ait Nuhians* performed these rituals with great care and joy. They all sang in *Tamazight*[57] and when the long-awaited band came in, they too sang well-known *Amazigh* songs. My informant, Saeed, explained that previously things were done differently. Now young *Ait Nuhians* wear jeans and T-shirts, whereas before young people of the *douar* wore adorned traditional costumes and rode elegantly embroidered horses. Many sheep were then killed, and sometimes the ceremony went on for more than a week. According to Saeed, the people of Ait Nuh have changed. The drought, which the *douar* endured for many years; the government's disastrous policy of centralisation, which has led to the cultural and economic stagnation and the marginalisation of the countryside; not to mention the advent of a new alienating mode of production, can all be said to contribute to the dissatisfaction of young *Amazighs* with life in the *douar*. Weddings and the celebration of a new born have become some of the rare occasions on which *Ait Nuhians* can enjoy themselves. Most young *Ait Nuhians* leave school at the ages of 12–15, sometimes before, to help their parents farm the land. They work under very harsh conditions and most of them are not paid for their hard work. By the time they are adults they will have no qualifications and nothing to hope for, but inheriting a small piece of land, and, in the case of the girls, marriage. Young Ait Nuhians mistrust the Moroccan government, its politicians and the Moroccan media. They are also discontented with the centralisation of the big city, which remains the core of political, cultural and economic life in Morocco. No one has access to a landline phone, though more people now have access to mobile phones[58] and a small number of households have access to satellite. Those with no access to satellite have no choice but to watch the two Moroccan channels: TVM and 2M. Both the channels dedicate only a very marginal portion of airtime to *Amazigh* programmes. They do not reflect the material realities of the young *Amazigh* throughout Morocco. This, along with the bad quality of its programmes (especially those of TVM), makes them irrelevant to the majority of young people. Young *Ait Nuhians'* dissatisfaction with Moroccan television is reflected in the discussion, below, that took place during a focus group discussion:

> **Moderator:** 'Do you enjoy watching the two Moroccan channels?'
>
> **Musa:** 'We have two channels full of nothing.'
>
> **Bashir:** 'They are full of news.'
>
> **Muhammad:** 'What news? Nobody wants to watch the news…they are so boring. If it is not the

	king, it is the government, if it is not the government it is the king...all these Members of Parliament are crooks anyway. In the last election, we helped an MP...we worked with him day and night for two months...we even lied for him...he promised us jobs and a lot. It is six months since he won. We have not seen him since, not even once.'
Musa:	'What's on TV anyway? *Omo,* 'a soap product.'
Group:	*Laughter*
Aziz:	'*Omo* and Always....'
Moderator:	'What's *Always*?'
Aziz:	'Women's thing when it is the time of the month, you know?'
Hamid:	'It's embarrassing. You sit down with your mother and father to watch television and they start showing *Always* ads...not only that, they show how they put them on and everything...There are no good educational programmes.'

Many Young *Ait Nuhians* perceive Moroccan television to be a mere vehicle for advertising and the platform for a corrupt and irresponsible regime. Moroccan media, television especially, are made for political economy reasons, to target the mass of Urban Morocco, which is more Westernised and more likely to afford the commodities of modernity. When people of the Atlas appear on Moroccan television, it is often with the aim of entertaining the urban, modernised mass. They are objectified, 'folklorised' (Zubaida, 1987: 155) and reified, as their existence becomes synonymous with the old, the exoticised and the traditional. They become part of the 'live ontological museum of the other' (Gassous, 1988: 48). A range of factors influences young *Ait Nuhians'* conceptions of the West. These include: education, history, the family and long-term consumption of Western media texts. We can also add communicative interactions with the Westerner, the *Ait Nuhian* émigrés (most of whom live in France) and also the latter's material possessions and changing appearance. Most of the *Amazighs* I talked to in the *douar* had never ventured beyond Khunifra. So isolated they are that, since the installation of electricity in the mid-1990's, television had become their main window on what they call the 'people of the outside', which comprises Westerners, émigrés living in France and Moroccans living in big cities such as Casablanca and Rabat. With the exception of the odd group of tourists making their way to Fez or Mekness, television is, for the young *Ait Nuhian*, the window to Western modernity. Here, I will concentrate exclusively on examining meanings of the West as they are read by the young *Ait Nuhians* through their consumption of Western media texts. The West transfixes young *Ait Nuhians*. For most of them, the West is the *kharij*, meaning the outside. Westerners are referred to as the *Eromens*, from the Arabic *Roumy*, which means Roman[59]. Many young Ait Nuhians associate and define the West as France, largely because historically most people who migrated from the *douar* went to France. Hardly any described the West as a space outside France or Europe.

> 'The West is in France'
> 'People in Europe are happy'
> 'They [Westerners] have paradise in life'
> 'Westerners are rich and lead satisfactory lives.'
> 'In Europe they have everything.'
> 'The West can give us leisure...time to enjoy life'.

From the above-mentioned conceptions, *Ait Nuhians* have used the words happy, satisfactory, enjoy, leisure, rich, paradise to describe not only Westerners but also the way they lead their lives. Most of the young *Ait Nuhians* I talked to described Westerners and the West in a positive light. These conceptions of the West as decoded from the Western media text, and other channels of communication (I will discuss later), are better understood and analysed through an exploration of Young *Ait Nuhians'* socio-economic strata. Young *Ait Nuhians* are much poorer than young Casablancans from the working class. The subsistence economy on which their parents and grandparents relied for centuries can no longer sustain, or satisfy, the new needs and desires brought about by the advent of a new mode of economic production: capitalism. In this new system, land that has sustained *Ait Nuhians* for centuries, has now become irrelevant, even a burden. The fulfilment of new desires and needs brought about by the advent of capitalism and its new technologies of comfort (the fridge, washing machine, radio, television, the car, the oven) has become far more important to the young *Ait Nuhians* than land, as this extract from a discussion illustrates:

Ahmad:	'We have nothing here.'
Moderator:	'You have land.'
Ahmad:	'What can the land do for us? We work from 6 am till 6 pm…we get burned in the sun, for what? Working in my land is not going to buy me a new car…it won't allow me to put money in the bank. I work so hard to plant coriander, for example,…it takes me months of hard work before it is ready. When I finally go to the souk 'traditional market' to sell it, people want to haggle!' (A look of disbelief and anguish)

For the young *Amazighs* of Ait Nuh, happiness is now measured and conditioned by the fulfilment of new desires and needs. The kind of happiness they have encountered through their consumption of Western media texts is a new kind of happiness. It is unlike the happiness the elderly of the *douar* have talked to me about. It is not based on traditional care-structures such as intimacy, friendship, singing and strong family ties, but based on the material possessions of industrial society, of goods that make the life of necessity obsolete. Young *Ait Nuhians* share the conception that everyone living in the West is rich and happy. The happiness of the Westerner, according to them, is not only due to material richness but also due to their access to leisure time. The idea or concept of leisure is especially attractive to young *Ait Nuhians* because it is a rare commodity in the *douar*. Young *Ait Nuhians* fantasise the idea of a holiday, free time where they can enjoy life. The average daily wage for an adult working in the *douar* is no more than 50 *Dirhams* (£3.50). Besides, opportunities for work are very scarce and there is no welfare system to support the unemployed. The whole area, as is the case with most of the Moroccan countryside, is marginalised both culturally and economically. This is why the idea of leisure is appealing to them and is more important than it is for other young Moroccans who live in the city and do not have to work from a very early age. When young *Ait Nuhians* watch Western programmes on Moroccan television, they compare their material realities to those of the young Westerner, who is often portrayed as *happy*, rich and with a lot of leisure time to enjoy life. Ahmad and Mustapha, two young Ait Nuhians, remarked:

> **Ahmad:** '... it is impossible to make anything happen here, we can barely afford to buy meat, in Europe they have everything. They are happy.'
>
> **Moderator:** 'How do you know this?'
>
> **Mustafa:** (interrupting) 'come on, you see them in films.'
>
> **Ahmad:** 'I see them [Westerners] on television sleeping on soft beds made of cotton and silk...when I look around me, I see my bed full of *halfa* "hay".'

The role of the 'traditionaliser'

Significations of the West such as freedom, happiness, progress, luxury and others are the invisible materials and the basis on which a mental geography of the West and the *Eromens* is built or drawn by the young *Ait Nuhian*. It is also through the inter-section between *encounters* with the West and the material real-ities of *Ait Nuhians* that new dynamics of selfhood and new ways of *being* in the world are constructed. Below is an interaction that took place between the moderator and a group of young *Amazighs*. The communicative extract illustrates what happens when young *Ait Nuhians* encounter Pamela Anderson from the American Series *Baywatch*.

Mohammed:	'When I watch *Baywatch*, I go mad.'
Group:	*Laughter*
Mohammed:	'Those women they show everything… they are so beautiful…their shape, their breasts.'
Group:	*Laughter*
Moh:	'Where can you find that beauty in here? The women here are so unattractive. They spend all the time cooking and making bread.'
Mohammed:	'In our religion you are not supposed to look at a naked woman.'
Aziz:	'Yes, but girls in big cities are already imi-tating these women (Baywatch) and the way they dress when they go to the beach.'
Moh:	'Now men are looking for something dif-ferent in a woman…they are not content with a woman wearing a hijab or a tradi-tional dress.'
Abdelwahed:	'Beauty is not in the face…if you want the truth beauty is in the heart. Allah does not

	look at your images or pictures but your hearts and deeds. In Islam, if your eye meets that of a woman, you should not look up twice.'
Musa:	'This is ridiculous, we already live in hardship, no money, no nice clothes, no holidays and you are asking me not to look at a girl if she passes by.'
Abdelwahed:	'That is not Islam.'
Musa:	'I agree with what you are saying, but it is not easy to follow.'
Musa:	'Tradition in the *douar* is dying.'

When young *Ait Nuhians* encounter Pamela Anderson, (the sexualised *gawria par excellence*) traditional *douar* values about the female body, sexual desire and beauty are challenged. Abdelwahed acts as a traditionalist and a channel of resistance to the discourse carried by the Western media text. His role within this particular mental migratory trajectory is indispensable. It is one of intervention and resistance. Young *Ait Nuhians*' consumption of the American series *Baywatch* has enabled them, for the first time, to view almost naked women on Moroccan television. The series, whether its producers admit to it or not, is considered to be soft pornography; it is an intentionally produced Scopophilia (see Mulvey, 1989, 16) for the world's 'male gaze'. Here, as Mulvey argues, 'the determining male gaze projects its fantasy onto the female figure, which is styled accordingly' (Mulvey, 1989: 19). The young Amazighs did not know Pamela Anderson by name, but were able to describe some of her physical features to me. What the stylisation of Pamela Anderson, and her American[60] female co-artists, epitomises for the young Amazigh is not only the new object of sexual desire *par excellence* but also a new kind of aesthetics, a different kind of beautification: that of the Western woman, the *gawria*: a woman who reveals almost all is more desirable, more beautiful. The *gawria* is sexual; she is blonde, slim and sexy. The women of the *douar*, who because of Islamic and *Amazigh* tradition have to cover their bodies, are by contrast seen as less desirable, less attractive and therefore less sexual. Unlike the female lifeguards of *Baywatch*, young women of Ait Nuh 'spend most of their time cooking or making bread'. Here Abdelwahed, the young traditionalist intervenes to remind his peers of the wisdom of Islamic culture by quoting from the Koran. Abdelwahed's intervention echoes Johnson's notion of 'multiplex ideologies' and how they can 'combat conceived cultural erosion by being at once both emotionally compelling and ambiguous enough to adjust to rapid changes without losing an appearance of continuity' (Johnson, 1987: 171). However, in this case the traditionaliser's 'multiplexity', as the comments show, is challenged strongly. Abdelwahed's role within this symbolic trajectory – that of countering Western discourse – may or may not be successful, what it does, however, is confirm that tradition is not what many Western sociologists consider it to be – that is, a social fact often associated with 'ruralism, passivity and ahistoricity' or, as in the case of Weber, a 'simple fidelity to the past' (Laroui, 1974: 35). A better understanding of tradition necessitates that we deal with it not only as a social fact but also and most importantly as a social process: that of traditionalisation. As the Moroccan historian and sociologist Abdullah Laroui (1974) observed in his book *The Crisis of the Arab Intellectual*: 'In a traditional society the obstacle to progress is not entirely internal; rather it is a resultant, composed of an outside influence, always manifested as a threat, and a reaction peculiar to the society in question. If the outside pressure persists or intensifies, traditionalisation also intensifies. That is why all the static models proposed by the sociologists – models that do not take into account this factor of outside pressure – must show tradition as an insurmountable obstacle' (Laroui, 1974: 43). Laroui also argues that 'a rigorous, well founded analysis of this mode of tradition has nowhere been undertaken; the ostensible studies to be found in the works of sociologists', he adds, 'are merely reverse images of modern industrial society' (Laroui, 1974: 42). However, regardless of Abdelwahed's intervention, a kind of mental emigration has already occurred: from one kind of aesthetics to another. It is an emigration from the appreciation of the unseen (beauty in modesty) to the appreciation of the seen (beauty in revealing all). The first wisdom – that of Islam and Douar custom – teaches that a woman must dress modestly, the second wisdom – proposed by the model of *Baywatch* – champions beauty that lies in extravagance, the bareness and nakedness of the human flesh.

Ait Nuh is, regardless of the shock of modernity and its encounters with the West through television, still governed by socio-cultural relations that are inherently traditional. Using participant observation as an ethnographic method, I was careful not to undermine the customs practiced in the *douar*, which meant I could not speak to the women about their media consumption. Women in Ait Nuh deal in commerce, ride horses, farm the land and share almost similar roles with the men of the *douar*, but they are not supposed to socialise with, or talk to, strangers. This unfortunately means that their views and voices are silenced in this research. Here I was pressured, as a last resort, to observe the women of the *douar* while sitting by the trough, getting water and performing different domestic chores (washing dishes, clothes). I also prompted the boys of the *douar* into speaking about the girls and their media consumption.

Musa:	'These Mexican soaps have put fire into the young girls here.'
Group:	*Laughter*
Musa:	'They show all the love stuff, kissing, and the girls like the stuff…they show women with short skirts you know?'
Moderator:	'Do you think these soaps have an influence on the girls of the *douar*?'
Aziz:	'Definitely, when they are getting water from the trough, they sit and talk about what they

saw in the soaps…they use the same language like *'Bahebak'* ['Egyptian' dubbed from Mexican, meaning I love you'].

Moderator: 'I noticed nothing different about the way women and girls dress in the *douar*.'

Mohammed: 'They wear the Jellaba here, but once they make it into the town they get rid of it, put their lipstick and jeans on.'

Moderator: 'Girls from this village?'

Aziz: 'Yes, but only few of them.'

Musa: 'I was told about this girl who studies in Mekness…She wears the hijab when she is here. A friend told me that she changes all her clothes when she gets to the train station. She wears a short skirt and puts lipstick on. That's not Islam.'

The comment made by Musa that Mexican soaps have put fire into the young girls of the *douar* calls for an explanation. In the Moroccan cultural context, Musa's comment suggests that the girls of the *douar* have become less timid about expressing their sexuality and sexual desires. For *Ait Nuhian* young girls to utter the phrase 'I love you' in front of boys is unprecedented in the common culture of the *douar*. According to the boys, this change in attitudes about 'the sexual' and 'desire' has been brought about by the influx of Egyptian and South American Soaps, and very recently Turkish soaps, that are religiously consumed by the women of the *douar*. When the young Amazigh girls utter 'I love you' to tease and provoke the boys of the *douar*, they mimick an Egyptian accent, and not an *Amazigh* or Moroccan one. The suggestion that the consumption of Egyptian and South American soaps has affected the way young girls of the *douar* dress is, however, questionable, especially as this may be the influence not only of the media but also of a whole range of variables. The Ait Nuhian girl who studies in Mekness, the nearest big city to the *douar*, may have chosen to wear a skirt, not merely because of consuming Egyptian and South American soaps but perhaps also because of other socio-cultural variables. Girls in the city dress differently to those in the *douar* and so the young *Ait Nuhian* girl may have been pressured to dress in a modern and liberal fashion so she could fit in.

The changing appearance of the *Ait Nuhian* émigrés

Talk of and about emigration in the *douar* is rife. In one of my fieldwork trips to Ait Nuh (2005), Mulud had just been deported from France. He was very lucky, his friends told me, that he did not come back in a coffin. Mulud nearly died of suffocation when his French–Moroccan cousin tried to smuggle him into France in a suitcase. The story of Mulud had spread from France to *Khunifra* and from *Khunifra* back to Ait Nuh, where Mulud was born. His story had become a folk tale. I was told many other stories about other attempts at 'burning'. I was also told astonishing stories about the *Eromens'* machine that was used by imperialists from the French protectorate (1912–56) to recruit workers from the *douar* during the 1950s and 60s. 'This machine had a big chain... You had to pull it very hard to lift a piece of iron... The higher you lifted it, the better chance you had of getting a working contract in France. Only the strongest men of the *douar* made it and a lot of people from *Ait Nuh* went to France that way', a young *Ait Nuhian* told me. The strong *Ait Nuhians*, who had conquered the machine by their physical strength, had in turn been conquered by an even bigger machine in which they worked as alienated cogs for meagre wages and were, in the main, denied rights. Therefore, the story of emigration to the West from Ait Nuh is long and predates the installation of electricity and television in the *douar*. Hitherto *Ait Nuhians* relied on interpersonal communicative interaction with the émigrés to acquire information about France and the land of the *Eromens*. Even today, the second generation of *Ait Nuhian* émigrés often gather with young people of the *douar* and recount their adventures in France.

Fieldwork pointed me towards the fact that young *Ait Nuhians'* desire to emigrate to the West is not merely the product of drought or poverty but also the product of a complex communicative interplay between different channels of communication. The latter takes place between *Ait Nuhians'* interpersonal communication with the émigrés of the *douar* – including their wealth and changed appearance – and the conceptions they have cultivated about the West through their long-term consumption of Western media texts. These elements enter into a dialectical relationship that produces different meanings for young *Ait Nuhians*. Ahmed, a young *Ait Nuhian*, said during a discussion: 'those émigrés left here looking brown and came back looking white. They brought with them new expensive cars, clothes... they bought more land and opened shops in the city... they tell us everything about the other world' (Ahmed, 23, Ait Nuh: 2001). Many young members of the *douar* endorsed Ahmed's descriptions of the *Ait Nuhian* émigrés and their changed appearance. Ahmed's descriptions of the émigrés can be divided into three interrelational statements. The first statement made by Ahmed denotes the changing colour of the émigré: from brown to white. 'The whiteness' of the émigré is, in this context, a symbolic signifier, the decoding of which is anchored by confirmations in the second and third statements, and the socio-cultural milieu of the *Ait Nuhian*. 'Whiteness', as decoded by the young *Ait Nuhian*, connotes good health, richness, fortune and happiness. 'Whiteness', as a communicative knowledge, is anchored by Ahmed's second statement: 'they brought with them new expensive cars, clothes... they bought more land and opened shops in the city'. Whiteness of the émigrés is, for *Ait Nuhians*, proof of their good living conditions. Young *Ait Nuhians*, who are mainly of a white complexion, and some with blond hair and green eyes, only look brown because of hard-working conditions throughout the day without any protection from the sun. As such, whiteness (paleness) for the *Ait Nuhian* signifies less hard-working conditions and are signs of a comfortable and luxurious life. 'Whiteness' also signifies transformation, a transition and a change from one condition to another: from 'brownness' to whiteness. It is as if to say: they left here looking like us; simple, brown, poor, hard-working peasants, and came back looking white, sophisticated, rich, just like the *Eromens* 'Westerners' and the ways they appear on the magic box. This knowledge that is communicated through the changing appearance of the émigrés – whiter, healthier and richer – is a fetish that conceals the hardship, alienation and exploitation of the Moroccan worker in Europe, in this case France, and therefore acts as a myth. The last statement made by Ahmed – 'they tell us everything about the other world' – is a form of interpersonal communication and could either support the myth of the émigré's changing appearance and wealth or could demythologise it, depending on what they are told about life in exile. The three forms of communication – the changing appearances of the émigrés, their newly acquired material possessions and the stories told by them about the West to other members of the *douar* – are anchored by conceptions cultivated by young *Amazighs* about the West through their long-term consumption of Western media texts. In addition, the émigré is transformed into a fetishised commodity. Who they are in relation to members of the *douar* becomes less important than what they possess that other members of the *douar* do not. This is encapsulated in the following statements made by young *Ait Nuhians* about the Amazigh émigrés living in France. (Please note that some of the comments were made about members of family living abroad):

Moderator:	'What do you make of the émigrés?'
Musa:	'They are dogs; I swear they are dogs.'
Moderator:	'You can say what you like.'
Musa:	'I am not shy of anyone. They come here and will not bring you even a good pair of trainers. They'll bring a shirt and a small packet of cheap cigarettes. What would I do with these cigarettes? They have millions stocked in the bank.'

Mohammed:	'They change a lot.'
Moderator:	'Do you think their status in the *douar* changes because of what they have?'
Musa:	'Of course, they come back for that very reason, so they look and feel superior to you. They do not come to see you... they have to show off... "we come from France!"'.
Aziz:	'The girls, when they come back here, they do not want to even shake hands with you.'
Mohammed:	'The racists.'

The 'socialist' youth group: negotiating Western modernness

This subgroup consisted of active young members affiliated to the *Union Socialiste des Forces Populaires* party. The two groups I spoke to do not aspire to Morocco becoming a socialist country, but rather an open democratic country where freedoms (individual, social and media) and human rights are respected and corruption is controlled. The core of both discussions, held in the socialist youth hall in the working class area of Old Medina, centred on the state of Moroccan media, identity dynamics and meanings of Western modernity emanating from Western media texts. The question of identity arose out of a discussion about post-colonial Morocco and the ongoing French influence on Moroccan cultural life.

Adil:	'There's a big confusion in Moroccan culture... We want to be seen as French, Italian, Spanish, American and Moroccan all at once. I really wished we lived this cultural imperialism with a reconciled self... to be or not to be.'
Group:	*Laughter*
Adil:	'We either lose our identity completely by becoming French, or we remain Moroccan... We have

> to be true to ourselves… We have never been to France yet we have French habits… We live in a paradox, one that not all of us is conscious of…, this is because there's a clear absence of culture of questioning, questioning the self. The person who never questions his self or identity will never find true answers about his real self… not questioning the self does not help us become conscious of what we consume from western media.' (Adil, 24 years)

The problem of cultural identity as it emerges from the comment made by Adil, lifts the veil from a condition symptomatic, perhaps not only of Morocco but also of all societies that experienced the Western 'colonial system' (Sartre, 2001). It is a kind of *cultural schizophrenia*[61]: a postcolonial condition and a complex cultural space where two cultural identities, each with a different temporality coexist within the same cultural spatiality: the mind of the postcolonised. In the case of young Moroccans, it is about being Moroccan but speaking in French, thinking in French and doing other French things. This, as Adil points out, is a kind of 'paradox'. It is important to note, however, that the problematic here not only lies in this paradoxical coexistence, or in the problem of cultural time, but also in the structure of the relationship between these two cultural identities and temporalities. What emerged from comments made by participants from the Socialist Youth Group is a complex set of dynamics, symptomatic of a postcolonial country existing in a postcolonial spatio-temporality and caught, like many previously colonised countries, in a double-identity: two sets of cultural dynamics; traditional and Western modernity, mental colonisation and mental de-colonisation. Adil's insistence on questioning his 'culture', identity and the 'self' captures the essence of Giddens's 'late modernity' subject: 'In the settings of what I call 'high' or 'late' modernity – our present day world – the self, like the broader institutional contexts in which it exists, has to be reflexively made' (Giddens, 1991: 3). At the heart of Adil's questioning stands the constitutive problem of postcolonial identity *par excellence*, thus his assertion: 'we either lose our identity completely by becoming French, or we remain Moroccan'. Giddens's analysis of 'late 'modernity, however, does not tackle colonialism's dynamics or its effects on the modern-subaltern subject. Self-reflexivity, in this context, is the product of a far more complex and intricate process. The ontological quest for understanding the postcolonial-self, as reflexively understood/interpreted by Adil and his postcolonial generation, operates in a confused, paradoxical and unsettled state of modernness, perpetually oscillating between different reference points and ways of being in the world. The extract below shows a conversational confrontation between two female participants from the Socialist Youth Group, which highlights contradictions inherent to the structure of feeling of the young Moroccan. The subject of the discussion was relationships, as they appear for young Moroccans in the popular American sit-com *Friends*. There was a clear emphasis on the issue of freedom, which I believe is well encapsulated by the confrontation that took place between Siham, a Westernised, modern young Moroccan woman, and Zeinab, the only member of the Socialist Youth who wore a *hijab*.

> **Siham:** 'There's nothing such as a friendship between a man and a woman in Morocco…I think this is wrong. Men and women can enter relationships which are platonic…I do not think there's anything wrong with that…on the contrary, we will get to learn more about each other. That's why I think the relationships in *Friends* set a good example' (Siham, 20 years old, Casablanca).
>
> **Boshra:** 'A programme like *Friends* comes in the form of messages…this sort of programme creates a lot of questioning among our young people. They start questioning their own situation…the girls, when they watch *Friends*, I am sure, they start to look at the style of clothes, make-up,

hair-style; a lot imitate these things and wish they lived such a free lifestyle' (Boshra, 19 years old, Casablanca).

Siham: 'I think it would be great to live with a man without having to marry him.'

Zeinab (The only female participant wearing a *Hijab*):

'But these sorts of programmes contradict our tradition and way of life. Islam teaches us to dress modestly and respectfully and not to wear mini skirts or reveal all God gave us' (Zeinab, 22 years old, Casablanca).

Siham: 'How can I now suddenly wear the hijab after 24 years of Western influence? Young people are afraid of growing beards and talking about Islam. You say American and Western film has an influence on us. We take from the Americans; they never ask us to. They never impose things on us. I am going to be frank here, I will touch on a point many of my brothers and sisters ignored, or are maybe shy to talk about... There's an enigmatic and contradictory relationship between our culture, tradition and our nature as human beings. We are taught that to be true Muslims we have to wear the *Hijab*, hide our head, our legs and what ever maybe attractive to a man. We cannot have sex until we are married. Having sex beforehand is a big sin... Most of those who marry do so in their 30s (have to get good jobs first)... If you have a sexual relationship beforehand, society points its finger at you. Our society is against us; our tradition is clearly not helping, so where do we go?'

The confrontation between Siham and Zeinab symbolises the ontological dilemma and the rupture inherent to the cultural structure of Arab-Islamic societies. One part aspires to join the 'modern world' and enjoy its secular freedoms; the other adheres to tradition and religious teachings, which it claims promise a different and higher stage of emancipation. One sees Western modernity as an alternative to the cultural hegemonic practices inherent in Arab society; the other sees Western modernity as a sickness and a threat to collective consciousness. The debate here revolves around two main issues – the questions of cultural identity and of gender roles, or male/female dynamics within Arab society. Siham draws on the meanings of Western modernity embedded in *Friends* to make her case against tradition and the Islamic cultural hegemonic practices intrinsic to Arab-Islamic society. Siham's argument can be encapsulated in the following questions: How are we supposed to restrain our natural sexual urges in a changed desegregated Islamic society where, for economic reasons, women cannot marry until they are in their 30s? What happens between our teens and 30s? Siham proposes the relationship models in the American series as an alternative to hegemonic Islamic practices. In a social study (Mernissi, 1975) examining the anomic effects of modernisation on male/female dynamics in Moroccan society, Mernissi came to the conclusion that 'sexual segregation, one of the main pillars of Islam's social control over sexuality, is breaking down. And ... that the breakdown of sexual segregation allows the emergence of what the Muslim order condemns as a deadly enemy of civilisation-love between men and women in general, and between husband and wife in particular' (Mernissi, 1975: 58). Desegregation has increased in Moroccan society and much of the Arab world since the 1970s, with men no longer dominating all public spaces. Women represent more than 35 per cent of the workforce in urban Arab societies. They inhabit the same space as men at work do in colleges, universities, the beach, the swimming pool, the café, the discothèque, cinema and so on. The only conspicuous places where men and women are segregated are at the mosque and the Turkish bath. This change, a product of both endogenous and exogenous factors, has managed to break down Islamic control over sexuality. With this breakdown comes a kind of sexual frustration, confirmed by Siham's propounding of the relationship model in *Friends* as an alternative to fixed hegemonic Islamic cultural particularities: 'I'd love to live with a man without having to marry him' said Siham. It is crucial to add that what Siham is negotiating through her self-reflexive comments is not only the right to sex before marriage, which incidentally happens behind closed doors, but also, and most importantly, a removal of the taboo on premarital sex so that it becomes, as in *Friends*, the norm. Siham calls for the normalisation of premarital sex/romance/love. She desires to live in a society where individual choices, such as premarital romance, are accepted and respected as an individual choice. Zeinab's position as a traditionalist and a traditionaliser is undermined by Siham's outcry for what she, Siham, believes is her natural right. The *Friends* model, regardless of Zeinab's attempts at traditionalising, remains for most participants, in this group, a better alternative to traditional hegemonic practices. What comes from the popular Western media text *Friends* is, Siham argues, an 'alternative' to the traditional male/female dynamics at play within Moroccan society. Zeinab, the female traditionalist who questioned the version of modernity championed by Siham, argued that modernity and our desire to be free in the world are not inherently Western characteristics, but are innate to all human beings. She, however, called for a different, creative and more ethical modernity that does not alienate tradition or the values it teaches, reflecting Taha Abdurrahman's take on what it means to *be* differently 'modern' (see Chapter 2).

The Islamist group and the coherent rejection of Western modernness

> Without the media there will be no West.
>
> (A young female Islamist)

The Islamist group, unlike the other subgroups, had a good overall knowledge of the world's geopolitics. For most of them,

Western modernity is, with the exception of two female participants, a kind of sickness, a threat to Islam and its culture, and so
a threat to the Moroccan's consciousness, culture, and identity.
They perceived Western modernity as the culture of capitalism,
imperialism and globalisation, a culture erected on the principles of greed and an unjust economic system, which they thought
was both reifying and alienating. As a young female Islamist
remarked,

> For me, the West conveys *silb*, because the West
> has denied us so many things: our youth, our
> identity, and our culture…I understand the West
> as meaning *silb, silb* in the negative sense.

Young Islamists saw Western modernity as a coherent, historical, and organised attack on Islam and its civilisation, deploy-
ing both coercive and non-coercive methods to annihilate and
humiliate a part of the world, which, they argue, refuses to bow
down to the West's imperialist motives. Their critique of Western
modernity extends to Morocco and its media, which they believe
have become an extension of the West and its interests. They thus
see the threats of Western modernity as being both external and
internal:

> There's nothing worth watching in local television.
> Nothing broadcast is relevant to our realities and
> this surely is intentional. 2M reproduces Western
> discourses. It is mainly broadcast in French and I
> think it has cheated Moroccan people out of their
> culture.

Islamists perceived the Moroccan ruling classes as collabora-
tors with the West and its project. They insisted that Morocco
was ruled by Francophiles who serve capitalism and its culture,
and deepen the Moroccan people's dislocation. In their critique
of Moroccan media, Islamists argued that, rather than working

towards creating an alternative Islamic and ethical modernity, the Moroccan ruling classes use the media to annihilate Islam's heritage and reproduce discourses of Western hegemony. Describing the image of the West in Western media texts, a young Islamist observed:

> What do Western media present us with? The purpose of western media texts is that of 'making purer'... it is that of cleansing the image of the West or, in other words, cleansing our perceptions of the West... Western film and cartoons carry with them a discourse. This discourse is not innocent, for films and cartoons are not detached from culture, politics or military orientation. Hollywood is an institution that propagates American and western discourse in general. This discourse is targeted at the Third world in general, and the Islamic world in particular. The idea propagated by Western media is that Western nations enjoy absolute freedoms and that the West is the place where dreams are turned into realities. They also propagate the idea of luxury and that the West means luxury. This discourse is false and conceals many realities. The West is not always as strong as it purports and it is not always a society of luxury. There are European countries that make big contributions to the world economy, but still have high levels of poverty and deserted children. The picture that arrives from the West about the West is flawed.

While this comment is the antithesis of most of the conceptions cultivated by young Moroccans from other subgroups about the West, it also reinforces the position of the Islamist vis-à-vis the West and its discourses. Although critical voices from the Socialist

Group argued that Western media texts carried meanings of Western modernity, they strongly believed that individuals were able to negotiate, refute or accept meanings. Islamists, however, downplayed the ability of the individual to critique, blaming the media for ceaselessly reifying and annihilating the young Arab's Islamic heritage. As a young, female Islamist commented:

> Western media have the effect of annihilating our past. They annihilate our past and therefore the past of our Islamic civilisation. Young people seem to think that we are rootless, without roots or civilisation and that civilisation started with the West. The West wants us to break with our past and adopt their present.

The Islamist group expressed the view that Morocco had already become an extension of the West and that it was now a Western, rather than a Muslim, country. This shared view is illuminated by the Islamists' comments below:

> 'We already have a West within Morocco.'
> 'We have become an extension and addition of the West.'
> 'Morocco is qualified to be a Western country...,
> it has reached a point of no return and where only a miracle can change things'.
> 'The West is trying to defame the picture of Islam and that of Muslims..., but the West or Western media should not worry so much, because we already have a West within Morocco'.
> 'As Moroccans, we purport that we have an Islamic identity, but, in reality, we have a Francophone identity. So, in fact, we are talking about two Wests... One is geographically outside the Muslim world... the other is internal and it is controlled by the Francophones within Morocco.'

According to Islamists, long-term consumption of Western media texts serves to annihilate the young Moroccan's past without which, they argued, the young Moroccan cannot have a coherent or strong identity. Young Islamists observed that the reason why the majority of young Moroccans are embarrassed by their own culture is largely because of the state of amnesia surrounding their Islamic cultural history, which both Western media texts and Moroccan media, they argued, are contributing to effacing. As a young Islamist observed:

> The young Moroccan is after all an Arab and a Muslim and western media are a direct threat to the young Moroccan's identity... They detach him from his past... and how can we have our identities if we do not have our past... If our past is annihilated and if our culture is constantly under attack, the result will be confusion... The human being is the product of his past and without it he cannot have an identity... and it would be true to say that a lot of Moroccans are embarrassed by their identities because they do not know their past... I'd rather they had no identities at all than have them and be embarrassed by them.

One young Islamist accused the West of making use of the Islamic heritage. Instead of acknowledging it, he argued that Westerners always discredit Islam and its culture and have ceaselessly used the media to defame Islam. It is not Western modernity, argued Islamists, which should have been globalised, but the culture of Islam: 'Islamic modernity'[62].

> The West made use of our civilisation and became more creative culturally, economically and scientifically. It is the culture of Islam that should have led Globalisation and not the West... The future is Islam.

However, when faced by Lenin's historical question: 'What can be done?' young Islamists' arguments became contradictory and less coherent. In fact, some of the arguments made by Islamists reflect a sense of ahistoricity and defeatism:

> Only a miracle can change things. Our position to the West is that of a corpse and a corpse cleaner...you cannot make demands when you are dead.

A young, and highly respected, Imam's answer to the problems facing Moroccan culture and society was:

> It is like a house (referring to Morocco); we have to destroy it and rebuild it again. We have to destroy all these systems and implement Islam again. Those who do not rule with what God has brought down are unbelievers. Undignified we will remain, unless we rule with the word of God.

But a female participant quickly challenged this view:

> The brother has used a poetic analogy..., but let me ask, do you mean by the house the rules and systems that caused all our problems, or do you mean the house and who lives in it? I do not think we will find it difficult to destroy things.... The real difficulty lies in changing people's thinking...and if we cannot change the way people think, what gives us the right to destroy the house with those who live in it as well?'

Another young, female Islamist went beyond the analogy of the Imam to argue:

> In my view, to face the West we need someone with the power of Hitler to lead us.

What these comments reveal is that while Islamists have in their critique of the West, Western media and the Francophiles of Morocco proved to be well informed, critical, coherent and above all, sharing, with the exception of few participants, unified ideological aims, their solutions proved contradictory, less coherent and ideologically unsound. Young Islamists agree that Islam is the only alternative to Western modernity, yet they disagree and are still unsure about the strategies that will see Islam and its culture reinstated at the core of the consciousness and culture of the Moroccan and the Arab. On a larger picture, these uncertainties, in turn, reflect the incoherence of some of the political programmes advanced by Islamist political parties in Morocco. Alongside all this, there is the issue of morality. All the Islamist participants shared the view that Western media texts, especially television programmes, constitute a corrupting force that threatens Moroccan ethical values embedded in Islam. A female participant reflected this position by commenting:

> My personal view is that Western media texts, be they music, film or television, all reflect a kind of *ebaha* 'laissez-faire'. The Western media champion perversion, a lack of ethics and moral decay...In Western media there's a sense of animalism, a championing of the profane that is degrading to the human being and ethics as a whole.

A minority of Islamists argued contrary to the critiques advanced by the majority of them. As a participant, representing this minority, commented:

> I personally find that Western media texts still have some advantages, there's a lot that young Moroccans can learn from scientific documentaries, but one needs to be able to separate the good from the bad.

Young Islamists share the view that young Moroccans from the bourgeoisie are the most likely to be influenced by the Western media text. This is something they put down to a liberal bourgeois upbringing, which prepares young people from the middle and upper classes for, and helps them integrate into, Western modernity's culture from a very early age. As two young Islamists put it, when I asked the group if they thought long-term exposure to Western media texts had any effect on the Islamic identity of the young Moroccan:

> I think those from a bourgeois background are most likely to be influenced by Western media… They are most likely to adopt a Western way of life because they can afford it and have already been brought up in a liberal Western environment…, but the poor will always think of the West in terms of money, not culture.
>
> Western media have executed their role successfully. Effect is manifest in the way young Moroccans dress. The Western dress code is something they take pride in. As for the Islamic dress code; it is traditional and backward…they take pride in speaking French, and those who speak in Arabic are treated as backward.

The *Gautier*[63] group and the coherent acceptance of Western modernness

For the middle class subgroup, whose members have all been raised in a liberal milieu, Western modernity is not perceived as a threat or problem, but as a way of life. As Moulay, a young Moroccan from *Gautier* – a Europeanised, middle class quarter of Casablanca, commented, 'We live in Morocco, but the way we speak, dress and everything else is European.' Young people from this group are introduced to Western modernity through

French, which they are taught in private schools from the age of 4 or 5. Their lifestyle is liberal in several ways. These characteristics are very uncommon among the Moroccan working class, which remains largely traditional. Western modernity is neither alien nor alienating for the young people of Gautier: they are brought up in it and it is part of their experience. Ironically, what they find alien and alienating is their own language, religion and culture. The Gautier group, unlike other groups, found local languages, such as *Tamazight*, *Dareja* and Arabic, the 'official' language of Morocco, to be both *passé* and uncivilised. French, however, is considered by the Gautier group to be the language of modernity, civilisation and the future. The extract below, from a focus group conversational interaction, sheds some light on the Gautier group's conceptions of local languages and French.

> **Moderator:** 'What language do you speak at home?'
> **Amin:** 'Mainly French.'
> **Moderator:** 'How about when you are with friends?'
> **Amin:** 'It depends, if you are speaking with a girl, you talk French.'
> **Moderator:** 'It's interesting, why?'
> **Widad:** 'Showing off, showing off.'
> **Amin:** 'French is *le style* 'the style.' It is like if you are coming from Paris or Lyon...she'll accept him if he speaks French.'
> **Moderator:** 'What if you spoke to a girl in *Dareja* or Arabic?'
> **Widad:** 'What would you say? *Bghit'n tsahb*! 'Moroccan *Dareja* for 'I'd like to make a relationship with you.'
> **Group:** *Big laughter.*
> **Amin:** 'There's nothing to say in Moroccan *Dareja*.'
> **Moderator:** 'Do you think there's something wrong with *Dareja*?'

Widad:	'It is unorganised…it has no base…it is like a bastard language.'
Amin:	'It has so many words that do not make sense, like *Tamazight* only very few people speak *Tamazight*; it is *passé.*'
Moderator:	'If *Dareja* is baseless, a bastard language, a *passé* language, how about Arabic?'
Amin:	'Kaifa Haluka ya Akhi? Arabic for "How are you Brother?"' (*Says Amin in a ridiculing accent*)
Group:	*Laughter*
Murad:	'We are not used to speaking in Arabic.'
Moderator:	'You prefer French, then.'
Group:	'Yes' (*nodding*).

Young middle class Moroccans speak French to each other because they think, among other things, that their language is inferior, *passé* and they, being young and 'modern', certainly do not want to be perceived as being either inferior or *passé*. Speaking French is a way of ridding themselves of the embarrassment of feeling '*being* inferior' – being Moroccan. These language-identity-games are clearly observable and were played out before me during my participant observation in Casablanca. When doing my fieldwork in Morocco, I used to frequent a modern café in Gautier[64] twice a day – during the morning for breakfast and later in the evening to mingle with and talk to young Moroccans. After a while, I realised that the café, though situated in quite a rich area of Casablanca, had attracted many young men and women from the poor working classes of Casablanca. This is where the game of *emulation* starts. Young, working class customers, who frequent the Café, engage in an identity game where they emulate belonging to the Gautier culture and experience. How do they do it? They do it by dressing according to Western codes of fashion, expensive though it may be, and by speaking mainly in French to the waiter, who perhaps can speak but not write French. I noticed that most of the orders given to the waiter were in French. For example: *Un jus d'orange, s'il vous plait, Un café noire, cassé, un panaché, s'il vous plait…L'addition s'il vous plait* and so on. Young, working class customers play out language games, as a way to integrate into the middle ground of Moroccan society – the *Gautier Culture* – and this is achieved through concealing their real identity from others who, perhaps comically, are playing the same game. Language games are anchored, besides appearance and the style of clothes – as we saw in the case of the Karaoke bar – by fetishised Western commodities displayed on the tables. The display, which consisted of mobile phones and packets of Western cigarettes, such as Marlboro, Winston and Benson, are part of the *emulation* game, for it authenticates the experience of belonging to the Moroccan *Gautier Culture*. These commodities are often displayed in front of young customers' tables and function as signifiers of wealth, class and status. Western cigarettes are expensive, and so many young people who cannot afford a whole packet buy single cigarettes, which are far cheaper, and place them in an empty Marlboro or Benson packet. A Moroccan brand of cigarettes, like any other Moroccan product, be it material or symbolic, would not do in the Gautier café; it has to be American, French or from another Western country. Of all the subgroups, young people from the middle classes of Casablanca were the least interested in Moroccan-Arab culture and religion. This is manifest in the following comments:

> **Moderator:** 'Do you like reading books?'
>
> **Farid:** 'Yes, I like French novels.'
>
> **Moderator:** 'How about books in Arabic?'
>
> **Farid:** 'No, even in class I refuse to read in Arabic…I refuse.'
>
> **Mahdi:** I go to a French school. I do not want to read Arabic…I am very bad at it…I read mainly French…*Des livres de poche*…I read Molière….'
>
> **Moulay:** 'The Koran' *he said sarcastically and burst into a fit of laughter.*

Group:	*Laughing hysterically, hands holding stomachs from the pain caused by laughter.*
Mahdi:	*Still laughing,* 'No, I do not know the Koran.... I know very very little about it.'
Moulay:	*Laughter*
Farid:	'I do not know it either.'
Moderator:	'What do you make of Islam as a religion?'
Moulay:	*Laughter*
Farid:	'Nothing.'
Mahdi:	'What? (*Laughter*)...How?...I am a Muslim, but we have a French teacher who tells us that everyone has their own belief systems...He tells us that hell does not exist..., that it is a myth...He makes me doubt the Koran and religion.'
Moulay:	'We are Moroccans...our blood is Moroccan, but the outside is European.'
Moderator:	'Could you say a little more about that?'
Moulay:	'I do not know...We live in Morocco, but the way we speak, dress and everything else is European.
Mahdi:	'Fuck the Arabs.'
Group:	*Big laughter.*

These comments show young Moroccans from this *bourgeois* corner of Casablanca as 'mental emigrants' *par excellence*. The middle and upper middle classes of Casablanca send their children to private schools where there is often far more emphasis on French than on Arabic[65]. When I went to ask for permission to conduct a survey in the Anfa Group Schools (a rich private school), I had to speak to the headmistress in French, for she knew hardly any Arabic; and this is the case in many private schools in Casablanca. Outside the school, young Moroccan children spoke in French and not Moroccan. The parents, who came to pick them up, spoke to them in French and not Moroccan.

Arabic and Islamic studies teachers, I was told by Moulay, Mahdi and Farid, are often humiliated at the Lyceé by young, bourgeois kids for being, according to them, 'backward' and part of a backward culture: the Arab-Islamic culture. This was very evident in the scornful manner in which Moulay, Farid and Mahdi spoke about Arabic books, the Koran and the Arabs. Moulay's comments illuminate what I mean by mental emigration and the condition of *'cultural schizophrenia'*: 'We are Moroccans. Our blood is Moroccan, but the outside is European.' Other comments from another middle class group shed light on an important migratory process: it is one where the mental trajectory progresses into a physical trajectory.

> **Moderator:** 'Do you think there are those among us who live in the West in Morocco?'
>
> **Amin:** 'I used to have a friend who was mad about America. In his room there was a massive poster which showed New York and which read: "The Promised Land"...He had a huge American flag. His clothes were all American made...He ended up going to the States.'
>
> **Amin:** 'What you are asking is true; we lead a Western life in Morocco ...'
>
> **Widad:** 'There's a guy called Hussein...He dreams about the States day and night...He watches so much rap and hip hop, he wants to go to the States and live that lifestyle...Maybe we are mental emigrants too. Look at Amin's hair..., and I would not have had a 'coup de Garcon' if I weren't influenced by Western lifestyle.'

These comments reflect cases where mental emigration develops into physical emigration. Among other things, they illuminate the importance of the mental or symbolic and its influence on the physical. It is important to note, however, that we are dealing with comments from young Moroccans belonging to the middle classes. In their case, the transition from mental emigration to physical emigration is not much of a problem, especially as they have more of a chance to obtain a Western visa than those from the working classes. In the case of the latter, mental emigration seldom progresses into physical emigration. The survey demonstrated that respondents from the upper middle and middle classes were by far the most prolific consumers of Western media texts. Sixty-seven per cent of respondents from the upper middle classes and 49 per cent from the middle classes said they preferred Western programmes to Arabic and Moroccan programmes. The survey also showed that no respondents from the upper middle classes watched TVM, Iqra and Al-Manar. Their dislocation and detachment from local culture and experience, which they perceive as uncivilised, makes them strangers in their own country. Western modernity is, for them, not merely a way of life, but a tool; one, which they use to establish their cultural superiority over the 'ordinariness' of Moroccan working class cultures. Amin referred to the working classes as 'dirt', whereas Farid referred to young people living in the Old Medina, (young people with whom I went to school) a working class quarter, as *hbash* – 'savages'. One of the main reasons why young Moroccans prefer to be seen and heard speaking French, rather than Arabic, Moroccan-Arabic or *Tamazight*, is because they believe these languages to be culturally inferior to French. Besides this 'cultivated' complex, there are other practical reasons, as Gallagher suggests:

> It may be stated flatly that in Morocco today the non-French-speaking candidate has no chance of getting a good government job or advancing himself in any ministry except those of Justice, Religious Affairs, or in specialised functions in the Interior (police work) or Education. High

> level posts in key ministries like Foreign Affairs, Commerce and Industry, Planning, Public Health, Defence... and Agriculture, as well as in the many specialised offices dealing with production and technical matters, are virtually closed to the monolingual Arabo-phone, not to mention jobs in important commercial or industrial enterprises in private business.
>
> (Gallagher, 1968: 143, as quoted in
> Bentahila, 1983: 15)

Gallagher's analysis is now perhaps even truer than when it was first written. Since then, there has been no strategic, structural change in the way Moroccan institutions operate. Today's Morocco, as a market, is even more open to capitalist forces. It has attracted many European and American businesses where business is done not in Arabic, but in French and English, and where the demand is not for monolingual Arabo-phone labour, but for Francophone and Anglophone labour. This is one of the main reasons why the Moroccan bourgeoisie teaches its children French from a very early age and sends them to expensive schools with an emphasis on French or English. Working class families cannot afford these schools, and their children therefore continue to be disadvantaged. This disequilibrium deepens the stratification of Moroccan society and produces a culture reducing Arabic, ironically, the language of science, even in Europe, until the fifteenth century, to irrelevance. Language is an indispensable constituent of culture, for with language, culture expresses its experience and creates and grows. A culture where the common language is subordinated or perceived by its people as such is doomed to stagnation, if not to cultural suicide. The subordination of Moroccan and classical Arabic in Morocco has deepened the stratification of its society into a crude and a dangerous cultural rupture – that between the Moroccan perceived as an *Arubi*, 'uncultured' speaker of Moroccan-Arabic or *shlh*, speaking *Tamazight*, and that of *Alipa*: 'Moroccan high society' who speak mainly in French. To be modern in Morocco has become partly synonymous to being able to speak and read French, not Arabic, and where French is perceived as 'une langue civilisée,' Arabic has taken the rear seat and become the language of the non-modern, or those yet to embrace modernity. French in Moroccan society is also perceived as the language of 'prestige and prosperity,' whereas Arabic is perceived as the language of 'poverty and the past' (Gassous in Bentahila, 1983: 28). As Gellner observed: 'I believe the impact of French culture in North Africa to be profound and permanent...In his heart, the North African knows not merely that God speaks Arabic, but also that modernity speaks French' (Gellner in Bentahila, 1983: 15).

Modernness as a multiple narrative-category

Discussions with the five different groups have shown that aspects of modernness (or what it means to *be* modern in the world) are, for young Moroccans, inextricably linked with stratification in class, *habitus* and, in the case of the young Islamists, ideological formation. It is on the harsh economic reality, together with the young *Ait Nuhians'* long-term exposure to Western media texts and their encounters with the *Ait Nuhian* émigrés living in France, that their 'structure of feeling' about modernity is constructed. Their poverty and lack of education encourage young *Ait Nuhians* to see promises of the wealth, comfort and luxury, they so desperately desire in modernity. Modernity manifests itself, for the young *Ait Nuhian*, as a promise of happiness that is wholly built on, and motivated by, the possession and accumulation of material goods: cars, money, new Western clothes, shops, businesses and the like, and luxury time to enjoy them. Their encounters with the West, through television and through the stories recounted by the émigrés of the *douar*, have not only altered their structures of feeling about their world and their position within it, but have also transformed their very world, by altering its pre-capitalist social structure. Those from the *douar* who immigrated to the land of the *Eromens* have come back looking different. They came back looking like the *Eromens* they see on television: whiter, modern and prosperous. This has had a destabilising effect on what could previously be described as being the 'democratic social structure' of the *douar*, which was not always motivated by wealth or material possessions, so much as by structures of care, trust and play. Of course, there has always been the odd feudal lord and the *makhzan* who exploited ordinary farmers and stole land through coercive measures. I heard many such stories from the *douar's* elderly. It is the 'organic solidarity' of the *douar* that has been affected. To use modern terminology, the ordinariness of the social structure of the *douar* has altered as the relationships within it moved from *Gemeinschaft* to *Gesellschaft*. The 'émigrés are dogs'; 'they are racists', said the two angry young *Ait Nuhians*. The *Ait Nuhian* émigrés are all, shockingly, in one way or another, related to both angry *Ait Nuhians*. Young *Ait Nuhians* are aware of the change that is taking place in the *douar* and of what has caused it. None-the-less, their aspirations to become as rich as, if not richer than, the émigré and his family are undiminished. For many young *Ait Nuhians*, this is the dream promised by modernity, and its realisation, it is believed by many, regardless of the difficulties, could only materialise if they crossed the border, to the land of the *Eromens*. Being Modern, for the young *Ait Nuhian*, is part of a 'long revolution' (Williams, 1961) overcoming necessity and subsistence economies, owning a mobile phone, a washing machine, clean running water, a car and all those commodities/luxuries that are now taken-for-granted in the West, but which were, in so many ways, the precursors of its long and modern revolution.

Discussions with young people from the Socialist Youth of Casablanca disclose another narrative of modernness; one that is more sophisticated, perhaps, given their in-depth, self-reflexive articulations on freedom, identity dynamics and sexuality. Unlike the young Islamists, the Socialist Youth Group was not anti-Western. Its participants strongly believed in democracy as a system and see the Western model of democracy as an alternative to the Moroccan political system. Their political struggle is driven, in the main, by a desire for social and individual emancipation from authoritarian power structures in Morocco and, as such, the West, for them, is positioned as a civilisational model, rather than an ideological enemy. Although all participants from this group agreed that Western media texts played a hegemonic role, they still believed in the individual's ability to negotiate meaning. The American series *Friends* that triggered a lot of heated debate was, for this group, not only a funny programme but also an alternative discourse to male/female dynamics in a traditional society. Their relationship to modernity was thus one of negotiation and *dialogism*. However, the Islamist group's position to modernity and its discourses are, as the material showed, framed within discourses of power. It is one of resistance and coherent rejection. The West, for them, constitutes an ambivalent and contradictory project, which not only promises happiness and progress, but which is also, due to its colonial project, inherently de-humanising, alienating and exploitative. The coherence of their position materialises in Islam and its teachings as a better, less ambivalent narrative of human happiness. However, in their attempt to resuscitate a golden Islamic renaissance, most young Islamists emigrate mentally to a past, a 'timeless' historical-cultural temporality, which they idealise and present as the only 'true' and viable alternative to modernity's project. In their attempt to articulate questions of the present with answers from the past, they alienate lived Arab secular realities, creating a rupture, if not confusion, within their own cultural temporality, and falling, therefore, into the trap of the cultural salafist. The middle class group encapsulates the case of the mental emigrant *par excellence*. Their deracination and detachment from the material realities of the Moroccan working classes, which they described as 'savages', their indifference to local languages, and the Arab-Islamic cultural repertoire, is symptomatic of a parasitic and arrogant bourgeois culture, mimicking the superiority of the colonial master. They live in the West in Morocco, speak and read mainly in French, and possibly, love and fuck in French.

'Mental emigration', perhaps the closest thing to what Daniel Lerner called 'psychic-mobility'[66], is a lived experience that discloses itself as a daily occurrence and phenomenon, in self-reflexive speech, the ontological, behaviour, dress code, language and thought. When Knadi[67], a young Moroccan, says he feels Western music in his blood and that it makes him feel as though he were there (in the West), only he truly knows what he means and what it feels like. The same could be said about the young Moroccan who said, 'Our blood is Moroccan, . . . but the outside is European.' Mental emigration is a structure of 'feeling' about the world and an active desire to be different in it. It is consequential of the massive penetration of Western culture, cumulatively encountered and cultivated by young Moroccans through Western carriers of meaning and a whole history of institutional modernisation, driven by the colonial and nationalist governments that followed. Mental emigration is a cultural consequence of *encountering* in a globalised world and the product of local problems internal to Morocco (as a microcosm of Arab society), for example, authoritarianism and poverty. Mental emigration is also an ambivalent and complex cultural space that accommodates different, and at times contradictory, problematic structures of feeling and narratives of modernness, and to describe it, therefore, merely as a negative socio-cultural phenomenon, the object of which is the ceaseless erosion and colonisation of consciousness, would be misleading in several ways. As evidence from my fieldwork shows, encountering the 'modern' through television brings with it the promises of change, emancipation and, most importantly, an 'alternative' to the hegemonic cultural practices inherent to a traditional society. It is the paradox and perpetual oscillation between secular realities lived in the modern Arab world and the fetishisation of heritage/tradition that makes the assessment of the young Arab's structure of feeling problematic. The problematic nature of this symbolic trajectory is further problematised by the complex structure of its reference points: departure and destination. Mental emigration, like physical, takes place within a trajectory with two reference points: departure and destination. In mental emigration, these are replaced by symbolic migratory reference points. It departs from cultural hegemonic practices that are inherent to Moroccan/Arab culture and heritage, with Islam as a major constituent, to ideas of freedom, emancipation, progress and wealth deeply embedded in discourses of Western modernity. At no stage, however, is mental emigration total or complete, and to argue otherwise would be an aberration. Young Moroccans may feel that Moroccan-Arabic is inferior to French, and consequently prefer to speak and read French, yet many still speak Moroccan-Arabic most of the time. Young Moroccans may emigrate mentally from certain archaic Islamic cultural practices, yet they remain Muslim. This conclusion – that mental emigration is neither complete nor final – backs Giddens's argument: the 'disembedding mechanisms intrude into the heart of self-identity; but they do not empty out the self anymore than they simply remove prior supports on which self-identity was based' (Giddens, 1991: 148–9). To argue that, for young Moroccans, mental emigration takes place from a fixed 'discourse' of Islam to a fixed 'discourse' of Western modernity would be misleading. It would be a simplification and a rarefaction of what is a far more contested and problematic phenomenon. What are my reasons for saying this? All require an examination more thorough than we have the space to undertake, so only the major reasons are examined. The mental flight from Islam/tradition and its teachings to Western modernity and its documentary is never total and perhaps never will be; rather, it happens at different levels. How is it possible to mentally emigrate from Islam, when the latter has often been manipulated as an ideological tool? The history of Morocco's *makhzan* shows that Islam has largely been implemented, not so much to rule with justice (a fundamental prerequisite for ruling in Islam), but as an ideological tool, the aim of which has been the gaining and maintenance of power (see Munson, 1993). Furthermore, Al-Jabri argues that the absence of rules for the public sphere has created a deep asymmetry in the whole Islamic legal system and 'made it a means of

submission to the ruler rather than for control of political power'
(Al-Jabri in Ansari, 1998: 169). In the same vein, the Islam lived
and experienced by the ordinary Moroccan/Muslim/Arab differs
from that preached by the theologian, the Islamist and the cultural *salafist*, or that rationalised by the anti-essentialist thinker.
To unpick Islam as a reference point of the mental migratory trajectory, it is thus important to differentiate between Islam as a
belief; 'a collection of rules of behaviour obeyed by the believer',
and the 'over-Islamization of Islam: the view that Islam is a single,
clearly established fact, unchanged and unchanging' (Al-Azmeh,
1993: 56). All arguments made here point to the fact that Islam,
as a symbolic 'repertoire', is not fixed. And the same could be said
about the purified discourses of 'Arabnness' and 'Moroccanness'.
Mental emigration can, in this context, only take place from one
kind of discursive hermeneutics[68] of Islam/Arab identity, and not
from Islam or Moroccanness/Arabnness per se. To problematise mental emigration's trajectory further, it is important, when
assessing its symbolic reference points not to perceive them as
being two entirely oppositional historical entities, which would
be an aberration. Arab-Islamic civilisation, argues Al-Jabri, was
not merely a link between Greek and European civilisations, but
was also a reworking and reproduction of Greek culture. Al-Jabri
insists: 'The presence of Arab-Islamic culture in international
European cultural history was not a mere temporary intermedi-
ate; its presence was that of a necessary and crucial constituent'
(Al-Jabri, 1991: 48). To speak of the Arab world as non-modern or
outside the modern world is to exoticise it, denying it its modern
history. As Al-Azmeh put it: 'The idea widespread in the Orient
as well as in the West, that the Arab population is Muslim by
essence and certain to return to a form of Islam embodied in the
shari'a...is contradicted by the modern history of the Arabs'
(Al-Azmeh, 1993: 53). These arguments blur the line between
modernity and the Arab-Islamic 'repertoire' and place them, culturally at least, within the same parameter of human heritage/
history. The penetration of the 'disembedding mechanisms' by

'distanciated' encountering in young Moroccans' everyday experience strengthens their self-identity; complexify, displace, enrich, trouble and subvert it, but never, according to evidence produced here, weaken it. Manifestations of modernness are inherent to the kind of dialectics that are produced through intersectional encounters between different cultural temporalities, and making sense of such *being* in the world, reflecting on it, refuting, negotiating it – is symptomatic of a modern self-reflexivity *par excellence*, a state of being-modern-in different ways in the world.

Conclusion

The ambivalence, duality and the kind of double-identity that is produced by the 'disembedding mechanisms' of encounter (colonialism included) need not be a handicap or a burden forever, nor should it be a question of choosing one repertoire over the other or, indeed, of reconciling the two. The problem, argued Al-Jabri, lies in the duality of our position towards the modernity/tradition duality (Al-Jabri, 1989: 13). This is where the real handicap is, and that is what needs to be straightened, adjusted, sorted and dealt with. Khatibi's answer to this problematic: a *double-critique*, where both the modern and traditional, as parts of a double Self-identity, are perpetually questioned, subverted and troubled (the positioning here is one of différance and distanciation), and it seems to me to be the best solution on offer from this cul-de-sac. It is through this perpetual self-critical and creative project that Arab modernity can truly fruitify, but this necessitates an organised and systematic exploration of the Arab everyday, the Arab present cultural tense. That's a task I would like to rehearse in the next and concluding chapter.

6

Still Searching for the Arab Present Cultural Tense: Arab Cultural Studies

> We often borrow from the Western cultural repertoire
> its results and fruits, ignoring its principles and *origina-*
> *tions*. We import from it to consume only and not to
> plant, knowing that the latter task requires a fertile soil,
> which cannot be imported.[69]

(Al-Jabri, 1989: 35)

I am aware that the foregrounding of Arab modernness through
contemporary Arab thought, the everyday and self-reflexivity, to
which the last chapters were dedicated, barely touches the surface
of what is a much more varied and complex phenomenon: being
Arab in a 'runaway' world, in changing times, when fixity has given
way to the liminal, certainty to doubt and where 'structures of feeling' are the results of interplay between competing cultural repertoires, intersectional temporalities and different discourses of
becoming. Manifestations of *being* modern in the Arab world are, of
course, far more diverse than I have attempted to show. However,
as I stated in the opening chapter, it was never intended that this

book be an exhaustive or, for that matter, a complete exposé of Arab modernness. A lot, I have no doubt, remains unsaid and 'unthought' about other aspects, such as those inherent to new forms of artistic expression: architecture, music, political discourse, literature, not to mention the uses of postmodern communication technologies and the new *dialogic*/self-reflexive spaces they have opened up. There is also a lot more to be said about intersections between ontic/self-identities and institutional reflexivities, different 'sequestrian experiences'[70], new forms of ontological security and the ways in which these produce different dynamics/meanings of *being* modern in the Arab world. Rather, what I had intended that the book be and do was far more modest: to initiate debates on the question of 'Arab modernity' in a way that moves beyond *Cartesian* conceptualisations of the 'modern' as they appear in contemporary Arab thought, in the minds of Arab thinkers and philosophers, to a conceptually ontological idea of the 'modern', so that the Arab cultural repertoire is reconnected with Man – the *subjectum* of modernity *par excellence* – and so that the taken-for-granted everyday, the carnivalesque – where manifestations of social relations, artistic expression, culture (its anthropological and aesthetic aspects) are taken seriously as a new arena of empirical research. The other objective, or intellectual task, that of *dislocation*, aimed to free the category 'Arab culture' from the clutches of ideologised discourses of *authenticity*, thus making space for new discursive formations and hermeneutics. However, the tasks of *bridging* and *dislocating* can only begin to make sense when seen and framed within a process, a long-term intellectual project, rather than within a conclusion. The question remains: How do we turn the phenomenon of Arab modernness, its double-identity and Khatibi's method of *double-critique* into an intellectual project and thereby a subject of systematic study and exploration? This concluding chapter attempts to deal with exactly these questions. It argues that for such a project to materialise in any meaningful way it is necessary to have a new and interdisciplinary epistemic space/home; one where studies of contemporary Arab cultures and Arab modernity can become the objects of organised empirical enquiry. The case I make here is for Arab cultural studies. This chapter's content was inspired by a London seminar series organised by the University of Westminster's Arab Media Centre between 2003 and 2005. The series, which tackled a range of issues on contemporary Arab media, culture and society, and the meta-discussions I had with colleagues on these topics, were fundamental in helping me think seriously about the project of Arab cultural studies. Throughout the series I was very much interested in the spatial and temporal situatedness – the 'where' and 'when' – of what was being said about contemporary Arab media, culture and society, and by 'whom'. The question 'by whom?' is one that deals with narration in the sense of who narrates whom, in what way and from what position or cultural moment. Despite its importance, the question of narration is one I am prepared to suppress momentarily in order that I can turn my attention to, what I believe to be, far more important and pressing issues. By the 'where' and 'when', *deixis*, I refer to the spatiality and temporality of the scholarly work presented in the series. In dealing with the 'where' and 'when' of what was said, I hope to engage in a meta-series discussion, and provide a platform for continuity and further debate. As I reflected on the series and its content, I became more and more preoccupied with questions of an epistemological nature, the most persistent being: how does the cultural material presented in the series relate to and inform 'contemporary' articulations (both sociological and philosophical) of Arab culture and society? To put it differently: What are our points of reference for what was said, and to what epistemic space 'paradigm' did the series contribute? What do we call it? How do we connect it to the existing body of intellectual work on Arab culture(s) and society? Here, I am not concerned with the question 'for whom are we writing?' as this was famously or, perhaps infamously, dealt with in Ahmad Aijaz's (1992) critique of postcolonial theory and its major intellectuals. Instead, the questions I pose seem to lie at the heart of a crisis that is deep-seated, not only in Arab 'culture' but also in prevalent modes of Arab reasoning. A meaningful articulation of contemporary Arab culture and society, I argue, requires us to build epistemological bridges to problematics inherent to contemporary Arab thought (see Chapter 2). For example, Habermas's 'public sphere' did not arise from nowhere and its articulation, as a normative concept, was not an accident, but a long and continuous philosophical argument that can easily be traced to Jean-Jacques Rousseau, or even to Plato. Habermas's work is part of a continual search for a rational society. To make connections between what can be said today about Arab media, culture and society, and contemporary Arab thought, I turn to what is perhaps the most important and influential Arab and Islamic philosophical treatise of the twentieth century, *A Critique of Arab Reason*, by the Arab philosopher Mohammed Abed al-Jabri. In this chapter, drawing on Al-Jabri's work, I explore three epistemological deficits in Arab reason[71] today. They stand in the way of the development of a contemporary and relevant cultural repertoire that is able to document, examine and communicate the 'cultural' as it is lived, experienced and thought in the present tense of Arab cultures. These, as the chapter will argue, are inherent to: the problematic structure of Arab reason, the problem of the unconscious in Arab cultural temporality, and Arab intellectuals' ceaseless undermining of the 'popular'. The chapter also investigates what might be learnt from the ongoing project of internationalising/de-Westernising the field of cultural studies, as a way to support the search for the Arab present cultural tense and also to further rehearse the questions that have previously been asked about Arab modernness.

Making use of work by André Lalande (1948), Al-Jabri distinguishes between two kinds of reason. One is 'la raison constituante' (Arabic: *al-aql al-mukawin*), which refers to the mental activity that creates knowledge, constructs meanings and decides on rules and principles. The second is 'la raison constituée' (Arabic: *al-aql al-mukawan*), which refers to reason that is already constituted and which encompasses a whole repertoire, including the arts and sciences (Al-Jabri, 1991: 15–16). Lalande defines the latter as 'the reason that exists, as it is, in a given moment...what it is in our civilization and epoch... we should also say in our profession'. This, he adds, presents us with two characteristics of great importance. 'On the one hand it assures the cohesion of a group, more or less large, that claims its ownership;... on the other hand, it can also be posed as an absolute by all those who have not yet acquired' *l'esprit critique nécessaire* (Lalande, 1948: 2). It is the dialectical relationship between these two categories of reason, Al-Jabri argues, that determines cultural repertoires and ways of reasoning. Al-Jabri attributes Arab reason's regression over the last 600 years to its preoccupation with reproducing the old (*raison constituée*) rather than creating the new. Al-Jabri argues that the death of philosophy (critical reason) as a project precipitated stagnation in Arab thought. This deficit in the structure of Arab reason has led, in turn, to another deficit: that of confusion in Arab cultural temporality or, as Al-Jabri puts it, 'unconscious cultural temporality' (Al-Jabri, 1991: 40). How does Al-Jabri articulate the problematic of 'unconscious time' in Arab culture? Using Jean Piaget's concept of *l'inconscient cognitif*, he calls for a structural reorganisation of the parts or phases of Arab cultural temporality, so that it can function in a linear fashion (Al-Jabri, 1991: 44). He shows how the structure of reason shares the temporality with the culture to which it belongs. As such, he argues that Arab reason's temporality is also the temporality of Arab culture. In the case of Arab culture, and unlike European cultural temporality, the old and the contemporary coexist on the same stage, hence the confusion in Arab cultural temporality (Al-Jabri, 1991: 47). As Al-Jabri observed:

> The temporal in recent Arab cultural history is stagnant... for it does not provide us with a development of Arab thought and its movement from one state to another; instead, it presents us with an exhibition or a market of past cultural products, which co-exist in the same temporality as the new, where the old and new become contemporaries. The outcome is an overlapping between different

> cultural temporalities in our conception of our own
> cultural history... This way, our present becomes
> an exhibition of our past, and we live our past in
> our present, without change and without history.[72]

The relationship between the old and the new, argues Al-Jabri, is unconscious, as what we forget of culture does not simply vanish but remains in the unconscious. In this case, reason as an epistemological tool produces and is constructed in 'an unconscious way' (Al-Jabri, 1991: 47). To illuminate this, Al-Jabri presents the contemporary Arab intellectual as a migrant through cultural time, who is able to change positions swiftly from Right to Left, from socialism to democracy and from Islamism to secularism[73] (ibid, 43). Besides this overlapping in Arab cultural temporality, Al-Jabri adds that the spatial and the temporal also overlap. Arab cultural history, he argues, 'is more connected to the spatial than it is to the temporal: our cultural history is the history of Kufa, Basra, Damascus, Baghdad, Cairo, Granada, Fez... which makes it a history of cultural islands'[74] (Al-Jabri, 1991: 47). To this assessment of the temporal and the spatial, we must add the exogenous elements downplayed by Al-Jabri, which I discussed at length in the previous chapter. These are manifested in the 'disembedding mechanisms' of global modernity, imposing/adding/inserting other temporalities and spatialities, which are then dissolved into Arab temporality. Contemporary Arab cultural temporality is not merely the product of the interplay between old and new elements in the same 'documentary' or repertoire, but also a product of a multiplicity of temporalities, both endogenous and exogenous.

A reworking/broadening of the idea of Arab and 'Islamic' culture is fundamental and should precede all attempts to theorise Arab/Islamic media, culture and society. The following extract from Raymond Williams's analysis of George Orwell's *Nineteen Eighty-Four* encapsulates what I mean when I refer to the broadening of the notion of 'Arab-Islamic' 'culture', a task I began to deal with in Chapter 3. Williams writes of Orwell: 'He went to books, and found in them the detail of virtue and truth. He went to experience, and found in it the practice of loyalty, tolerance and sympathy.' 'But in the end', Williams continues, quoting directly from Orwell's novel:

> it was a bright cold day in April, and the clocks were striking thirteen. Winston Smith, his chin nuzzled into his breast in an effort to escape the vile wind, slipped quickly through the glass doors of Victory Mansions, though not quickly enough to prevent a swirl of gritty dust from entering along with him.[75]

Williams writes of the dust that:

> it is part of the case: the caustic dust carried by the vile wind. Democracy, truth, art, equality, culture: all these we carry in our heads, but, in the street, the wind is everywhere. The great and humane tradition is a kind of wry joke; in the books it served, but put them down and look around you. It is not so much a disillusion, it is more like our actual world.[76]

It is this grittiness in culture, the ordinary, the everyday, the profane, that must be articulated and not only what Matthew Arnold once described as 'the *best* knowledge and thought of the time' (Arnold, 1994: 79). What is required, in our pursuit of the present cultural tense in the Arab world, is a re-articulation of culture, where the concept denotes not only a fixed set of aesthetics or values but also a system of relations, which takes into account the gritty nature of lived experience (the social/anthropological) as well as the best that has been written and said. Re-articulating the concept of culture so that it draws from the present tense of Arab cultures is a way of dealing with and changing what the present of Arab cultures holds, in terms of power relations between, for example, male/female, ruler/ruled, rich/poor, Arab/non-Arab as well as other power structures.

However, it is not only the temporal (endogenous or exogenous) that brings change but also what we put into it. As Immanuel Kant said: 'it is not temporality itself that changes, but something that is in it'.[77] This observation leads to the third epistemological deficit: that of Arab intellectuals' ceaseless undermining of the 'popular' in Arab cultures. Arab intellectuals' interpretations of culture, as I discussed in Chapter 3, are ideologised and largely elitist. With few exceptions, and without exaggeration, their 'take' on culture can be compared to those of the Spanish philosopher José Ortega y Gasset (1932), Matthew Arnold (1869) and other modernists, who could not hide their abomination of the masses and their ordinary cultures (Carey, 1992). Arab intellectuals are, in general, more aristocratic than the aristocracy. Arab popular culture, for example, is still considered by many prominent and influential Arab intellectuals to be profane, unconscious, irrelevant and consequently unworthy of study. This view is symptomatic of the vast majority of Arab intellectuals who constantly downgrade spoken *ammeya* (colloquial languages) and for whom, to use Orwell's analogy, what goes on in the vile and gritty wind – the *souk* (marketplace), *makha* (café), the television pop music contest – is classified as profane. All that is, therefore, *of the people*, whether music, television programmes or just ordinary everyday experience, remains largely underexamined[78]. The phrase, the 'Arab street', which is commonly used by Arab media and Arab intellectuals, reflects this elitist stance and its distance from the majority of the population. Why should there be an Arab street when there is no talk of a European, American or Indian street? The constant massification and homogenisation of Arab audiences into this redundant term – 'the street' – is proof of a major lack of understanding about how complex and stratified audiences are. There is today no substantial research using empirical methods that examines how Arab audiences interact with the media or which investigates the relationships between Western media consumption and dynamics of imperialism. Audience research in the Arab world is fragmentary and largely underdeveloped (Al-Gammal, 2003). The present chapter does not permit a lengthy exploration of the reasons for this lack. Suffice it to say that it is not just a political economy problem that is at the heart of this deficit (Sakr, 2009)[79] but also an epistemological problem that is inherent to the Arab cultural repertoire and which has yet to accommodate and articulate ordinary culture as a part of scientific enquiry. Unlike their counterparts in Western countries, especially the UK and the USA, Arab academics, it seems, have not yet grasped the need for a coherent field of cultural studies. There is no cultural studies in the Arab world as such, only fragmented works in the area, which remain largely unconscious parts of an incoherent whole. This inadequacy has wider implications for the poverty of audience research in the Arab world, most of which is quantitative, commercially driven and tells us hardly anything about who Arab audiences are, or about how they interact with and read media texts. It is important to add, as Jon Alterman has noted, that even the quantitative data emerging from surveys on Arab audiences 'tend to be developed for marketing studies, and thus concentrate on wealthier populations and remain proprietary' (Alterman, 2005: 203–8). What is required is qualitative research with the potential to investigate the ontic/social world of Arab audiences and their interpretations of it. In dealing with the threat of cultural imperialism, Arab scholars too often take audiences for granted. Al-Jabri argues for the importance of understanding 'the phenomenon of cultural 'infiltration', not only as an outside action, moved by a desire for hegemony, but also through the negative implications it has for our present cultural reality' (Al-Jabri, 1994: 209). 'Cultural infiltration', he adds 'is in principle an infiltration of identity' (ibid, 214). Rather than unpacking how this infiltration actually takes place, Al-Jabri moves directly to remedy. 'The answer to the question: what can be done is to work inside our culture by renewing it from within. The beginning is to understand this 'inside' by reorganizing its parts so it is reconnected to us and we are reconnected with it in a modern and contemporary way' (ibid, 223). The reason we need to start work from within 'our culture', Al-Jabri argues, is because, 'were it not for its weakness, the action [cultural infiltration] coming from without could not have carried out its effects in a way which makes it a danger' (ibid, 226). Al-Jabri's proposition, albeit genuine and stirring, tells us absolutely nothing about where and how cultural infiltration occurs. Nor does it deal with the kind of channels that facilitate it. Arab scholars[80] have generally dealt with 'cultural imperialism' as a taken-for-granted phenomenon, its conclusiveness never brought into question, so that we are never told empirically how this 'effect' or 'action' takes place. This uniform approach gives rise to serious concern, for it seems to render superfluous any empirical enquiry into implications of imperialism for Arab culture and structures of feeling. The danger in this line of thinking is that it risks, unwittingly, masking the very dynamics of the imperialism it purports to understand.

Internationalising cultural studies and the problem of translation

The working out of the idea of culture and what it means to be modern in the Arab world has to be seen as a process, an ongoing intellectual project that is ready to accept and deal with the three deficits described above. However, this reworking of the idea of culture also requires a space or, to use Deleuzian language, a 'plane' where the study of contemporary culture can become a legitimised scientific practice where 'culture', as a category, is re-articulated and unpicked as the product of a system of relations, and as a 'process, not a conclusion' (Williams, 1958: 295). Such space must also allow for 'an articulated expression...of new forms of aesthetics in Arab cultures' (Berque, 1972: 739). As for the urgent and pertinent questions of how such an intellectual project might be possible, and under what epistemological umbrella it would operate, Al-Jabri's answer to the problems of Arab 'reason' and 'culture' is a return to critical reason through the vehicle of philosophy. He has taken up the immense task of retracing where the Arab philosophical project was abandoned, by revisiting and re-articulating the contribution of Ibn Rushd, who is known in the West as Averroes. In this manner, Al-Jabri hopes not only to resuscitate the project of rationality in the Arab and Islamic worlds but also to reconcile the past with the present. While a return to the philosophical project is clearly indispensable in dealing with the deficits Al-Jabri identifies, other intellectual disciplines must also be allowed to work towards the same purpose. Philosophy alone is not enough, at least not the kind of philosophical discourse that refuses to ontologise its critique in order to make it current and relevant. The question is really one of hermeneutics: upon what bases do we reinterpret Arab cultures and societies today? I propose that we base our reinterpretation on the social and the cultural, and, since the existential precedes them both, the existential should be added as a third category. These three categories or determinants would form the basis upon which we can rely in our search for the present tense of Arab cultures. The articulation of these categories would take place within a new field of research that, unlike sociology, has yet to be fully introduced to the Arab world: Cultural Studies. Due to its interdisciplinary nature, drawn from philosophy, sociology, psychology, history, political science, anthropology and others, cultural studies is better equipped to deal with questions of Arab modernness. It would be naïve, however, to think that such a field could have the effect of a magic ring, which has only to be touched for all the problems of Arab thought and culture to vanish. What cultural studies will guarantee, if added to Arab university curricula, is the space for a whole new body of intellectual work on contemporary Arab cultures and societies. The field of cultural studies is, above all, an epistemic space that situates the category of culture at the centre of its inquiry. It is not a 'fixed body of thought that can be transported from one place to another, and which operates in similar ways in diverse national or regional contexts' (Ang and Morley, 1989: 135). Cultural studies can be moulded and reshaped to adapt to different historical and cultural situations. As Ang and Morley have argued, the place and relevance of cultural studies 'varies from context to context, and has to be related to the specific character of local forms of political and intellectual discourse on culture' (ibid, 136). There are literally hundreds of studies, textbooks and articles on cultural studies as a paradigm and field of study, many of which revisit its beginnings in Britain after World War II, emphasising the role of the Centre for Contemporary Cultural Studies at Birmingham University and its intellectuals, of whom Stuart Hall was a leading figure, in shaping this distinct and relatively new project. So much has been written, in fact, that I see no need to retell this story. Here, instead, I am more interested in shedding light on the internationalisation/'de-Westernisation' of cultural studies, including the problem of translation and whether cultural studies, as an episteme, can be useful in our pursuit of the present cultural tense in Arab cultures. Cultural studies has been defined as a radical project, a movement, a fashion and sometimes, because of its interdisciplinary nature and boundless intellectual geography, simply as 'nobody-knows-anymore'. Since the 1980s it has managed to migrate to other parts of the world. Yet the term usually evokes the British, Australian, American or European incarnations of cultural studies, restricting the field's geography mainly to the West.[81] Regardless of its claim to internationalisation, at the end of the 1980s Ang and Morley observed that it remained 'largely restricted to the developed world, reflecting the fact that it is in the West that the cultural dimension of politics has been foregrounded, as a result of transformations in the social formation brought about by post-industrial and post-Fordist capitalism' (Ang and Morley, 1989: 136). One of the distinctive characteristics of cultural studies is 'its desire to transgress established disciplinary boundaries and to create new forms of knowledge and understanding not bound by such boundaries' (Stratton and Ang, 1996: 362). It is the 'open-ended and experimental' nature of cultural studies that guarantees its distinctiveness...as a particular discursive formation and intellectual practice' (Stratton and Ang, 1996: 361). Interviewed by Kuan-Hsing Chen, Stuart Hall emphasised the need to increase the overlap, rather than police the boundaries of cultural studies (Chen, 1996: 400). But Stratton and Ang argue that these qualities hide an implied 'unproblematic liberal pluralism'; they point out that cultural studies is not exempt from power relations' (Stratton and Ang, 1996: 361–2). Abbas and Erni expressed similar concerns in the introduction to their anthology *Internationalizing Cultural Studies* (2005), stating that:

> a certain parochialism continues to operate in cul-
> tural studies as a whole, whose objects of and lan-
> guage for analysis have had the effect of closing off
> real contact with scholarship conducted outside its
> (western) radar screen. In the current moment of
> what we call 'the postcolonial predicament' of cul-
> tural studies, in which a broad hegemony of western
> modernity is increasingly being questioned among
> cultural studies scholars from around the world,
> we must consider any form of internationalisation
> as an effort – and a critical context – for facilitating
> the visibility, transportability, and translation of
> works produced outside North America, Europe
> and Australia.
>
> (Abbas and Erni, 2005: 2)

Their attempt to de-Westernise cultural studies is, in their own words, 'a political and intellectual intervention into a state of unevenness in the flow and impact of knowledge' within the field (Abbas and Erni, 2005: 2). In this context, the internationalisation of cultural studies is not regarded as the propagation of another universal body of knowledge like, for example, sociology, which is legitimised through Western discourse (Stratton and Ang, 1996), but as a resistance to universalism and intellectual imperialism.

What an Arab cultural studies project may look like, or how it will develop in, let us say, Palestine or Algeria, is difficult to predict. What is clear is that with the body of intellectual work on Arab culture and society already to hand, Arab cultural studies will quickly establish unique, yet different, characteristics and particularities[82]. However, national or cultural differentiations and distinctiveness must not be the basis from which a whole intellectual project is defined. It is not the 'Britishness' or 'Englishness' of cultural studies that defines the field, but its radical rethinking of the relationship between culture and society. Similarly, it is not the 'Arabnness' of cultural studies that should define its intellectual agenda, but the opposite. When asked to elaborate on the internationalisation of cultural studies and the problem of translation, Stuart Hall replied:

> I use 'translation' in quotation marks...translation as a continuous process of re-articulation and re-contextualisation, without any notion of a primary origin...whenever it [cultural studies] enters a new cultural space, the terms change; and, exactly as you find in any re-articulation and disar-ticulation some elements remain the same, because there clearly are certain points, certain terms and concepts in common, but then there are also new elements which change the configuration.
>
> (Hall, 1996: 394)

The appropriation of 'British' cultural studies in different locales has largely been influenced by local cultural particularities. Ang and Morley observed in 1989 that in the Netherlands, for example, cultural studies had been most influential in departments of education, where Paul Willis's 1977 study of anti-school culture had found more resonance than Dick Hebdige's 1979 study of subculture, which offered a 'less institutionally-focused emphasis on the politics of style' (Ang and Morley, 1989: 137). The explanation, Ang and Morley suggested, lay in the fact that: 'from a generalised social democratic perspective, interest in forms of cultural resistance is cast in the desire to (better) *teach* 'the people', not to learn from popular experiences' (Ang and Morley, 1989: 137). Notwithstanding the importance of re-articulation and translation as necessary intellectual processes, some elements must remain the same. In Hall's words, cultural studies 'is *always* about the articulation – in different contexts...between culture and power' (Hall, 1996: 395). It is, if anything, this relationship that needs to be maintained if Arab cultural studies are to be credible. Indeed, maintaining such credibility depends on the ability to articulate and assess not only the dynamics of power as they emerge in the cultural text but also the economic structures that govern and influence cultural production in the Arab world (see Sakr, 2001, 2007). What I am trying to emphasise here is the importance of political economy, which should not necessarily be seen as an oppositional or rival paradigm, as is the case in Western academe, but as a complementary and crucial component of Arab cultural studies, one that enhances our understanding of cultural production in the Arab region.

The problem of arbitrariness between intellectual formations and historical 'moments'

The establishment of new academic fields is not accidental, nor does it develop outside history. Stuart Hall's early writings, where he makes the case for the media's centrality to experience, confirm this. The media, he argued with Whannel:

> are not the end products of a simple technological revolution. They come at the end of a complex historical and social process; they are active agents in a new phase in the life history of industrial society. Inside these forms and languages, the society is articulating new social experiences for the first time. In fact, the emergence of new art forms is closely linked with social change.
>
> (Hall and Whannel, 1964: 45)

The question that must be asked in the Arab context is: are the historical and socio-cultural conditions in the Arab region suited to the development of an academic field that takes culture and the media as the objects of its enquiry? If so, what are these historical events, and what shape should this field take? What ought its main concerns to be? One of the important lessons learnt from the historiography of studies into media and communication, especially the development of Mass Communication in the USA in the 1930s, and Cultural studies in Britain in the 1960s and 70s, is that their development was not accidental, but was rather the product of historical moments. They are 'a determinate effect of the historical process; responses to the pathologies (the disorders) of modernity' (Scannell, 2006: 4). A study of the development of these fields, any academic field, cannot take place outside the historical, political and socioeconomic contexts that determined them, nor the historical formations that shaped them. Scannell observed that academic fields:

> Show up, in particular times and places, as one response to contemporary anxieties about the world. The form that such responses take is an effect of history in the first place, not of the founding institutions and their founding fathers. Thus, if the two key moments in the academic study of the media in the 20th century are Columbia in the 30s and 40s and Birmingham in the 60s and 70s then what must be accounted for, in the first place, is why each moment took the form that it did: why did it appear as a *social* question in 30s America and as a *cultural* question in 70s Britain and why in that order (i.e., why does the social question appear, historically, before the cultural)?... Thus there are two quite distinct and separate historiographies to the formation of intellectual fields: the endogenous histories of particular developments (sociology at Chicago, say) and the exogenous history to which they are a response. The former is a plurality, the latter a singularity: histories and History.[83]

If we are to accept Scannell's reasoning as a more sophisticated and useful way of *doing* media and communication historiography, how then do we appropriate it to make sense of study and enquiry into media, culture and society in the Arab world? What do we know about the intellectual formations of the scholars who are now engaged in the study of the region's media and culture? Upon what hermeneutics do they rely to interpret the world? What paradigms, if any, have emerged from their enquiries? To what historical moment are they responding? Answering these questions is certainly beyond the scope of this chapter; what follows, however, is not entirely detached from the problems they pose. If I am contributing a paper, let's say, on Jordanian, Tunisian or Egyptian popular culture, or the political economy of Sudanese media, to what epistemic space will I be contributing? This question is apposite for both the Arab scholar who writes in Arabic and publishes his work mainly with an Arab audience in mind, and for the scholar dealing with similar issues in English, French or German in different Western academic locales, with a mainly Western readership in mind? It is not so much the 'geographical' situatedness of the 'field' that is concerned here, but its 'epistemological' situatedness. One problem that emerges from the situatedness question is methodological. Since the development of academic fields is partly shaped, as we learn from Scannell, by intellectual formations that are in turn affected by certain historical 'moments', then how will this affect the structural and methodological development of a field such as Arab media and cultural studies, to which both Western and Arab scholars have been contributing, not only from different geographical spaces but also from different historical/cultural/ political moments? Here, the problem is one of confusion caused by the arbitrariness between the cultural temporality and the historical 'moment' within which knowledge is produced about Arab media, culture and society. Arab and Western scholars contributing to the field may not share similar intellectual formations or motives, in fact many of them are likely to be unaware of the work of others, since what has so far been produced on the region's media and culture is polarised, isolated work, exhibiting little linearity of thought and argument. This is not to say, of course, that established academic fields, such as British cultural studies, were clearly defined from the outset or were even 'coherent'. The field of British cultural studies was, and still is, the product of competing paradigms, different intellectual formations and even endless turf wars. Nevertheless, what brings this field together in a way that may not be possible for Arab cultural studies, is inherent to the commonality of the historical moment and the cultural temporality within which it operates. To this we also need to add the existence of sustained debate, not only about media, culture and society, but about how these are thought and rethought within this field. It is a debate about the field itself, which is also an evidence of its maturity (Morley and Chen, 1996; Curran and Morley, 2006; Garnham, 1986, 2000; Hall, 1986; Silverstone, 1999; Scannell, 2007; Sparks, 2000). If the cultural 'turn' was, according to Scannell, the result of a shift in the nature of Western political discourse (from a politics of poverty to a politics of abundance), and if this was also to play a part in shaping British cultural studies in the 1960s as an intellectual discipline, then to what 'moment' or political shift do we attribute the rationale for an Arab cultural studies? Are the transformations brought about by capitalism, and/or the modernisation and standardisation of everyday life enough? In the same vein, since a shift in political discourse implicates change in meanings ascribed to 'politics', should we not also be rethinking what is meant by *politics* in the Arab context today? Scannell's analysis is rather plausible, but his justification for the shift in political discourse is clearly framed within a Eurocentric context, and cannot therefore be generalised. In the case of the poor South, of which the Arab region is part, the politics of poverty is still dominant, and so is the emancipatory discourse with all its different struggles. South American and African Cultural Studies emerged in societies where the politics of poverty were predominant. They still are. I think it is thus safe to say, at least in the case of these geographies, that a shift from the politics of poverty to the politics of abundance was not a prerequisite for the establishment of African or South American cultural studies. The intellectual formations that shaped African cultural studies in the 1950s and 60s (especially Frantz Fanon, Ngugi wa Thiong'o and Kiamani Gecau's) shared a common experience: colonialism. Their work was a response to anxieties caused by colonialism and its aftermath. Here, again, we can also say with some certainty that the postcolonial was the 'moment' that shaped African cultural studies. The Arab region, like Africa, was spared neither the physical nor the mental brutality of the colonial system. It is therefore required of Arab cultural studies to explore not only the dynamics of postcolonial consciousness but also imperialism and its consequences on people and culture in the region.[84] It is interesting to note, from a historical viewpoint, that although African and British Cultural studies were shaped during the same period (mainly the 1960s), both their reference point and the historical moments to which they responded were different, and this is a reason to raise the problem of arbitrariness between intellectual formations and historical moments.

'De-Westernisation' as discourse

The events of 9/11 have had major effects on global and local politics. They have triggered two wars[85], toppled regimes, and have spawned an undefined and timeless war, now known to everyone as the 'global war on terror'. Some have even dared to define our world and age through two headings: pre-9/11 and post-9/11. The effects on the study of Arab media, culture and society, are not unnoticed. 9/11 has certainly rekindled the West's interest in the Arab and everything that is Arab: media, culture, society, politics and more. If fields of enquiry are indeed, as Scannell (2006) suggests, the product of *endogenous* and *exogenous* events, then 9/11 (as an external historical event) has certainly played a part in the morphing of Arab media, culture and society from an almost negligible area of interest to becoming a hot topic. Evidence of this is visible in the plethora of academic publications, courses, seminars and conference panels dedicated to the study of the subject. The outcome is a rather rich and varied scholarship that covers a range of areas including, but not limited to, the political economy of Arab media, media and democratisation, Arab satellite broadcasting and Arab popular cultures. Notwithstanding the importance of this work, a lot of which is, incidentally, concentrated in British and US academia, little attention has been given to either the *epistemological* problematics that usually come with the development of new fields of enquiry or the dreaded burden of representation from which Orientalists have yet to recover. A key question that has yet to be rehearsed is: how does the mushrooming of recent literature on Arab media, culture and society relate to or, even better, inform Arab contemporary thought and *vice versa*? Here, I situate my argumentation on Arab cultural studies within the intellectual process of 'de-Westernisation', which has been described by Curran and Park as the 'growing reaction against the self-absorption and parochialism of much Western media theory' (2000: 3). The media theory 'de-Westernisation' debate can easily be traced back to the late 1980s, one decade after the inception of British media and cultural studies. Terms commonly used to describe the debate included intellectual concerns, such as 'appropriation', 'translation', 'localisation', 'authentication' and so on (see Ang and Morley, 1989, Stratton and Ang, 1996, Sparks, 2000, Chen, 1996, Curran and Park, 2000, Abbas and Erni, 2005). Since I am concentrating primarily on the Arab case, it is important to note that the development of Mass Communication Theory in the USA in the 1930s and 40s also triggered heated discussion on 'de-Westernisation' in Arab academic circles, mainly in Egypt, where the first mass communication department was established as early as 1939. Glass traces this debate to the 1950s at the University of Cairo. In his article, entitled: 'The Global Flow of Information: A Critical Appraisal from the Perspective of Arab Islamic Information Sciences', Glass (2001) stratifies Arab media and communication scholars into five different intellectual traditions:

Group 1: (1950s–1996) Their work was concerned with public opinion and the social functions of communication and was largely influenced by American communication models.

Group 2: Also established in the 1950s, this group worked hard to institutionalise the teaching of media practice.

Group 3: Was established in the 1960s and was mainly concerned with classical Islamic theories of communication.

Group 4: Was established in the 1970s and called for the re-Islamization of Arab information.

Group 5: Described as the product of the 1980s, advocated an 'Arab conceptualisation of information'

(Glass in Hafez, 2001: 220–2)

The 'de-Westernisation' debate is also part of a much older and broader intellectual tradition that questioned the universality of the values and grand narratives of the Enlightenment. This critical tradition, as far back as Nietzsche, has resulted in a whole body of work, since embraced by subsequent generations of scholars in their efforts to unpick and critique frames of knowledge and thought that assumed the universality, and thus the superiority, of the Enlightenment and its ideas. Abdullah Laroui's *Histoire du Maghreb* (1970) and Edward Said's *Orientalism* (1978) are two good examples of such critical work. 'De-Westernisation' in the field of media/cultural studies is rapidly becoming an intellectual project in its own right. It is also emerging as a 'discourse' with layers of meanings that require ceaseless troubling and subverting. Discourses of 'de-Westernisation' have been driven by both *endogenous* and *exogenous* elements. The former are manifest in articulations and debates emerging from within the discourse in relation to problematics of translation, appropriation and localisation (as intellectual processes). The latter are concerned with a number of external elements, inextricably linked, that are the results of worldwide changes (globalisation being a key factor), the demands of the education market and the changing nature of student intake. I chose to deal with this 'growing reaction' of 'internationalisation' and 'de-Westernisation' as 'discourse', and not merely as a framework or debate, due to its heterogeneous nature – the discourse of 'de-Westernisation' is multilayered – and also because attempts at 'de-Westernisation' are driven by a multiplicity of processes, including the intellectual, the pedagogic, the demagogic and the economic. Economic development, especially in China and East Asian countries such as South Korea and Japan, has encouraged the middle classes of these countries to invest large sums of money so that their offspring can continue their higher education in the USA or the UK. For some British universities that offer undergraduate and graduate courses in the fields of media/cultural studies, the intake of International students has increased exponentially, so much so that in certain MA courses international students outnumber British students. It has now occurred to academics who teach media and cultural studies in Britain that the changing nature of the student intake dictates a fundamental change in: a) the content of their taught courses (which had hitherto focused mainly on British and American media), and b) how such content is delivered pedagogically. A number of media and communication departments in British universities, for example, have, as a consequence, sought globalising/internationalising as a survival strategy for both intellectual and economic reasons. The dictum now is: internationalise or perish. How much of this, however, is driven by intellectual concern (which we see in the development of international media centres and changes in teaching content), the logic of the market, or both, is unclear.

Towards 'de-Westernisation' as *double-critique*

In their book *De-Westernising Media Studies*, rather than tracking 'particular aspects of media globalisation' through descriptive methods followed in 'American textbooks', Curran and Park, who are more interested 'in extending communication theory', opted for a more 'interpretive orientation' and so decided to organise their edited collection around comparative perspectives of different 'national media systems' (Curran and Park, 2000: 12). To achieve this, they set their contributors a 'global' exam paper made up of four key questions, which I quote below in full (ibid):

> How do the media relate to the power structure of society?
> What influences the media, and where does control over the media lie?
> How has the media influenced society?
> What effect has media globalization and new media had on the media system?

There is no doubt that the answers to the set of 'imposed' questions made for a huge improvement over the conventional or, dare I say it, the rather descriptive American textbook-style, which Curran and Park criticise. In this case, it is fair to say that the book not only provides a good and comprehensive account of different media systems from different cultural contexts, but is also an important contribution to the growing discourse around 'de-Westernisation'. In setting the agenda, however, the authors have unwittingly reproduced the very kind of 'self-absorption and parochialism' from which they intended to steer, for, in dictating the parameters of discussion, no matter how good their intentions were, the editors have limited what could be said about the media in different cultural contexts to a set of questions which *they* (as scholars from the centre) thought were relevant and important. Framing the questions within presupposed hermeneutical categories, such as the 'social' and 'power structure' (again regardless of their importance) are ways to police the debate. What is more, the editors also assume that the hermeneutical and methodological tools necessary for the articulation of such important questions are already there and available to all contributors. The discourse of 'de-Westernisation', I am afraid, must dig deeper than this. If the media constitute the 'modern' phenomenon *par excellence,* and if their study has largely been a way to come to terms with 'modernity's pathologies' (Scannell, 2007), then, surely, their study has to be informed by, and be answerable to, the philosophical discourses of modernity in different local cultural contexts. In this way, the study of media is joined to and relocated within a cultural repertoire that it can enrich and from which it can learn. The study of the media in the West does not stand alone; it is interdisciplinary and part of a linear philosophical argument, and of a critical tradition that can be traced from Hegel to Habermas. This relocating and reconnecting task is, I would argue, fundamental. It is, I dare say, the basis upon which our thinking around media and communication should be built. Furthermore, 'de-Westernisation' of media and communication theory is better unpicked as *discourse,* because the claims to 'authenticity' that often accompany such an intellectual process are themselves encrusted in *discourses* that require unpacking and subverting (see Khiabany, 2006). In this case, the *discourse* of 'de-Westernisation' would be far more effective were it to function through a *'double-critique' structure,* one mechanised through a dual intellectual exercise that is able to oscillate between 'de-Westernisation' and de-de-Westernisation, authentication and de-authentication. However, the discourse of 'de-Westernisation', as it stands, is still in its infancy: a stage where more intellectual effort is channelled towards *authentication* than to the questioning and subverting of the claims that come with such process. This causes disequilibrium in the structure of the 'de-Westernisation' discourse, making it less critical.

'De-Westernisation' or 'dialogism'

Is it possible to have an Arab media and cultural studies without an Arab critical theory? In other words: is it enough to rely on Western critical theory as a knowledge frame for the articulation of a whole field of enquiry into media, culture and society in the modern Arab world? The point in asking such a question is not an attempt at authentication. Rather, the question I pose is more concerned with highlighting the necessity for thinking about a localised form of critical theory that is conscious of its time; its cultural and historical specificities and the philosophical problematics that it poses. Looking at the philosophical discourse of modernity in the West, from Hegel to Habermas, one is struck by the linearity of the *argumentation* on modernity, especially the problematic of time-consciousness and self-reassurance. The question of time-consciousness was paramount to the articulation of Western modernity as a concept, and modern time-consciousness was constantly revitalised by Western thinkers, including Hegel, Nietzsche, Adorno, Benjamin, Heidegger, Baudelaire and others (see Habermas, 1987). In the Arab case, and with the vantage point of hindsight, the intellectual task of coming to terms with modernity's 'self-reassurance' and 'time-consciousness' must not be left solely to philosophical analysis. This exercise must be complemented by a culturalist approach, which, in my view, is (without the intention of belittling the role of philosophy) more equipped to deal with the *nowness*, or the present tense, of everyday Arab cultures in all their 'ordinary' and artistic manifestations. In his book *Contemporary Arab Thought*, Abu-Rabi' accentuates the importance of Western critical theory and the social sciences in making sense of modernity in the Arab region, arguing that since:

> the Muslim and Arab worlds have for the last two centuries been shaped by two main forces: colonialism and global capitalism...a theorisation of social life in the Arab-Islamic worlds cannot take place outside Western Critical Theory and its critique of Capitalism...neither the intellectual nor social nor economic history of the modern Arab world can be understood in isolation from the totality of world processes in the economic, political, and intellectual fields.

(Abu-Rabi', 2004: 3)

Although I share Abu-Rabi's view that the Arab situation, and indeed any other situation, can no longer be examined through the prism of the local alone, I think relying solely on Western critical theory to make sense of what it is to be modern in the Arab world today is somewhat problematic. Is it possible to speak of, or imagine, a quintessentially 'Arab' critical theory, when most of the Arab philosophers and thinkers who have led the debate on modernity have done so through their encounters with the West and Western frames of thought? The cultural and historical affinities shared between the West and the Arab world (especially vis-à-vis cultural exchange) can be traced back to the Andalusian civilisation and even further. It is also important to add that, more recently, in the Arab *Nahda* (Renaissance) of the late nineteenth and early twentieth century, Arab 'culture' reconstructed itself on the basis of the 'rediscovery'[86] of European culture. 'Far more than Japan', argued Kassir, 'where modernization concentrated on reproducing the technological, military and financial mechanics of the West's supremacy, the Arab world, nowadays described as inherently closed, embraced all the intellectual debates that came from Europe' (Kassir, 2006: 49). Today, most Arab philosophers and thinkers are not unaware of the Western episteme; in fact, the majority of them have incorporated it into their work as a methodological tool. The four positions of Arab thought, described in Chapter 2, have all encountered, and in different conjunctions, appropriated Western episteme (structuralist and post-structuralist) and methodology in their work.[87] The Arab world's historical and cultural affinities with the West make it naïve, if not misleading, for us, to engage in a facile discourse of *authenticity*. This is why I tend to favour a 'dialogical' approach, to use Bakhtin's term, that goes beyond the one-way, monologic frames of thought, where one is able to acknowledge and, most importantly, learn from the other's modalities and ways of interpreting the world. 'De-Westernisation', as a term, is also inherently negative; since it is based on the elimination and exclusion of the other and does nothing else than reproduce suzerain, orientalist, oppositional discourses of 'us' and 'them'. To situate, as a prerequisite for a critical discourse of 'de-Westernisation'/internationalisation, this 'dialogical' approach within the *double-critique structure*, articulated earlier, it is imperative that Arab/Western 'dialogism' also becomes a constant object of critique and reflection. The 'dialogical approach' may present us with a better alternative to the one-way asymmetrical discourses of 'de-Westernisation', but this must not place it above critique or reflection. The 'dialogic' must also be constantly subverted and troubled. In the Arab context, what we need to ask is: in what ways will the field of media and cultural studies help answer, or at least deal, with questions inherent to the contemporary philosophical discourse of modernity, as conceived by Arab thought?

This question has so far been downplayed, if not ignored, for two main reasons. On the one hand, the philosophical discourse of modernity, as conceived and thought by contemporary Arab philosophers and thinkers, has yet to consider the media and their role in society the subject of serious academic enquiry. On the other, the media theory 'de-Westernisation' discourse, as it thus far appears in Arab-Islamic scholarship, has yet to recognise the epistemological significance of reconnecting their discourse of 'de-Westernisation' with the Arab or local philosophical discourses of modernity.

The 'postcolonial' and problems of method

The Arab world is a postcolonial place and its people, like the remaining 'three quarters of the people living in the world' [have] 'had their lives shaped by the experience of colonialism' (Ashcroft, Griffiths and Tiffin, 1989: 1). Nevertheless, the 'postcolonial' question, with the exception of a range of literary texts that come mainly from countries of the Maghreb, is seldom posed in the Arab world today in relation to the identity and lived realities of Arabs. It is as if the aftermath of colonialism had washed away completely, or perhaps Albert Memmi's long-awaited 'new man' had finally arrived: 'The colonized lives for a long time before we see that really new man'[88]. Unfortunately neither has happened and we still know very

little about the ways in which imperialism has altered the ordinariness of culture and the structures of feeling of people in the region.
An enquiry into the Arab's structures of feeling is thus in many ways
also an enquiry into the consciousness of a postcolonial region. The
postcolonialised live in different and liminal cultural temporalities, simultaneously. They have no choice in the matter. They live
in a 'third space' (Bhabha, 1994), constantly in flux and perpetually in a struggle to be born. It is only through working out what
this 'third space' is, and how it operates (not just metaphorically but
also empirically) that the 'new man', Albert Memmi (1974) so famously talked about, can emerge. Working out what this third space
may be is also, in many ways, about coming to terms with what it
means to be modern in the world, for the two things are historically intertwined. In their seminal work *The Empire Writes Back,*
Ashcroft, Griffiths and Tiffin use the term 'postcolonial' 'to cover
all the culture affected by the imperial process from the moment
of colonisation to the present day. This is because there is a continuity of preoccupations throughout the historical process that
was initiated by European imperial aggression (Ashcroft, Griffiths
and Tiffin, 1989: 2). Robert Young defines the term as: 'a dialectical
concept that marks the broad historical facts of decolonisation and
the determined achievement of sovereignty – but also the realities
of nations and peoples emerging into a new imperialistic context
of economic and sometimes political domination' (Young, 2001:
56). Leela Gandhi defines the term as: 'a theoretical resistance to
the mystifying amnesia of the colonial aftermath' (Gandhi, 1998: 4).
According to the three definitions above, postcolonialism is 'continuous', a 'dialectical concept' and a 'theoretical resistance' against
the 'amnesia of the colonial aftermath'. Where the first definition
emphasises the temporal continuity of postcolonialism to the present day, the second accents the raison d'être of postcolonialism as a
discourse. According to the third definition, it is also a kind of 'theoretical resistance' against the many covert and continuous dynamics of imperialism, which spell out the words 'theory' and 'resistance'
against what may be otherwise rephrased as our *indifference* to the

aftermath of colonialism. What we understand from the three definitions is that postcolonialism and the postcolonial extend to the present, and that they ought to 'cover' and 'mark' not only the history of colonialism but also the *now* and present material 'realities' of postcolonised peoples throughout the world. These definitions of the postcolonial invite the following critical questions: Does the prefix '*post*' in the postcolonial refer to the end of colonialism? Who speaks for the postcolonised, in what language and from which location? Does postcolonialism, as a theory of 'resistance', deal with the material 'realities' of postcolonised people? If so, what does it teach us about the 'structure of feeling', or the consciousness of the postcolonised? Does this, as a field, teach us anything about power relations inherent in postcolonial countries? Postcolonial theory has had so far too many critics from both *within* and *without* the field, but none more poignantly direct and effective than the Indian critic Aijaz Ahmad, who commented in his book *In Theory*:

> To the extent that both 'Third World Literature' and 'Colonial Discourse Analysis' privilege coloniality as the framing term of epochal experience, national identity is logically privileged as the main locus of meaning, analysis and (self-) representation, which is, in turn, particularly attractive to the growing number of 'Third World Intellectuals' who are based in the metropolitan university. They can now materially represent the undifferentiated colonized other – more recently and more fashionably, the post-colonial other – without much examining of their own presence in that institution, except perhaps in the characteristically postmodernist mode of ironic pleasure in observing the duplicities and multiplicities of one's own persona. The East, reborn and greatly expanded now as a 'Third World', seems to have become, yet again, a *career*.
>
> (Ahmad, 1992: 93–4)

Implicit in Ahmad's statement is an array of criticisms, which he especially directs at the postcolonial theorist as a 'diaspora' within the Western academy. According to Ahmad, representing the post-colonial has become the activity of privileged (postmodern) intellectuals from the third world, 'intellectuals who are based in the metropolitan university'. Ahmad's reference to the theorists' representations of the postcolonised as being 'undifferentiated', hints at the postcolonial theorist's deracination and detachment from 'real' postcolonial struggles. Ahmad's critique extends from the postcolonial theorist's *locality* and affiliation to the academy as a Western institution, to the very kind of knowledge the theorist uses to rationalise the 'postcolonial'. The use of post-structural, post-modern methodology by postcolonial intellectuals to rationalise the 'postcolonial' is, for Ahmad, a way to abandon political engagement and to consolidate discourses of Western hegemony. The East, argues Ahmad with a stinging sense of irony, now reborn as the 'Third World', has become a '*career*', not only for the Orientalist but also for Said himself, Bhabha, Rushdie, Spivak and others. As Stephen Slemon and Helen Tiffin put it:

> When reading for textual resistance becomes entirely dependent on 'theoretical' disentanglement of contradiction or ambivalence within the colonialist text – as it does in deconstructive or new historical readings of colonialist discourse, – then the actual locus of subversive agency is necessarily wrenched away from colonised or post-colonial subjects and re-situated within the textual work of the institutionalised western literary critic.
>
> (In Moore-Gilbert, 1997: 17–18)

Slemon and Tiffin, like Ahmad, criticise 'postcolonial' theory for its lack of political agency, as it puts more emphasis on deconstructing the complexities of the 'postcolonial' text than on the 'postcolonial' subject per se, he/she whose condition and material realities they ought to be representing. Rather than it being a 'theory of resistance' against the 'amnesia of the aftermath of colonialism', postcolonial theory is accused of rendering 'non-western knowledge and culture as "other" in relation to the normative "self" of western epistemology and rationality' (Gandhi, 1998: ix–x). I take issue with postcolonial theory, not because of its privileged locale, nor because of its choice of theory: Marxist as well as Foucauldian approaches are both valuable. In other words, adhering to determination and human agency as the 'motors of history' in one's work is as important as theorising 'entrapment', 'in-betweeness', 'alienation', 'dislocation' and 'hybridity'. Rather, my own objection lies with postcolonial theory's nonchalant privileging of complex 'postcolonial' texts over the 'real' material conditions and 'realities' that govern and influence the lives of the 'real', living, breathing postcolonial subject. Silencing the 'subaltern' by arguing that they cannot speak positions the postcolonial theorist as the immediate speaker for the subaltern. This role has, however, been effected with little care for listening to what the subaltern can tell us, and this, in turn, deepens the fissure between the postcolonised and the theorist, abstracting the field further from the material realities of the postcolonial. My answer to the question 'Can the subaltern speak?' is 'Yes, the subaltern can speak, but have we listened to them?' To speak of the 'subaltern' in a homogeneous fashion, furthermore, masks the local material realities of the postcolonised. There is, in fact, no such thing as a 'subaltern', but there are 'subalterns' whose structures of feeling are not merely the product of colonialism, but are also the product of the power dynamics and social relations inherent to their postcolonial societies (see Chapter 5). Furthermore, while postcolonial theory's preoccupation with concepts of 'hybridity', 'diasporas' and 'liminality' have enriched the field of cultural studies, these concepts remain mere abstractions, for, with very rare exceptions (see Kraidy, 2006), these conceptualisations are never accompanied by empirical evidence, nor by real reference points reference that support them. What is required of a critical Arab cultural studies is an empirical approach to the study of the 'postcolonial', and a transition from postcolonial literary criticism to a postcolonial critique, based on evidence and empirical research. Edward Said warned that colonial discourse analysis risked 'falling into a premature "slumber" if it did not continue to develop' (Cited in Moore-Gilbert, 1997: 186). For it to develop as a component of Arab cultural studies, postcolonialism needs to escape its literary confines and open itself up to other disciplines and to more innovative methodologies. The Arab's postcolonial experience intersects with another – that of Arab modernness. The two experiences are inextricably linked, and the dynamics they produce are largely what make Arab identity what it is.

The case against Arab cultural studies

An Arab cultural studies project may be critiqued or rejected on a number of premises. Here, I content myself with addressing just two. One is that, since Arab societies have not undergone the same historical conditions that have influenced and shaped the cultural studies project in the industrialised West, cultural studies' applicability as a paradigm in Arab academia is questionable. The second is that since the 'dominant paradigm' in cultural studies'[89] interprets the world as a social and cultural phenomenon, alienating the existential aspect, it would be problematic to translate cultural studies into a world-structure where experience is determined through dialectics between the social, cultural *and* 'existential'. Although it is a truism that the historical conditions that shaped cultural studies in the West have no parallels in the Arab world, or indeed in the remainder of the world, it can be argued that, under the auspices of globalisation and its ceaselessly homogenising machinery, the world is increasingly, and despite ongoing fragmentary resistance in some areas, becoming a homogeneous place. By homogeneity, I refer to the spread and globalisation of modernity's institutions[90], which is described by Giddens in *The Consequences of Modernity* (1991). How the world reacts to the latter is a different question altogether. What is clear, however, is that globalisation and its postmodern technologies, including television, satellite, the Internet and their worldliness,[91] have definitely made our world more connected. Needless to say, this does not suggest evenness or balance. On the contrary, our world is one of unevenness and imbalance. So, the historical conditions that inspired change in the Western conception of culture are now compensated for by the relentless globalisation of modernity and its institutions. This perhaps justifies the call by Abbas and Erni (2005) for an internationalist paradigm of cultural studies that tackles not only local but also global and trans-local issues. The Arab world is, like the rest of the global south, subject to the dynamics of the global capitalist order and its hegemonic culture. Besides, in today's globalised world, we really cannot afford to conceptualise or theorise an Arab cultural studies through the prism of the local alone. The Arab region has long (two centuries to be precise) been subject to the globalising structures, temporalities and institutions of modernity, so, just as critical theory was a response to what Adorno and Horkheimer called the 'dialectics of the Enlightenment', Arab cultural studies must also intervene to describe, make sense of and theorise the region's reaction to modernity and its disorders. It is through the prism of the *glocal* that Arab cultural studies must position itself and not merely through the local. As such, I do not see the historical argument as an obstacle. As for the problem of the 'dominant paradigm' in cultural studies, the answer lies simply in 'translation' and re-appropriation. The hermeneutics upon which Arab cultural studies will rely in the future to give meaning to the world, and to our experience in it, should account for the 'social', the 'cultural' and the 'existential'. The last category is crucial, not because it will appeal to, or be inclusive of religiosity/the metaphysical, and even of fundamentalist discursive formations, but because the omission of the existential will make it difficult for us to think outside the 'social' and the 'cultural', which would be limiting and be contrary to Lalande's and Al-Jabri's ideal of *l'esprit critique nécessaire*. Paddy Scannell, who has no interest in propagating any type of religiosity, put this succinctly in his critique of

British cultural studies' hermeneutics:

> Is 'life' (human existence) then, coterminous with
> the social? Is human being more or less equivalent
> to social being? Is 'man' a 'social animal', and if so,
> is that the most fundamental thing about him? I
> do not want to rush to the bluntly obvious answer.
> Rather, to pose this question is to ask (obliquely)
> whether or not sociology and cultural studies
> have an outside. More exactly, can they think out-
> side of themselves? If there is no outside of the
> social/cultural 'in thought' then thought cannot
> imagine human being as anything other than the
> socio-cultural. Social being is an intimate aspect
> of the being that I, in each case, have. But it is not
> definitive of that being. 'Life' is not so much a more
> encompassing term than society/culture. Rather it
> is earlier than such terms.[92]

It is difficult to raise the issue of culture in the Arab context without a reference to religiosity, both scriptural and 'popular'. Religion
and its 'shared instrumental practices' (Zubaida, 1987: 142) play
an important, if not fundamental role in conceptualisations of
Arab everyday cultures. Religiosity is engrained in the everyday
structures of Arab societies. It is visible, heard and smelt, and it
is partly what binds Arab identity together. Walking down the
'popular' streets in the Arab world before the time of the *Iftar*
(breaking the fast) leaves one intoxicated by a wonderful mix of
food smells: *Harrera* (soup), cakes and other mouth-watering
delicacies. The care-structures with which Ramadan practices, to
give just one example, are observed, unveil intentional structures
that form a 'common experience' and a 'structure of feeling' which
reaches beyond the religious to permeate other spheres of everyday life. Here, the religious is enmeshed in and intertwined with
the 'social' and the cultural. The *Adan* (call for prayers), people's

greetings, language, popular jokes, satellite religious programmes, sounds of the Koran emanating from spice shops, church bells, not to mention, momentary encounters with the traditionaliser (the father, sister, friend, Imam, storyteller and the taxi driver – the quasi-prophets who see it their duty to remind their people of God's sacred words and the prophets' good conduct) are all evidence of the extent to which religious discourse permeates the temporal and the spatial in the Arab world, and they must therefore be studied as cultural phenomena. So, to grasp the totality of cultural experience, the hermeneutics upon which Arab cultural studies relies to interpret social and cultural reality in the region needs to incorporate a category that precedes both the social and the cultural, if not life itself, and that is the existential; a category much ignored in Western cultural studies because of the intellectual formations that shaped the field. Spiritual life in the Arab world and its transformations in 'modern times' make for a very important object of study. In his *Islam Observed: Religious Development in Morocco and Indonesia*, Geertz made a strong case for the objectification of religion within anthropological enquiry, arguing that:

> Alterations in the general complexion of social life, in the character of religious sensibility, are more than just intellectual reorientations or shifts in emotional climate, bodiless changes of the mind. They are also, and more fundamentally, social processes, transformations in the quality of collective life. Neither thought nor feeling is, at least among humans, autonomous, a self-contained stream of subjectivity, but each is inescapably dependent upon the utilization by individuals of socially available 'systems of significance' cultural constructs embodied in language, custom, art and technology – that is to say, symbols. This is as true of religiousness as it is for any other human capacity.
>
> (Geertz, 1968: 18–19)

However, notwithstanding the importance of religiosity as a component in the study of contemporary Arab cultures, it is important to add that at the very moment we confine the analysis of culture or limit it to the realm of the 'sacred'/metaphysical, we destroy not only its ontological nature but also the prerequisite for a creative and critical consciousness. By enveloping culture in the realm of the *sacred* alone, we risk losing sight of its gritty and profane nature. Although religiosity and, indeed, the 'systems of significance' available to social individuals remain important components of cultural studies, Arab cultures, or any culture, must not be defined or determined solely through religiosity or the sacred. Reworking Arab-Islamic culture through its *ontologisation* requires us to record its present expressive powers in their 'sacredness' and 'imperfections', and to this we should also add their 'dialectical deformations' (Berque, 1983: 24). The 'quest for an original approach' to Arab-Islamic modernity, or *being* modern in the world, cannot be abstracted or removed from 'the contemporary culture that Arabs are already constructing for themselves' (Berque, 1983: 69). This, as I see it, is a role for a hermeneutically flexible, and critical Arab cultural studies.

Conclusion

The task that lies ahead, however, is greater than 'de-Westernisation' or internationalisation: it is one of 'creativity'. It is, to use Lalande's distinction again, to be able to think of and rehearse different ways of activating *la raison constituante* (the mental activity that *creates* knowledge, constructs meanings and decides on rules and principles). This intellectual task is possible only through troubling outmoded *modalities* of Arab thought inherent to its *raison constituée* (that part of reason that is already constituted). This process has already begun: Fatima Mernissi and Nawal Sadawi's troubling of male/female dynamics in Arab-Islamic societies; Abdullah al-Ghathami's revolt against the return of the *fahl* in Arab poetic aesthetics and his call for the democratisation of Arab culture;

Mustafa Safouane's championing of the *Vernacular* as a liberating force from the dictatorship of classical Arabic (Safouane, 2007) as well as Khatibi's *double-critique* (1980) are just a few examples from critical projects that operate exactly where cultural activity and creativity is now required. Their work is a step in the right direction.

Notes

1 On Encountering and Modernness

1. *Baraka* is a small sum of money, usually given to holy men. The term is also used in a different context to denote the metaphysical powers attributed to the *shurfa* (saints), who mostly claim to be descendents of the prophet Mohammed. See Geertz' *Islam Observed* (1968) for a detailed definition of *Baraka*.

2. From the German word '*Da-sein*', literally meaning: being-there. In *Being and Time*, Heidegger uses the term to refer to beings for whom *being* in the world is a matter of concern and an object of reflection. As he put it: 'to work out the question of Being adequately, we must make an entity – the inquirer transparent in his own Being. The very asking of this question is an entity's mode of Being; and as such it gets its essential character from what is inquired about – namely, Being. This entity which each of us is himself and which includes inquiring as one of its possibilities of Being, we shall denote by the term "Dasein"' (Heidegger, [1962] 2007: 27).

3. Heidegger's concept of *fallnness* is embedded in a particular metaphysics of the Christian faith, where it is believed, that humans have come into the world as sinners, thus Adam and Eve's fall from paradise to earth. The Muslim narrative, however, refutes the concept of *original* sin and puts man in an historical standing. My use of the term *fallnness* has no religious significance. Instead, I use it in a symbolic way.

4. One of the fundamental techniques that revolutionised pottery making in Morocco, I was told in an interview with an old Moroccan potter from Asfi, is the introduction of the oven, a technique he introduced since his visit to Italy in the 1960s. This simple introduction helped increase the production of pottery and even improved its quality.

5. I use the term communication in its broad sense to include media and other forms of expression. This includes ordinary talk, style, jokes and other means. However, the main focus in later chapters will be on television as a medium of encountering.

6. I use the preposition 'on' instead of 'of' because I am not yet convinced that the body of work available on the question of the 'modern' in the Arab repertoire is substantial enough (here I am referring to the linearity and systemacity of the arguments dealing with the question of modernity) to say that there is an Arab discourse of the 'modern' or 'modernity'. So, for now, and to avoid any confusion, I settle for the preposition 'on'.

7. An earlier Arab awareness of the West was discussed by Bernard Lewis in his 'The Muslim discovery of the West'. See the SOAS Bulletin, Volume: xx, London 1957 (pp. 407–19). See also Albert Hourani's *Arabic Thought in the Liberal Age: 1798–1939* (Chapters 3 and 4).

8. See also, towards the end of the chapter, a discussion on Tahtawi's justification for and concerns of emulating the European French educational system. It's especially interesting how he advises that those wishing to read the French's philosophical work, needed, as a prerequisite, for fear they lose their faith, to be well versed in the Koran and its sciences.

9. See David Macey (2000: 257–8) for these different definitions, 257–8.

10. While doing fieldwork in Morocco in 2008, I conducted a pilot questionnaire, asking 100 Moroccans from different social strata: 'What does modernity mean to you?' The response was, interestingly, not different from key articulations of the 'modern' as they appear in contemporary Arab thought. Much of the definitions depicted a *Baudelairian* take on the 'modern', where secular realities, the transient and the new coexist with the sacred and the timeless. A lot of the definitions described modernity and *being* modern as being able to 'adapt to new times' without losing sight of religious ethics and morality. Also, a lot of the respondents identified being modern with being fashionable, being able to use modern technology and having the freedom to act as an individual.

2 Contemporary Arab Thought and the Struggle for Authenticity: Towards an Ontological Articulation of the 'Modern'

11. I use Arkoun's term here to invoke the 'unthought' as a deliberate and an intentional omission. Arkoun explains his use of the terms

'unthought' and 'unthinkable' in the extract below from his book, *Islam: To Reform or to Subvert* (2006):

> This work [referring to his book] in effect comes up against the limits and arbitrary aspects of hegemonic reason and is involved in the most useful debates on the passage from the *Phenomenology of the Mind*, trapped in the mytho-historico-transcendental thematic, to '*the social institution of the mind*'. Like all high-profile thinkers in the contemporary West, the young researcher J. De Munck never mentions hegemonic reason, or the **unthinkable**; when he refers to the **unthought**, it is only to announce the schedule for procedural reason; but the **unthinkable** and **unthought** are inherent in the linear structure of any discursive statement, and also in the fact that any proposition is an act of power whether followed by a result or not; for a proposition implies selection from the range of significations in any tradition, thus an orientation of meaning in a particular direction from all possible horizons of expectation of any given speaker of a particular language.'
>
> (Arkoun, 2006: 31)

12. Author's translation from Arabic.
13. For a comprehensive guide to key debates dealing with the *assala* and *mu'assara* problematic in Arab thought, see *aturath wa tahadeyat al-'assr fi al-watan al-Arabi: al-assala wa al-mu 'assara* (1985), Beirut: The Centre for Arab Unity Studies. This 872-pages-long book is based on a conference organised by the same Centre and provides useful interventions on the topic by some leading philosophers and thinkers from different parts of the Arab world.
14. The concepts that this Arab historian/philosopher articulated in his books: *Mafhum al-ideolujeya* (The Meaning of Ideology) (1980), *Mafhum al-hurreya* (The Meaning of Freedom) (1981), *Mafhum Addawlah* (The Meaning of the State) (1981) *Mafhum attarikh* (The Meaning of History) (1992) and *Mafhum al-Aql* (The Meaning of Reason) (1996, 2001), all dealt with modernity.
15. Author's translation from French.

16. A more expansive discussion on the *historicisation* of the category 'Arab culture' is provided in Chapter 3.

17. Although known for being a 'moderniser' and against *taqlid* (opting for imitation rather than independent reasoning), Mohammed Abduh, the highly influential nineteenth-century 'reformist' from Egypt, equated 'reform' with learning from the lessons of the past (from *al-salaf al-salih,* to be precise), which seems to contradict the whole logic of *reform,* and which should be understood in terms of change, progression and a move away from past methods, structures and ideas (Al-Jabri, 2005). Muhammad Abduh divided the raison d'être of his 'reform' into two main purposes: a 'restatement of what Islam really was' and a 'consideration of its implications for modern society' (Hourani, 1983: 140–1). Describing the first purpose, Abduh observed: 'First to liberate thought from the shackles of *taqlid,* and understand religion as it was understood by the elders of the community before dissention appeared; to return, in the acquisition of religious knowledge, to its first sources' (See Hourani, 1983: 140–1). I have used the case of Abduh here to highlight the intricacy and fluidity within the four key intellectual positions described in this chapter. The case of Abduh is certainly an ambivalent one, but since he understands and seeks reform through a return to the past (regardless of the 'timelessness' of its ideas) it places him, intellectually, as a 'cultural salafist'. What it also highlights is the difference between the ways in which the concept 'reform' has been used/articulated by scholars from the four different intellectual positions.

18. *Ahl al-salaf al-saleh* refers to the companions of the prophet Mohammed (pbuh).

19. Abdelkabir Khatibi (1938–2009) is a Moroccan sociologist, literary critic, novelist and poet. His work, both fictional and non-fictional, is, in many ways, an exploration of complex postcolonial traits, such as 'double-identity' and 'hybridity'. 'Double-critique', a method he uses to reconcile and deal with his own double-identity, is conspicuous in his literary work. This includes: *La blessure du nom propre* (1974); *La memoire tatotée* (1979) [an autobiographical piece, also his most acclaimed literary work]; *Amour bilingue* (1983); *Maghreb pluriel* (1983); [articulating the diversity and plurality of cultures in the Maghreb]; *Un été à Stockholm* (1990); *Le livre de sang* (1979);

Ombres japonaises (1988); *Le prophète voilé* (1979); White vomit (1974); [criticizing Zionism] *Le même livre* (1985); [exploring the similarities between Arabs and Jews; *Le roman maghrébin* (1958); *L'art calligraphique arabe* with Mohammed Sijilmassi (1976) and *Le livre de l'aimance* (1995).

20. I was introduced to the idea and concept of *tajawuz* 'transcendence' (meaning the transcendence of the duality problematic between *turath* and modernity) by two of its advocates, during an interview in Marrakech 2008: Abdul-Aziz Boumesshouli and Abdessamad Ghabass.
21. Author's translation from Arabic
22. A liberal movement for reform in late nineteenth-century and twentieth-century Egypt (Eikelman and Anderson: 1999: 203)
23. Abdurrahman, *The Question of Ethics*, 179 in Sheikh, 2007: 143.

3 Arab Popular Cultures and Everyday Life

24. See the Centre's list of publications for examples of academic publications dealing with the subject of 'Arab culture', published in 2005.
25. See also analytical works by Ben Shekroun, 1980; Tarabeshi, 1993; Binabdal'ali, 1994; Al-Jabri, 1994; Belqziz, 2000; Abu Zaid, 2002; Bundoq, 2003; Ussfur, 2003; Wakidi, 2007; Oumlil, 2005.
26. Sabry, Tarik (Interview with Abdul-Aziz Boumesshouli and Abdessamad Ghabass, Marrakech, September, 2008).
27. I borrowed the term *une terre brûlé* (a burnt land) from Riad Ferjani, who used it in a symposium on Media and Migration in the Institute of the Press, Paris (March 2009).
28. Undoubtedly, Abdullah al-Ghathami, a Saudi scholar, is one of the earliest and most important advocates of Arab cultural studies. His book *Cultural Criticism* (2000), which I discuss at length in the next few pages, is a very important contribution to the field. Among his many key contributions are *Feminizing the Poem and the Different Reader*, 1999 (in Arabic); *Women and Language*, 1996 (in Arabic); *The Poem and the Oppositional Text* 1994 (in Arabic); *Writing Against Writing*, 1991 (in Arabic); *The Culture of Illusion*, 1998 (in Arabic); *The Story of Modernity in Saudi Arabia*, 2005 (in Arabic); *Deconstructing*

the Text, 1987 (in Arabic). His most recent book is entitled: *Television Culture*, 2006 (in Arabic). He is a feminist and a champion of women's rights too.

29. Nizār al-Kabānni and Adonis, two highly celebrated Arab free verse poets, have, however, regardless of their claims to modernity, been held responsible by Al-Ghathami for the return of the *fahl* (chauvinist) and for altering Arab modernity's revolutionary course against the *nassaq* and its anti-modern discourses.

30. Author's translation from Arabic.

31. See an excellent study by Helga Tawil-Souri (2007) entitled: 'The Political Battlefield of Pro-Arab Video Games on Palestinian Screens', where she explores the uses of Hezbollah Video-games by young children in Ramallah. Instead of analysing 'the apparatus exercising power' of the oppressor as occupier, she investigates the resistance mechanisms (in the pro-Arab video games) and how they reverse/ reorganise, albeit virtually, the functioning of the occupier's power.

4   The Bridge and the Queue as Spaces of Encountering

32. Naguib Mahfouz used to frequent many cafés in Cairo. In fact, a lot of his literary work (e.g., *Khan al-Khalili*) was a result of the time he spent in different cafés, reading, smoking Shisha and observing ordinary men and women doing everyday things.

33. According to Herodotus' observations, this spectacle is a continuation of an old Pharaohnic cultural tradition and arguably a precursor to modern Egyptian belly dancing, as an art form (see Hammond, 2007).

34. Raafat, Samir (2000) http://www.egy.com/landmarks/00–11-01.shtml, accessed 2009.

35. Michel de Certeau makes an interesting and useful distinction between place [lieu] and space [espace]. A place, he observes, 'is the order ... in accord with which elements are distributed in relationships of co-existence. It thus excludes the possibility of two things being in the same location (place). The law of the 'proper' rules in the place: the elements taken into consideration are *beside* one another, each situated in its own 'proper' and distinct location, a location it defines. A place is thus an instantaneous configuration of positions. It implies an

indication of stability. A *space* exists when one takes into consideration vectors of direction, velocities, and time variables. Thus space is composed of intersections of mobile elements…Space occurs as the effect produced by the operations that orient it, situate it, temporalise it, and make it function in a polyvalent unity of conflictual programs or contractual proximities.' (de Certeau, 1984: 117). De Certeau's distinction fits very well with my primary observations of the bridge, as an architectural place, and my secondary observations, where the bridge changes into a geometrically complex and intersectional space.

36. Neither is it an Italian or a German thing (or in fact a Western thing *per se*). I think queuing is a quintessentially British cultural trait. Ironically, when I went to the British Embassy to do some fieldwork, I found no queue at all. I overheard queuers outside other embassies saying that the British were too efficient and organised to allow such chaos to unfold outside their embassies.

37. Since I conducted fieldwork in queues outside different Western embassies in Casablanca, including the US, Belgian, Spanish, French and Italian Embassies (2003), I found that almost all embassies prohibited queuing for security reasons post-9/11. Those wishing to apply for visas now have to write to the embassy and can visit only through appointment. This can be said to have, interestingly, transformed my fieldwork on the everyday to historical ethnography/ anthropology by default.

38. Dareja is the colloquial everyday language spoken by most Moroccans. It's a mix of Arabic, French, Spanish, Portuguese and perhaps other influences.

39. Of all the work written on *Heimat* in the English language, I found Peter Blickle's (2002) book: *Heimat: A Critical Theory of the German Idea of Homeland* to be the most useful. According to Blickle, the term *Heimat* comprises two German words: *Heim* (home) and *Mut* (courage). The term has, however, historically been used to mean different things. If we 'consider the various translations of *Heimat* into English, we find such diverse results as 'home,' 'homeland,' 'fatherland,' 'nation,' 'nation-state,' 'hometown,' 'paradise,' 'Germany', 'Austria',…'native landscape'…'birthplace,' 'homestead' (Blickle, 2002: 4). The plural of the word *Heimat* is *Heimaten*. However, to have a *Heimaten* rather than a *Heimat* can also mean *Heimatless* or *Heimatlessness*. The

philosopher Vilém Flusser once wrote: 'I am *Heimatless* because too many *Heimaten* are stored inside of me' (ibid, 63). In the same vein, Nietzsche's character, *Zarathustra*, from his novel *Thus Spake Zarathustra* (1883–91), leaves his *heimat* for the mountains, where he becomes a wise man. He becomes wise because he was brave enough to leave his *heimat* behind. In this context *Heimatlessness* can be associated with wisdom or the pursuit thereof (ibid).

I use the term *Heimat* in the case of Knadi, a young Moroccan from the Old Medina, as a spatiality that allows him, and many young Moroccans to whom I spoke, to be and feel temporarily different in the world. The 'interrelationship between a sense of self and the perception of one's world' argues Blickle 'is a central aspect in the formation of a sense of *Heimat*'. He also adds that *Heimat* provides 'a world where the experiences of alienation are magically healed' (ibid, 62). This 'world' is, in the case of Knadi, the Western music text. The latter provides him with an escape from the harsh realities of life in the Old Medina and the hegemonic fixed cultural practices he finds alienating, into a different temporality and spatiality. The Western media text as *heimat* is, for Knadi, a 'frontier…between the mental and the physical' (ibid, 63). It is an intermediary, imaginary space that lies between the *here* (Morocco) and the *there* (the unreachable West).

5   *Modernness* as a Multiple Narrative-Category: Encountering the West

40. *Gur* is Moroccan Dareja for Westerners. It is not clear what the origin of the word is.
41. Islamists (3 groups), Casablanca,
    The Socialist Youth Group (2 focus groups), Casablanca,
    Young Moroccans of Ait Nuh (2 focus groups), Khunifra, Atlas Mountains
    Young Moroccans from the middle classes (2 Focus groups), Gautier, Casablanca
    Young Moroccans from the working class quarter of the Old Medina and Olfa, (2 focus groups), Casablanca
42. The six colleges were chosen to represent different areas of Casablanca. *Anfa* College, for example, is situated in one of the richest areas of

Casablanca and attracts students from the upper middle classes, whereas *Ibn al Haitm* and *Ibn Toumart* are located in poorer areas of Casablanca and therefore attract students from working class backgrounds. The colleges targeted by the survey are coed with the exception of *Ibn Toumart*, which is for boys only and El *Khansa*, which is for girls only. I have used the demographic category 'A' to refer to *Anfa* and 'E' to refer to *Ibn Toumart*. I have also used categories B, C1, C2, and D to reflect other socio-economic structures within Casablanca. It is important to note, however, that these social categories are only roughly approximate to social categories used in the West and might therefore not adapt correctly.

The questionnaires were distributed by teachers at the beginning of the class and collected by them immediately after they were completed. This guaranteed a successful return rate (891 of 1000). The questionnaire, which is divided into two parts, comprises 15 questions. The first part dealing with access to media technology and the consumption thereof, the second part dealing with emigration and its causes. The SPSS (Statistical Package for the Social Sciences) programme was used for the purpose of storing, coding and manipulating the survey data.

43. By Arabic programming, I mean programmes made in the Middle East (mainly Egypt, Syria, Lebanon and Saudi Arabia).

44. Since I conducted the survey in Casablanca (see Sabry, 2003), there has been a considerable rise in the consumption of MBC channels (MBC1, MBC2, MBC3, MBC4 and MBC+). *Sanawat al-Daya'* (The Lost Years) and *Nour*, two Turkish soap operas broadcast by MBC1, have been hugely popular with Moroccan and other Arab audiences. MBC2 and MBC action, which show Hollywood movies, are popular with young audiences. MBC3, which shows cartoons, is hugely popular with Arab children. Another substantial change in viewing habits has also occurred with the big increase in Arabic music video channels. I expect MBC's audiences and the Arabic music video channels to be substantially higher now than when the survey was first conducted.

45. Islamist translates into the Arabic word *Islamy* (sing) and *Islameyoon* – its plural. An *Islamy* is someone who adheres to the implementation of the *Shari 'a* –'the Muslim code of religious law'. Participants from the group I label as 'Islamist' are mostly activists from the *al-'adl wa*

al-ihssan party, and they share common ideological formations that distinguish them from the rest of the subgroups. For a historical exposé on Moroccan Islamists see Mohammed Dareef (1999).

46. Because of the similarities between the material that emerged from young people of the Atlas and those from the working classes living in Olfa and Medina and not to be repetitive, I focus in my concluding remarks, on the *Ait Nuhian* youth with whom I conducted 2 focus groups and whom I met over a period of eight years (between 2001 and 2009). Material from the focus groups conducted with young people of the Olfa and the Medina is, however, used sparsely through the chapter. Young people from the Old Medina told me the stories about 'burning' and the Couscoussière.

47. It is crucial to note that there are problematic sociological differences between what is defined as working class or middle class in Britain and what is perceived as working class or middle class in Morocco. It is equally important to note that the class system in Morocco was a colonial imposition, a structure totally alien to precolonial Moroccan society. In other words, the stratification of Moroccan society into a small bourgeoisie and a large working class came into existence as an effect of Western colonialism and its new economic mode of production: capitalism. However, the Moroccan bourgeoisie and its counterpart in the West do not, for socio-political reasons embedded within the structure of Moroccan society, share the same historical consciousness. The Moroccan, and indeed the Arab, bourgeoisie may share some characteristics with its counterpart in the West, yet where the latter engaged in an adventurous and organised historical project, the former is known to have been less adventurous, disorganised and without a sense of history (see Al-Heimr, 2001). Furthermore, the Moroccan Bourgeoisie was never totally independent of the *Makhzen*. The distinctions that Pierre Bourdieu (1984) makes between bourgeois and working class tastes in his sociological study of French society – *Distinction* – become very problematic when applied to Moroccan or Arab society. In the latter, which is perceived as 'high culture' or 'middle class taste', is far more complex, especially as it resides outside Arab-Moroccan culture and its value systems. Middle class taste in Moroccan society, for example, feeds from and claims its superiority over other Moroccan popular cultural tastes

by its incorporation and mimicking of the culture of Balzac and Chateaubriand.

48. Octopus is used, as a metaphor, to depict Western domination.
49. The term commonly used by Western scholars is 'tribe'.
50. The term *Ait Nuh* means the people of Noah, named after a Saint called *Sidi 'Eissah w Nuh*, whose body rests in a tomb with a chamber and an imposing dome, situated in the main and oldest mosque of the *Douar*. According to the douar's elderly, the saint is known to have performed miraculous acts and was the first to introduce Islam in the area. Mainly the women of the douar visit his tomb and usually stay overnight with the hope of having a dream with a message/advice from the Saint. According to Brett and Fentress (1996–7), who have conducted substantial historical research on the history of the Berbers (*Amazighs*), this tradition, predates Islam and, 'was one of the distinguishing characteristics of the Berbers in antiquity. The dead were certainly connected with the fertility of the soil and probably exercised some control over the future … provision of chambers for this practice is a standard trait of Berber tombs'. Brett and Fentress also quote Pomponius Mela on the topic, who observed that: 'The Augiliae consider the spirits of their ancestors gods, they swear by these and consult them as oracles, and having made their requests, treat the dreams of those who sleep in their tombs as responses' (Brett and Fentress, 1996, 1997: 35). This is an example of cultural encountering and 'hybridised tradition' par excellence, as the prayers in the chamber are not just addressed to *Nuh* as oracle or an ancestry god but also as a descendent of the prophet Mohammed and thus a provider of Baraka. But why is it that only women mainly visit the chamber is not clear to me. I collected a number of statements about the Saint's life from the elders of Ait Nuh, who told me that the Saint was the descendent of Moulay Driss I (a descendent of the Prophet Mohammed who fled Arabia in 787) and the founder of Fez, later built by His son Moulay Driss II. When I queried about the origin of the name Nuh (joking there might be a chance that *Ait Nuhians* could be the descendents of the Prophet Noah), some stated that Noah was an aberration and that the real name was '*Bulluh*', meaning the Man with the 'Koranic wooden Plaque'. For more information on Saints in Moroccan Culture see Chtatou, 1996.

51. From the Arabic adjective *silbi*, meaning, 'negative.' It is also from the verb *salaba*, meaning to deprive or deny someone something.

52. I use the words brothers and sisters here to reflect how the young Islamists addressed each other during the focus groups. When young Islamists introduced themselves, they always begin with either: 'your brother in God/Islam' or 'your sister in God/Islam'.

53. 'Self-identity is not a distinctive trait or even a collection of traits, possessed by the individual. It is *the self as reflexively understood by the person in terms of her or his biography*. Identity here still presumes continuity across time and space: but self-identity is such continuity as interpreted by the agent' (Giddens, 1991: 53).

54. See Scannell, 2009, *Television and the Meaning of Live* (2010).

55. *Gawri* is dareja working class term for a Western male. *Gawria* is the feminine equivalent.

56. Circular drums

57. One of the languages spoken by *Amazighs* (meaning free people).

58. Since the last 5 years (between 2004 and 2009), I noticed a great increase in access to mobile phones. Practically every family in Ait Nuh now has one. The average price for a mobile phone set in Morocco is 500 Dh (£40), which is extremely expensive for people of the *douar*, most of whom survive on farming. In a lot of the households I have been to, in Ait Nuh, it is mainly the young women who manage the mobile phone.

59. North Africa (including Morocco) was Roman for a total of seven centuries. The majority of *Amazighs* resisted Roman Imperialism. According to Michael Brett and Elizabeth Fentress, Amazigh culture and religion were only 'partially influenced by the hegemony of Rome (1997: 50). For further academic sources on the history of the Romans in Africa (in the English language) see Raven's *Rome in Africa* (London, 1984) and Warmington's *The North African Provinces from Diocletian to the Vandal Conquest* (Cambridge, 1954).

60. Not that it matters that much, but I am aware that Pamela Anderson is proudly Canadian!

61. In his book *Cultural Schizophrenia: Islamic Societies Confronting the West* (1992), Iranian philosopher Daryush Shayegan, observes: 'we who were born in the periphery are living through a time of conflict between different blocks of knowledge. We are trapped in a fault-line

between incompatible worlds, worlds that mutually repel and deform one another. If accepted consciously, lucidly, without resentment, this ambivalent situation can be enriching; it can amplify the registers of our learning and broaden our sensibility. But the same ambivalence, when sheltered from the critical field of knowledge, causes mental blocks and lacunae, mutilates perceptions and fragments realities and mental images alike' (Shayegan, 1992: vii).

62. When interviewing the philosopher Mohammed Abed al-Jabri in his home in 2002, I asked him whether he thought an 'Islamic Modernity' was feasible. Below is an extract from the dialogue which took place between us:

> Al-Jabri: 'Ok, let us assume, for a minute that there is something we can call "Islamic modernity". What would you say is the most sacred and authoritative source in Islam?'
>
> T: 'The Koran', I replied.
>
> Al-Jabri: 'Sure, since we believe that the Koran is the word of God, [a revelation from God] and since we also believe that the Koran is a timeless text, written for every place and time, isn't it logical to then deduce that God, the creator of the Universe, a timeless entity and author of a timeless book, is beyond the modern and modernity, which is a mere phase in human history . . . ?'

63. Named after the French poet Théophile Gautier (1811–72).

64. I have to confess that I was brought up in Gautier, but by two trade unionists who practised what they preached. I was sent to state schools, which meant that I frequented mostly kids from the working classes. Plus, French was seen as a bourgeois language and was never spoken in the house.

65. In the Middle East, Egypt, Kuwait, Emirates, Jordan, Lebanon and other countries of the Mashreq, the bourgeoisie sends its children to American schools/Universities. Of late, the upper middle classes in Morocco are sending their children to American and English, rather than French, schools.

66. In his *Cultural Schizophrenia*, Daryush Shayegan uses the phrase 'ontological displacement' (1992: 33–50).

67. 'Abd Arrazak Knadi is an old friend of mine from *Bousbir* quarter. Knadi kindly agreed to be interviewed, and I have spent hours talking

to him about the West, migration and Western music. His dream to emigrate to the West materialised when he made it to Denmark in the early 1990s. However, his visa expired and he was deported back to Morocco. He is now in his early 40s and has given up hope of getting a visa. His English accent is so convincingly English, even Londoners confuse him for being British. Knadi has never been to the UK.

68. In his *Islam and Political Discourse of Modernity*, Armando Salvatore (1997: 17) uses the term 'hermeneutic circles' to refer to the community of interpreters, imposing different, and, in many cases, essentialised narratives of Islam.

6   Still Searching for the Arab Present Cultural Tense: Arab Cultural Studies

69. Author's translation from Arabic
70. According to Giddens, sequestration of experience 'refers...to connected processes of concealment which set apart the routines of everyday life from the following phenomena: madness; criminality; sickness and death; sexuality; and nature' (Giddens, 1991:156).
71. In the opening pages of *A Critique of Arab Reason: The Construction of Arab Reason* (Beirut, 1991), Al-Jabri justifies using the phrase 'Arab reason' instead of 'Arab thought'. He not only understands that the meaning of 'thought' overlaps with that of 'ideology', but is also aware that the word 'thought' can mean both the tool for producing thoughts and the ensemble of thoughts produced. His treatise, written in Arabic, is about thought as the tool (reason) that produces thoughts. As he later put it, in *A Critique of Arab Reason: A Critical Analytical Study of Knowledge Norms in Arab Culture* (in Arabic)(Casablanca, 2000: 11): 'In this book, I am not interested in thought or thoughts as such, but the tool that produces them.'
72. Author's translation from Arabic
73. The failure of the pan-Arab project, which was precipitated by the collapse of the communist ideology and the disintegration of the Soviet bloc in the late 1980s, led a number of Arab intellectuals to rethink their political positioning, changing hats from one political position to another. This further complexifies the four positions of contemporary Arab thought. These positions (as discursive formations) are not fixed; they are dialectical and constantly changing.

74. Author's translation from Arabic
75. George Orwell, *Nineteen Eighty-Four* (1951: 5) in Williams, 1963: 276.
76. Raymond Williams, *Culture and Society 1780–1950* (1963: 276).
77. 'L'esthétique transcendantale ne peut compter le concept de changement aux nombres de ses donnés *a priori*, car ce n'est pas le temps lui-même qui change, mais quelque chose qui est dans le temps. Ce concept exige donc la perception de telle ou telle existence actuelle, où se succèdent certaines déterminations; et par conséquent il suppose l'expérience' (Kant, quoted in Lalande: *La Raison et les Normes*, 1948: 26).
78. In an interview I conducted with Mohammed Abed al-Jabri in the summer of 2002, I was surprised when he declared, in a rather Althusserian fashion, that Arab popular culture was 'unconscious' and that its study was unnecessary. Al-Jabri's intellectual project is, ironically, in many ways about reinstating/resuscitating the present tense of 'Arab culture'.
79. Here, I recall a brief intervention by Naomi Sakr on Arab audience research (in a Communication and Media Research Institute conference) at the University of Westminster, 30/31 March 2009. The theme of the conference was 'African and Arab Audiences: Shared Research Agendas'.
80. See al-Jabri, Abed Mohammed, 1994); al-Ghazali, Mohamed, 1998; al-Yahyawi, Yahya, 1997; Amin, Samir and Ghalyun, Burhan, 1999 and Manjra, Mahdi, 2001.
81. We can add African and Asian Cultural Studies to this list, but they are still in the early stages of their development.
82. I envisage that Arab cultural studies will develop in different ways, reflecting the diversity and the varied cultural experience of the Arab world. The idea of a shared 'Arab culture', or a shared frame of 'common injustice', is not undesirable, provided that they are not disguised in discourses of 'authenticity', which downplay difference and otherness. Making a claim to authenticity (any discourse of Arab authenticity) cancels out 'otherness', and that would defeat the whole point of critical cultural studies.
83. Scannell, 2006, unpublished manuscript (Ph.D. Thesis, University of Westminster).
84. I will revisit the 'postcolonial' question towards the end of this chapter.

85. A war in Iraq and another in Afghanistan.
86. For a good and thorough exposition on the Arab world's encounters with European culture in the nineteenth century, see Ibrahim Abu-Lughod's *Arab Rediscovery of Europe* (1963).
87. The work of Edward W. Said and Mohammed Abed al-Jabri, two hugely influential Arab thinkers, owes much to Foucault. Laroui's work, and that of many other influential Arab Marxists, is unimaginable without Weber, Althusser and Karl Marx's writings. Khatibi, Boumesshouli and Binabdal'ali, from the philosophy of *tajawuz*, are very influenced by the work of Derrida, Levinas and Heidegger. Taha Abdurrahman, who calls for a creative, ethical Muslim modernity, interestingly draws more from Western than Arabic academic sources, and there are many other similar examples that show how Arab thought and culture are enmeshed in Western thought.
88. Quoted in Leela Gandhi, *Postcolonial Theory: A Critical Introduction* (St. Leonards, NSW, 1998: 6).
89. See Hall, Stuart (1980): 'Cultural Studies: Two paradigms' in *Media, Culture and Society*, Volume: 2 (pp. 57–72).
90. In the case of the Arab world, the history or process of modernisation (including political institutions, education, commerce, transport and communications) has been ongoing for more than two centuries. Aziz Al-Azmeh makes the case, in his *Islams and Modernities* (1995), that the history of the modern Arab world is often subjected to amnesia, not only from the West (whose image of the Arab is still an exoticised one) but also by Islamist 'hermeneutics circles' that seek reform and answers to questions of the present in a glorified Islamic past.
91. See Paddy Scannell's forthcoming book (2010) *Television and The Meaning of Live*.
92. Paddy Scannell (1999), unpublished manuscript.

Bibliography

Abbas, Ackbar and Erni, John Nguyet (eds) (2005) *Internationalizing Cultural Studies: An Anthology*, Oxford: Blackwell.

Abdal'ali, Ghadah (2008) *'Aiza Atjawaz*, Cairo: Dār Shuruq.

Abdurrahman, Taha (2006) *Ruh al-Hadatha: al-Madkhal ela ta'ssis al-hadatha al-Islamiya*, Casablanca: The Arab Cultural Centre.

—— (2002) *al haqu al-Arabi fi al-ikhtilaf al-falsafi*, Casablanca: The Arab Cultural Centre.

Abu-Zaid, A, Mustapha (2002) *athakāfa asha'abeyah bayna atta'adudeyat allughaweyah wa attanawu'a athakāfi in Nadwat Mustaqbal athakāfa fi al-'ālam al-'arabi*, Riyadh: Maktabat al-Malik 'Abd al-'Aziz al-'Ama (pp. 1015–37).

Abu-Lughod, Ibrahim (1963) *Arab Rediscovery of Europe: A study in Cultural Encounters*, Princeton, N J: Princeton University Press.

Abu-Lughod, Laila (2005) *Dramas of Nationhood: The Politics of Television in Egypt*, London: The University of Chicago Press.

—— (2002) 'Egyptian Melodrama – Technology of the Modern Subject?' in Ginsburg, F.D., Abu-Lughod, L and Larkin, B (ed.) *Media Worlds: Anthropology on New Terrain* (pp. 115–33), London: University of California Press.

Abu-Rabi', Ibrahim (2004) *Contemporary Arab Thought: Studies in Post-1967 Arab Intellectual History*, London: Pluto Press.

Adorno, W. Theodor (1991) *The Culture Industry: Selected Essays on Mass Culture*, London: Routledge.

Adorno, W. Theodor and Horkheimer, Max (1972) *Dialectic of Enlightenment*, New York: Herder and Herder.

Aijaz, Ahmad (1992) *In Theory: Classes, Nations, Literatures*, London: Verso.

al-Aid, Yamna (2005) *On Meanings of Critique and the Movement of Arab Culture* [in Arabic], Beirut: Dar al-Farabi.

al-Azmeh, Aziz (1993) *Islams and Modernities*, Verso: London.

—— (1992) *al-Assala aw siyassat al-hurub mina al-waki'*, London: Dar al-Saqi.

al-Gammal, Rasem (2003), 'Broadcasting Research in the Arab World, 1952–2002: An Overview', a paper presented at the University of

Westminster's CAMRI conference on Arab Broadcasting, London, June 2003.

al-Ghathami, Abdullah (2005) *Attaqafa Atilivisyoniyat*, Casablanca: The Arab Cultural Centre.

—— (2000) *qiraa' fi annaqd athkafi*, Casablanca: The Arab Cultural Centre.

—— (1999) ta'neet al-qassida wa al-qaari' al-mukhtalif, Casablanca: The Arab Cultural Centre.

al-Ghazali, Mohammad (1998) *Cultural Imperialism Resides in our Emptiness* [in Arabic], Cairo: The House of Sunrise.

al-Heimr, Abdessalam. (2001) *Anukhbah al-maghrebiyah wa Ishkaleyat al-hadatha*, Casablanca: Al-Multaqa.

al-Jabri, Abed Mohammed (2005) *Fi naqd al-hajat Ila al-islah*, Beirut: The Centre for the Study of Arab Unity.

—— (2001) *al-'aql al-akhlaqi al-'Arabi 4: A Critical Analytical Study of Ethical Models in Arab Culture*, Casablanca: Dār al-Nashr al-Maghribiyah.

—— (2000) *Naqd al-aql al-'Arabi 3: Arab Political Reason*, Beirut: The Centre for the Study of Arab Unity.

—— (1996) *Naqd al-aql al-'Arabi 2: The Structure of Arab Reason*, Casablanca: Arab Cultural Centre.

—— (1994) *al-Mass'alat attakafeyah*, Beirut: The Centre for the Studies of Arab Unity.

—— (1991) *Naqd al-'aql al-'Arabi 1: The Construction of Arab Reason*, Beirut: The Arab Cultural Centre.

—— (1989) *Ishkaleyat al-Fikr al-Arabi al-Mua'ssir*, Casablanca: Banshra.

al-Khamissi, Khalid (2006) *Taxi*, Cairo: Dār Shuruq.

al-Rāwi, Salah (2001) *falssafat al-wa'y asha'abi: derassat ft attakafat asha'beyah*, Cairo: Dār al-fikr al-hadith.

al-Yahyawi, Yahya (1997) *The Arab World and Challenges of Technology, Media and Communication* [in Arabic], Kunitra: Boukili.

Alterman, Jon (2005) 'Arab Media Studies: Some Methodological Considerations' in M. Zayani (ed.) *The Al Jazeera Phenomenon: Critical Perspectives on New Arab Media* (2003–8), London: Pluto.

Amin, Galal (2004) *Whatever Else Happened to the Egyptians?* Cairo: The American University in Cairo Press.

Amin, Samir and Ghalyun, Burhan (1999) *The Globalization of Culture and the Culture of Globalization* [in Arabic], Beirut: Dar al-fiqr.

Ang, Ieng and Morley, David (1989) 'Mayonnaise Culture and Other European Follies' in *Cultural Studies*, Volume: 3, Number: 2 (pp. 133–44).

Ansari, Abdou Filali (1998) 'Can Modern Rationality Shape a New Religiosity? Mohammed Abed al-Jabri and the Paradox of Islam and Modernity' in Cooper, John et al. (eds) *Islam and Modernity* (pp. 129–56), London: I.B.Tauris.

Appadurai, Arjun. (1990) 'Disjuncture and Difference in the Global Cultural Economy' in Featherstone, M (ed.) *Global Culture: Nationalism, Globalization and Modernity* (pp. 295–310), London: Sage.

Arkoun, Mohammed (2006) *Islam: To Reform or to Subvert*, London: Saqi Books.

—— (1997) *Naz'at al-ansana fi al-fikr al-Arabi: Jeel al-messkawaih wal-tawhidi*, Beirut: Dār al-Saqi.

Armbrust, Walter (ed.) (2000) *Mass Mediations: New Approaches to Popular Culture in the Middle East and Beyond*, London: University of California Press.

Armbrust, Walter (1996) *Mass Culture and Modernism in Egypt*, Cambridge: Cambridge University Press.

Arnold, Mathew (1869, 1994) *Culture and Anarchy*, London: Yale University Press.

Ashcroft, Bill, Griffiths, Gareth and Tiffin, Helen (1989) *The Empire Writes Back: Theory and Practice in Post-colonial Literatures*, London: Routledge.

Aswāni, 'Alā' (2002) 'Emārat *Ya'kobyan*, Cairo: Mirit lil-Nashr wa-al-ma'lumat.

Augé, Marc (1995) *Non-Places: Introduction to an Anthropology of Supermodernity*, London: Verso.

Awad, Lewis (1972) 'Contemporary Arab Culture: Motivations and Ends' in *Cultures: International Review, Journal of World History*, Volume: XIV (pp. 756–70).

Ayish, Mohammad (2003) 'Beyond Western Communication Theories: A Normative Arab Islamic Perspective' in *Javnot*, Volume: 10, Number: 2 (pp. 79–92).

Barthes, Roland (1972) *Mythologies*, London: Vintage.

Baudrillard, Jean (1983) *In the Shadow of the Silent Majorities*, New York: Semiotext.

Bauman, Zygmunt (1998) *Globalisation*, London: Polity Press.

Belkbir, Abdessamad (1991) 'On the Meaning of Popular Culture' [in Arabic] *in Attakafa Asha'beya Ihda Rakaez Wahdat al-Maghrib al-Arabi*, a paper presented at the conference of Nadour, pp.15–27, Morocco: Moroccan Cultural Centre.

Belkqziz, Abdalelah (2000) *Nihayat al-Da'eyat: al-Mumkin wa al-mumtana' fi adwari al-Muthqafin*, Casablanca: The Arab Cultural Centre.

Ben Shekroun, Mohammed (1980) *La Culture Marocaine Populaire*, Casablanca: The Moroccan Cultural Centre.

Bentahila, Abdelali (1983) *Language Attitudes among Arabic-French Bilinguals in Morocco*, Avon: Multilingual Matters Ltd.

Bentley, Nick (2005) 'The Young Ones: A reassessment of the British New Left's Representations of 1950s Youth Cultures' in *European Journal of Cultural Studies*, Volume: 8, Number: 1 (pp. 65–83).

Berman, Marshall (1983) *All That Is Solid Melts into Air: The Experience of Modernity*, London: Verso.

Berque, Jacques (1983) *Arab Rebirth: Pain and Ecstasy*, London: Saqi.

—— (1978) *Cultural Expression in Arab Society Today*, London: University of Texas Press.

—— (1972) 'Vers une culture arabe contemporaine' in *Cultures: International Review, Journal of World History*, Volume: XIV (pp. 729–55).

Bhabha, K. Homi (1994) *The Location of Culture*, London: Routledge.

Binabdal'ali, Abdal-Salam (2002) *Baina al-ittisal wa al-Infissal: dirassat fi al-Fikr al-Falssafi bi al-Maghrib*, Casablanca: Dār Tubqal.

—— (2000) *al-Fikr fi 'assr al-Techneya*, Casablanca: Ifrequiya al-Sharq.

—— (1994) *thakkafat al-udun wa thakafat al-'ain*, Rabat: Dār Tubqal.

—— (1983) *al-Fikr al-Falssafi fi al-Maghrib*, Beirut: Dār attali'a.

Blickle, Peter (2002) *Heimat: A Critical Theory of the German Idea of Homeland*, New York: Camden House.

Boumesshouli, Abdul-Aziz (2007) *al-qā'in wa al-matahat (Being and Loss) attafkir fi azzaman al-mu'assir*, Marrakech: The Moroccan Centre for Philosophical Research.

—— (2006a) *al-Falssafa al-Maghribeya, Sua'l al-Kawneya wa al-Mustaqbal*, Marrakech: The Moroccan Centre for Philosophical Research.

—— (2006) *al-Falssafa al-Maghribiyah*, Marrakech: The Moroccan Centre for Philosophical Research.

Boumesshouli, Abdul-Aziz (2005) *Akhlāqu al-ghair: Nahwa falssafa Ghair-iyah*, Marrakech: The Moroccan Centre for Philosophical Research: Walili Printers.

—— (2001) *al-ussus al-falsafeyat li nadareyat nihayat al-akhlaq*, Marrakech: The Moroccan Centre for Philosophical Research: Matba'at Walili

Boumesshouli, Abdul-Aziz and Ghabass, Abdessamad (2003) *Azzamān wa al-fikr*, Casablanca: The Centre for Philosophical Research: Dār attakafa.

Bourdieu, Pierre (1984) *Distinction: A Social Critique of the Judgement of Taste*, London: Routledge and Kegan Paul.

Brett, Michael and Fentress, Elizabeth (1997) *The Berbers*, London: Blackwell.

Bundoq, Mahdi (2003) *Tafkik attakāfat al-'arabeyah*, Cairo: al-majliss al-a'la littakafat.

Carey, John (1992) *The Intellectuals and the Masses*, London: Faber and Faber.

Centre for Arab Unity Studies (1985) *Aturath wa tahadeyat al-a'ssr fi al-Watan al-Arabi: al-Assala wa al-mua'ssara*, Beirut: Centre for Arab Union Studies.

Chtatou, Mohammed (1996) 'Saints and Spirits and Their Significance in Moroccan Cultural Beliefs' in *The Journal of the Society for Moroccan Studies*, Number:1 (pp.62–84).

Clifford, James and George, Marcus (eds) (1986) *Writing Culture: The Poetics and Politics of Ethnography*, London: University of California Press.

Coleman, Simon and Collin, Peter (eds) (2006) *Locating the Field: Space, Place and Context in Anthropology*, Oxford: Berg.

Curran, James and Morley, David (eds) (2006) *Media and Cultural Theory*, London: Routledge.

Curran, James and Park, Myung-Jin (eds) (2000) *De-Westernizing Media Studies*, London: Routledge.

Dareef, Mohammed (1999) *The Moroccan Islamists* [in Arabic], Casablanca: al-Jadida.

de Certeau, Michel (1984) *The Practice of Everyday Life*, London: University of California Press.

Deleuze, Gilles and Guattari, Félix (1994) *What is Philosophy?* New York: Columbia University Press.

During, Simon (2005) 'Popular Culture on a Global Scale: A Challenge for Cultural Studies' in Abbas, A and Erni, N (2005) *Internationalising Cultural Studies: An Anthology* (pp. 439, 453), London: Blackwell.

Eickelman, F. Dale and Anderson, W. Jon (eds) (1999) *New Media in the Muslim World: The Emerging Public Sphere*, Bloomington: Indiana University Press.

Fetterman, David (1989) *Ethnography Step by Step*, London: Sage.

Foucault, Michel (2008) *The Archaeology of Knowledge*, London: Routledge Classics.

Gandhi, Leela (1998) *Postcolonial Theory: A Critical Introduction*, Edinburgh: Edinburgh University Press.

Garnham, Nicholas (2000) *Media, Modernity and Emancipation*, Oxford: Oxford University Press.

—— (1986) 'Contribution to a Political Economy of Mass-Communication' in Collins et al., *Media, Culture and Society: A Critical Reader* (pp. 9–32).

Gasset, José Ortega (1932) *The Revolt of the Masses*, S.I: Allen and Unwin.

Gassous, Mohammed (1988) 'Observations on Transformations in Contemporary Moroccan Popular Culture' in *Popular Culture: One of the Principles of Maghribi Unification* [in Arabic] (pp. 33–56), Kunitra: Manshurat al-Majlis al-Baladi.

Geertz, Clifford (1973) *The Interpretation of Cultures*, London: Fontana Press.

—— (1968) *Islam Observed*, London: The University of Chicago Press.

Gellner, Ernest (1981) *Muslim Society*, New York: Cambridge University Press.

Georganteli, Eurydice and Cook, Barrie (2006) *Encounters: Travel and Money in the Byzantine World*, London: The Barber Institute of Fine Arts.

Giddens, Anthony (1999) *Runaway World: How Globalization Is Reshaping Our Lives*, London: Profile Books.

—— (1991) *Modernity and Self-Identity: Self and Society in the Late Modern Age*, London: Polity.

Glass, Dagmar (2001) 'The Global Flow of Information: A Critical Appraisal from the Perspective of Arab Islamic Information Sciences' in Hafez, Kai (ed.) *Mass Media, Politics and Society in the Middle East* (pp. 217–40), New Jersey: Hampton Press.

Goffman, Erving (1959) *The Presentation of Self in Everyday Life*, England: Penguin Books.

Golding, P and Harris, P (ed.) (1997) *Beyond Cultural Imperialism: Globalisation, Communication and the New International order*, London: Sage.

Habermas, Jürgen (1987) *The Philosophical Discourse of Modernity*, Massachusetts: The MIT Press Cambridge.

Hall, Stuart (1986) 'Cultural Studies: Two Paradigms' in Collins et al., *Media, Culture and Society: A Critical Reader*, (pp. 33–49).

—— (1980): 'Cultural Studies: Two Paradigms' in *Media, Culture and Society* 2 (57–72).

Hall, Stuart and Whannel, Peter (1964) *The Popular Arts*, London: Hutchinson: Educational.

Hamada, Basyouni (1994) 'Islamic Culture Theory, Arab Media Performance and Public Opinion' in Splichal, S (ed.) *Public Opinion and Democracy: Vox Populi – Vox Dei* (pp. 215–39), London: Hampton Press.

Hammond, Andrew (2007) *Popular Culture in the Arab World: Arts, Politics and the Media*, Cairo: The American University in Cairo.

Hanafi, Hassan (2002) 'al-falsafa fi al-watan al-'arabi fi mia't 'am' in *al-falsafa fi al-watan al-'arabi fi mia't 'am*, (pp.17–41), Beirut: The Centre for the Studies of Arab Unity and the Egyptian Philosophical Association.

Hannerz, Ulf (2006) 'Studying Down, Up, Sideways, Through, Backwards, Forwards, Away and at Home: Reflections on the Field Worries of an Expansive Discipline' in Coleman, Simon and Collin, Peter (eds) *Locating the Field: Space, Place and Context in Anthropology* (pp. 23–41), Oxford: Berg.

Hawwas, Abdelhamid (2002) *Papers in Popular Culture* [in Arabic], Cairo: markaz al-buhut al-'arabeya.

Hebdige, Dick (1979) *Subculture: The Meaning of Style*, London: Methuen & Co. Ltd

Heidegger, Martin ([1962] 2007) *Being and Time*, Oxford: Blackwell Publishing.

Hoggart, Richard ([1957] 1992) *The Uses of Literacy*, Harmondsworth: Penguin Books.

Hourani, Albert (1991) 'How Should We Write the History of the Middle East?' in *International Journal Of Middle East Studies*, Volume: 23, Number: 2 (May 1991, p. 133).

—— (1983) *Arabic Thought in the Liberal Age: 1798–1939*, Cambridge: Oxford University Press.

Hussein, Taha (1975) *The Future of Culture in Egypt*, New York: Octagon.

Husserl, Edmund (1973) *The Paris Lectures*, The Hague: Martinus Nijhoff.

Ibn Khaldun (1967) *The Muquaddimah: An Introduction to History*, Princeton, NJ: Princeton University Press, Translated from the Arabic by Franz Rosenthal.

Jameson, Frederic (2002) *A Singular Modernity: Essay on the Ontology of the Present*, London: Verso.

Johnson, Nels (1987) 'Mass Culture and Islamic Populism' in Stauth, Georg and Zubaida, Sami (eds) (1987) *Mass Culture, Popular Culture, and Social Life in the Middle East* (pp. 165–87), Colorado: Westview Press.

Jorgensen, L. Danny (1989) *Participant Observation: A Methodology for Human Studies*, London: Sage.

Kassir, Samir (2006) *Being Arab*, London: Verso.

Khatibi, Abdelkabir (1980) *Annaqd al-Mujdawij* Beirut: Dār al-'Awdah.

Khiabany, Gholam (2006) 'Religion and Media in Iran: The Imperative of the Market and the Straightjacket of Islamism' in *Westminster Papers in Communication and Culture*, Volume: 3, Number: 2 (pp. 3–21).

Kraidy, Marwan (2008) 'Reality TV and Multiple Arab Modernities: A Theoretical Exploration' in *Middle East Journal of Culture and Communication*, Volume: 1, Number: 1 (pp. 49–60).

—— (2006) *Hybridization the Logic of Globalization*, Philadelphia: Temple University.

Kuan-Hsing, Chen (1996) 'Cultural Studies and the Politics of Internationalisation: An Interview with Stuart Hall' in Morley and Chen (1996) *Stuart Hall: Critical Dialogues in Cultural Studies*, (pp. 392–408) London: Routledge.

Kuhn, S. Thomas (1996) *The Structure of Scientific Revolutions*, Third edition, London: The University of Chicago Press.

Lalande, André (1948) *La Raison et Les Normes*, Paris: Librairie Hachette.

Laroui, Abdullah (2006) *'Awaeq al-tahdith*, Morocco: Manshurat Itihad Kutab al-Maghrib.

—— (2001) *Modernité et L'Islam*, Casablanca: Centre Culturel Arabe.

—— (2001) *Mafhoum al-'aql*, Casablanca: The Arab Cultural Centre.

—— (1992) *Mafhoum attarikh*, Casablanca: The Arab Cultural Centre.

—— (1981) *Mafhoum addawlah*, Casablanca: The Arab Cultural Centre.

—— (1980) *Mafhoum al-hurreya*, Casablanca: The Arab Cultural Centre.

—— (1977) *Les Origines Sociales et Culturelles du Nationalisme Marocain*, Paris: Maspero.

Laroui, Abdullah (1976) *The Crisis of the Arab Intellectual: Traditionalism or Historicism?* Berkley: California University Press.

—— (1973) *al-'Arab wa al-Fikr Attarikhi,* Beirut: Dar al-Haqiqua.

—— (1970) *L'histoire du Maghreb,* Paris: Maspero.

Lefebvre, Henri ([1984], 1999) *Everyday Life in the Modern World,* New Jersey: Transaction Publishers.

—— (1995) *Introduction to Modernity,* London: Verso.

Lerner, Daniel (1958) *The Passing of Traditional Society,* Illinois: The Free Press.

Levinas, Emmanuel (1978) *Existence and Existents,* London: Kluwer Academic Publishers.

Lewis, Bernard (1957) 'The Muslim Discovery of the West', *SOAS Bulletin,* Volume: xx, London (pp. 407–19).

Loomba, Ania (1998) *Colonialism-Postcolonialism,* London: Routledge.

Luhmann, Niklas (1998) *Observations on Modernity,* California: Stanford University Press.

Macey, David (2000) *Dictionary of Critical Theory,* London: Penguin Books.

Mahmmoudi, Abdellah (1997) *Master and Disciple: The Cultural Foundations of Moroccan Aauthoritarianism,* London: The University of Chicago Press.

Mahmmoudi, Abdelhamid (1998) *aturath al-sha 'abi wa al-rewayah al-'arabeyah al-haditha,* Baghdad: Dār al-shu 'un al-thaqafeyat al'ama.

Manjra, Mahdi, (2001) *The Intifada in the Age of Rule by Humiliation* [in Arabic], Kunitra: Boukili.

Memmi, Albert (1974) *The Colonizer and the Colonized,* S.I: Souvenir Press.

Mernissi, Fatima (1992) *La peur-modernité: Conflit Islam démocratie,* Paris: Albin Michel.

—— (1991) *Women and Islam,* Oxford: Blackwell.

—— (1975) *Beyond the Veil, Male-Female Dynamics in Modern Muslim Society,* London: John Wiley and Sons.

Meyrowitz, Joshua (1985) *No Sense of Place: The Impact of Electronic Media on Social Behavior,* Oxford: Oxford University Press.

Miller, Susan (1992) *Disorienting Encounters: Travels of a Moroccan Scholar in France in 1845–1846,* Oxford: University of California Press.

Moore-Gilbert, B. J. (1997) *Postcolonial Theory: Contexts, Practices, Politics,* London: Verso.

Morley, David (2000) *Home Territories, Media, Mobility and Identity*, London: Routledge.

Morley, David and Chen, Kuan-Hsing (eds) (1996) *Stuart Hall: Critical Dialogues in Cultural Studies*, London: Routledge.

Mowlana, Hamid and Wilson, J. Laurie (1990) *The Passing of Modernity*, London: Longman.

Mulvey, Laura (1989) *Visual and Other Pleasures*, Basingstoke: Macmillan.

Munson, Henry (1993) *Religion and Power in Morocco*, London: Yale University Press.

Murdock, Graham (1993) 'Communications and the Constitution of Modernity' in *Media, Culture and Society*; Volume: 15, pp. (521–39).

Ngugi, wa Thiong'o (1986) *Decolonising the Mind: The Politics of Language in African Literature*, London: James Currey.

Oumlil, Ali (2005) *Suāl attakāfat: attākafat al-arabeyah fi 'ālamin mutahawil*, Beirut: The Arab Cultural Centre.

Raven, Susan (1984) *Rome in Africa*, London: Longman.

Saadawi, Nawal (1997) *Why Keep Asking Me about My Identity?* New York: Zed Books.

Sabry, Tarik (2007a) 'An Interview With Paddy Scannell' in *Westminster Papers in Communication and Culture*, Volume: 4, Number: 3 (pp. 3–23).

—— (2009) 'Media and Cultural Studies in the Arab world: Making Bridges to Local Discourses of Modernity' in Daya Thussu (ed.) *Internationalizing Media Studies* (pp. 196–214), London: Routledge.

—— (2008) 'Arab Media and Cultural Studies: Rehearsing New Questions' in Kai Hafez (ed.) *Arab Media: Power and Weakness* (pp. 237–51), New York: Continuum.

—— (2007) 'In search of the Present Arab Cultural Tense' in Sakr, N., *Arab Media and Political Renewal: Community, Legitimacy and Public Life* (pp.154–68), London: I.B.Tauris.

—— (2005a) 'The Day Moroccans Gave Up Couscous for Satellite: Global TV, Structures of Feeling and Mental Emigration' in *Journal of Transnational Broadcasting Studies*, Volume: 1, Number: 1, (pp. 197–221).

Sabry, Tarik (2005) 'Emigration as Popular Culture: The Case of Morocco' in *Journal of European Cultural Studies*, Volume: 8, Number: 1 (pp. 5–22).

—— (2004) 'Young *Amazighs*, Migration and Pamela Anderson as the Embodiment of Modernity' in *Westminster Papers in Communication and Culture*, Volume: 1, Number: 1 (pp. 38–52).

—— (2003) *Exploring Symbolic Dimensions of Emigration: Communication, Mental and Physical Emigration*, Ph.D. thesis, Harrow: University of Westminster.

Safouane, Mustapha (2007) *Why Are the Arabs Not Free?* Oxford: Blackwell Publishing.

Said, W. Edward (2003) *Orientalism,* London: Penguin Books.

—— (1993) *Culture and Imperialism*, London: Vintage.

—— (1989) 'Representing the Colonised: Anthropology's Interlocutors' in *Critical Inquiry*, Volume: 15, Number: 2 (pp. 205–25).

Sakr, Naomi (2009) 'Arab Audience Research: An Intervention' in *African and Arab Audiences: Shared Research Agendas*, a conference organised by the University of Westminster's Arab Media Centre, March 30/31, 2009.

—— (2007) *Arab Television Today*, London: I.B.Tauris.

—— (2001) Satellite Realms: Transnational Television, Globalization and the Middle East, London: I.B.Tauris.

Salvatore, Armando (1997) *Islam and Political Discourse of Modernity*, Reading: Ithaca.

Sartre, J. Paul (2001) *Colonialism and Neocolonialism*, London: Routledge.

Scannell, Paddy (2010) *Television and the Meaning of Live*, London: Sage.

—— (2007) *Media and Communication*, London: Sage.

—— (2006) *Broadcasting and Time*, Ph.D. Thesis: University of Westminster.

—— (1999) 'Cultural Studies and the Meaning of Life', unpublished manuscript.

—— (2000) 'For-anyone-as-someone structures' in *Media, Culture and Society*, Volume: 22, Number: 1 (pp. 5–24).

Shayegan, Daryush (1992) *Cultural Schizophrenia*, London: Saqi Books.

Sheikh, Mohammed (2007) *Al-maghareba wa al-Hadatha*, Rabat: Ramsis.

Silverstone, Roger (1999) *Why Study the Media*, London: Sage.

Sparks, Colin (2007) *Globalization, Development and the Mass Media*, London: Sage.

—— (2005) 'The Problem of Globalization' in *Journal of Global Media and Communication*, Volume: 1, Number: 1 (pp. 20–3).

—— (2004) 'What is Wrong with Globalization?' a paper presented at the conference 'Epidemics and Trans-Border Violence: Communication and Globalization under a Different Light,' Hong Kong, December 16–18.

—— (2000) 'Media Theory after the Fall of European Communism: Why the Old Models from East and West Won't Do Anymore' in Curran, James and Park Myung-Jin (eds) *De-Westernizing Media Studies* (pp. 35–50), London: Routledge.

—— (1992) 'Popular Journalism: Theories and Practice' in P. Dahlgren and C. Sparks (eds) *Journalism and Popular Culture* (pp. 24–45), London: Sage.

Spivak, G. Chakravorty (1995) 'Can the Subaltern speak?' in Ashcroft, Bill, Griffiths, Gareth and Tiffin, Helen (eds) *The Postcolonial Studies Reader* (pp. 24–8), London: Routledge.

Sreberny, Annabelle (2008) 'The Analytic Challenges of Studying the Middle East and Its Evolving Media Environment' in *Middle East Journal of Culture and Communication*, Volume: 1, Number: 1 (pp. 8–24).

Sreberny-Mohammadi, A (1997) 'The Many Cultural Faces of Imperialism' in Golding, P and Harris, P (eds) (1997) *Beyond Cultural Imperialism* (pp. 49–69), London: Sage.

Stauth, Georg and Zubaida, Sami (eds) (1987) *Mass Culture, Popular Culture, and Social Life In the Middle East*, Colorado: Westview Press.

Stratton, Jon and Ang, Ieng (ed.) (1996) 'On the Impossibility of a Global Cultural Studies: 'British' Cultural Studies in an International Frame' in Morley and Chen (1996) *Stuart Hall: Critical Dialogues in Cultural Studies* (pp. 361–91), London: Routledge.

Tahtawi, Rifa'ah Rafi' (1834, 1835) *Takhlis al-ibriz ila talkhis Bariz,* Bulaq: Dār al-Tiba'ah al-Khidaywiyah.

Talal, Mohammed (2005) *Al-Ittisal wa al-mujtama'a fi al-'Alam al-'Arabi,* Casablanca: The Centre for Journalism and Communication.

—— (1993) *Al-Ittisal fi al-'Alam al-'Arabi: Qadaya wa-Muqarabat,* Rabat: The Moroccan Company of Print and Distribution.

Tarabeshi, George (1993) *Madbahat atturath fi attakafat al-'Arabeya al-Mu'assirat,* London: Dar al Saqi.

Tawil-Souri, Helga (2007) 'The Political Battlefield of Pro-Arab Video Games on Palestinian Screens', in *Comparative Studies of South Asia, Africa and the Middle East*, Volume: 27, Number: 3 (pp. 536–51).

Ussfur, Jaber (2003) *Cultural Papers: The Culture of the Future and the Future of Culture* [in Arabic], Cairo: al-Markez al-massri al-Arabi.

Wakidi, Mohammed (2007) *al-bu 'd attakāfi*, Kunitra: al-Bukili.

Warmington, B. (1954) *The North African Provinces from Diocletian to the Vandal Conquest*, Cambridge: Cambridge University Press.

Williams, Raymond (1976) *Keywords*, London: Croom Helm.

—— (1961) *The Long Revolution*, New York: Columbia University Press.

—— (1963), *Culture and Society 1780–1950*, London: Penguin Books.

—— (1958) *Culture and Society*, London: The Hogarth Press.

Young, Robert (2001) *Post-Colonialism: An Historical Introduction*, Oxford: Oxford University Press.

Zubaida, Sami (1987) 'Components of Popular Culture in the Middle East' in Stauth, Georg and Zubaida, Sami (eds) (1987) *Mass Culture, Popular Culture, and Social Life in the Middle East* (pp. 137–63), Colorado: Westview Press.

Zuhur, Sherifa (1992) *Revealing Reveiling: Islamist Gender Ideology in Contemporary Egypt*, New York: State University of New York Press.

Index

salafism, cultural, 30, 33, 35
salafist, cultural, 30, 32, 37–8, 41, 45, 47
satellite, 49, 96, 97, 99, 100, 102–5, 116, 176, 188, 190
Scannell, Paddy, 11, 27, 38, 50, 96, 172–5, 180, 189
schizophrenia, cultural, 4, 130, 156
science, 9, 19, 64, 148, 160, 167, 176, 181, 196
Scopophilia, 122
self-reflexivity, 131, 157
semantics, 16, 65
semiotics, 4, 33, 51, 59, 61
sex/sexuality, 51, 60, 75, 122–3, 125, 132–4, 150
Sheikh, Mohammed, 35, 199
silb, 110, 135
sociology/sociologist/sociological, 13, 18, 38, 54, 59, 80, 123, 159, 167, 169, 172, 190, 198, 204
space, third, 74, 184
Sparks, Colin, 7, 55, 98, 174, 176
spatial, 8–11, 63–4, 74–5, 91, 97, 107, 111, 130, 159, 162, 191
Spivak, G. Chakravorty, 186
Sreberny, Annabelle, 7
Sreberny-Mohammadi, 98
stratification, 43, 47, 61, 76, 93, 99, 100, 148–9
structure of feeling, 110, 112–13, 131, 149, 152, 185, 190
subaltern, 131, 187
subculture, 58–60

tajawuz, falsafat, 33, 39, 41
talk, 76, 78, 79–86
Tarabeshi, George, 199
television, 4, 7, 15, 21, 26, 48–9, 54, 68, 73, 96–7, 99, 100, 103, 105, 114, 116–20, 122, 124, 126, 135, 140, 149–50, 152, 164, 188, 195

temporality, cultural, 8, 10–11, 25–6, 28, 31, 97, 114, 151, 161–2, 173
temporal, 5, 8–10, 16–17, 66, 80, 114, 161–2, 184, 191
terrorism, cultural, 15, 73
theory, 28, 39–40, 59, 98, 159, 176, 178, 180–7, 189
time, unconscious, 161
tradition, 18–19, 33, 35–6, 41, 45, 52, 56, 64, 72, 74–6, 122–3, 152–3
traditionaliser, 121, 134, 191
traditionalist, 122–3, 134
translation, 166, 168–70, 177, 189
turath, 26–9, 31–2, 34, 35, 36, 41, 57, 197
turatheya, 30, 32, 35–6
turathaweya, 32, 35
turathi, 32, 41
Turkish soap opera, 125, 203

urban, 14, 61, 117, 133

West, 7, 9, 14, 21, 27, 29, 34, 36–8, 59, 79, 86–7, 90–3, 95–6, 98–9, 104, 106–12, 117–22, 124, 126–8, 130, 135–41, 146, 150–2, 154, 157, 166, 175, 182, 186, 188–9, 196
Western, 4, 6, 14, 18, 26–8, 30–1, 35–41, 47–8, 54, 55, 59–60, 65, 72, 76, 78–9, 82, 85–93, 98–9, 101–4, 109–10, 112, 114, 117–20, 122–3, 127–38, 140–7, 149–53, 157, 160, 164–5, 168–9, 171, 173–83, 186–7, 189, 191
"de-Westernisation," 28, 39–40, 168, 175–80, 182–3, 192
"de-de-Westernisation," 40, 180
Williams, Raymond, 50, 113, 150, 162–3, 166

Zionism, 48
Zubaida, Sami, 117, 190